AROUND AND ABOUT PARIS

FROM THE GUILLOTINE
TO THE
BASTILLE OPERA

THIRZA VALLOIS

Around and About Paris

FROM THE GUILLOTINE
TO THE BASTILLE OPERA

THE 8TH, 9TH, 10TH, 11TH
& 12TH ARRONDISSEMENTS

Bonne lecture!

Thirza

ILIAD BOOKS

First Published in 1996

New edition 1998

Reprinted 1999

Copyright © 1996, Thirza Vallois

ISBN 0 9525378 3 4

Iliad Books
5 Nevern Road
London SW5 9PG
Tel: 0973 325 468
Internet: http://www.wfi.fr/vallois

Designed and produced by Kitzinger, London
Printed in Canada by Webcom Limited

To my Parents and Nathaniel
with love

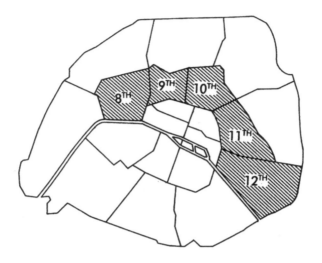

8TH 9TH 10TH 11TH 12TH

CONTENTS

In memory of Ella

ACKNOWLEDGEMENTS

I would like to express my deepest gratitude to Masha Schmidt, the illustrator of this book, who has captured so faithfully its atmosphere.

I would like also to thank the people who have worked with me specifically on this second volume of *Around and About Paris.* They are listed in alphabetical order:

Karim Boubekeur, Claire Carrier, Ingrid Cranfield who has given me invaluable advice in editing the book, Nicolas Georget, Tony Kitzinger who has designed the book with so much commitment and care.

Special thanks also to all my friends and colleagues who, in one way or another, have given me their support during this long adventure. They include:

Helen Braverman, Fifi Dosoruth, Roselyn Dery, Richard Dunn, Baba Gamet, Fleurette Havranek, Ena Langman, Eve Lauhouti, Dan Levy, Danielle Michel-Chiche, John Marriott, Gloria Moss, Karina Pierre, John Price, Susan Rosenberg, Andrew Russell, Ellie Santos, Ron Shepping, Gerry Silverman, Stephen Solomons, Claudie and Laurent Taieb, Barbara-Sue White, Sarah Wilkinson, Elizabeth, Caroline and Peter Wilson.

INTRODUCTION

Le mur murant Paris rend Paris murmurant
The wall that walls in Paris makes Paris rumble

On 14 July 1789 France entered the modern age unawares. Louis XVI had been hunting all day. On his return home he wrote in his diary, *'aujourd'hui, rien'* ('Today, nothing'). Symbols were the driving force of the French Revolution and one by one the emblems of tyranny and of social injustice yielded to the fury of a people in arms.

One such symbol was le Mur des Fermiers Généraux*, the notorious toll walls that had been erected around Paris between 1784 and 1787, 23 kilometres long, 3.30 metres high. Since the rickety toll barriers at the checkpoints of Paris had failed to control the movement and activities of Parisians, who were both unruly and resourceful, and always ready for a cat-and-mouse game with the authorities, it was decided to seal off Paris by means of solid walls and 60 toll-gates.

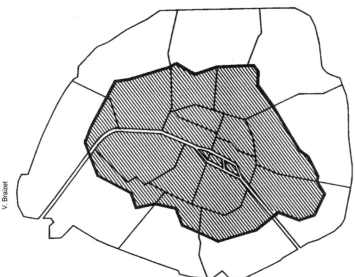

* *Fermiers Généraux* were the royal tax collectors

1

These were manned by vigilant customs officers, and no goods would get by them, it was hoped. The scheme only contributed to stirring up the people and feeding their spirit of revolt. Some smart Parisians set out at once to thwart the scheme and smuggled in goods through tunnels which they dug under the walls (vestiges of which have been found, notably on rue de la Glacière, north of Boulevard Auguste-Blanqui, in the 13th arrondissement). Others let off steam by writing satirical verse:

> *Pour augmenter son numéraire*
> *Et raccourcir notre horizon,*
> *La Ferme a jugé nécessaire*
> *De mettre Paris en prison.*

> To augment his wealth
> And to reduce our horizon
> The taxman deemed it expedient
> To put Paris in prison.

The people of Paris had good reason to resent the taxman, then known as the Farmer General (Fermier Général), for in the 17th and 18th centuries he held the most lucrative post in the kingdom and was able to amass immense wealth (thanks in particular to the salt tax in the 17th century), while most people were living in utter destitution. For Nicolas Ledoux the toll-gates provided an opportunity to give vent to his artistic imagination and create 45 different monuments (*propylaea*) around the city, a fact that strikingly illustrates the fathomless gap that separated the privileged from the masses in their daily preoccupations and of the insensitivity of the former to the plight of the latter.

The impatient people of Paris did not wait for the storming of the Bastille to express their frustration. On 12 July 1789 they unleashed their anger on the toll-gates, setting fire to some, damaging others. When the toll tax was abolished on 1 May 1791, they went into the streets to rejoice and plant May trees next to the barriers, while long queues of carts waited outside the gates for the guns to thunder midnight and signal freedom for the entry of goods into the capital. But the young Republic was desperately short of funds and by 1798 the toll tax was re-established.

In 1795 a new France emerged from the bloody turmoil. King and church were gone, replaced by new institutions. Paris too assumed a new aspect, divided for the first time into arrondissements – 12 at the time – but bounded by the toll walls bequeathed by the *Ancien Régime*. The circular Métro line no. 2/6, Nation-Etoile, essentially follows their course. Its large sections of elevated track provide clear markers as to where the city's limits lay less than 150 years ago. At times they correspond exactly to the border between the inner and outer arrondissements that were annexed in 1860; in other cases some adjustments were made during the 1860 annexation, as you can see from the map on page 1.

The present volume tells the story of the territory incorporated into Paris north of the river in 1795, where the new society that emerged after the Revolution was largely shaped.

A NOTE ON THE TEXT

So as to facilitate the reading of French names and titles, the use of capital letters follows English rules. When they are italicised, however, French rules have been retained.

Because Paris is a city of change, some of the places or exhibits mentioned in the text may have since disappeared or been transformed. If this is the case, please bear with the author.

THE 8TH ARRONDISSEMENT

THIS is the Paris of wealth and luxury, of palatial hotels and *haute couture* houses, the Paris of French gastronomy at its best and most expensive, of prestigious art galleries and pricey concert halls; a Paris that displays its world-renowned fashions along the Avenue Montaigne and the Faubourg Saint-Honoré and its fabulous jewellery in its Carré d'Or, (the flashy compound at 10 Avenue Georges V). From Christian Dior, Balenciaga and Givenchy to Louis Vuitton or Hermès, from Taillevent, Lucas Carton and Lasserre to Maxime's, from the Plaza Athénée, Georges V and La Trémoile to Fauchon, no arrondissement boasts such a concentration of renowned establishments. Here too stands the princely residence of the President of the Republic, the Palais de l'Elysée, once the home of the most luxury-minded of royal mistresses, the Pompadour, enjoying the close company of such venerable embassies as those of the United States and the United Kingdom.

Above all, this is the showcase of France, where French dreams of *grandeur* come true – running from the glorious Place de la Concorde on the eastern edge of the arrondissement, up to the Arc de Triomphe on its western edge, the Avenue des Champs-Elysées displays the most famous and spectacular urban vista in the world and, as such, has become the inevitable route of state visits to the capital and of Republican ceremonies meant for show, in particular the military parade of Bastille Day (14 July). On such occasions all the glory of the Republic is on show and no pains are spared to dazzle the world at large – and oneself!

Wallowing in self-aggrandisement, the French went all out to celebrate the 1989 bi-centenary of the Revolution, turning it into a billion-franc extravaganza to the benefit of privileged guests from far and wide, among whom could be noted the conspicuous presence of many an African leader who, though unconcerned by such revolutionary precepts as liberty, equality or brotherhood back home, did not spurn the glamorous festivities. Nor was the Socialist government embarrassed by its self contradictions when making up its list of honourable guests.

That 14 July 1989, at 9 pm French time, television stations throughout the world were mobilised to offer millions of viewers a French pageant at its best. The average Parisian, after the usual aggravations and hassle caused by the preparations, had to make do with packed pavements and poor visibility. Many preferred to depart for the countryside and leave more room to tourists. . . Summoned to concoct this highlight of the bicentenary, the trendy Jean-Paul Goude staged a mega-parade of 8,000 participants, including 3,000 musicians. All the provinces of France and all the regions of our planet were invited to take part in a parade which included British Horse Guards and American cheer leaders, Senegalese drummers and wailing Arab women . . . Russian snow storms, British rain, Scottish bagpipes, Irish gigs and Auvergnat *bourrée*, football stadiums, African zebras and Asian elephants, Soviet tankers and pyramids of light – an incredible mish-mash of perfect kitsch, crowned by a profusion of glorious fireworks and tricoloured smoke. The Chinese refused to cooperate with this hybrid project and declined to participate: why should the dancers of the Peking opera smurf and why should their martial arts be turned into a breakdance? Nor would they sport worn out clothing to stage the hardships of the Long March when everyone else was wearing their Sunday best. The Bretons would not have neon lights in their headdresses and other provincials refused to have Goude's bicoloured socks.

At the foot of the Obelisk, at Place de la Concorde, opposite the grand-stand with its 16,000 privileged guests, stood Jessye Norman, beautifully dressed by the Tunisian Parisian designer Azzedine Alaïa. Presiding over the ceremony, the black American soprano uplifted the multitudes with a vibrating *Marseillaise*, then faded away into the Jardin des Tuileries. Needless to say that French patriots were scandalised by the choice of an American – of all nationals! – and would have liked the anthem to be rendered by a Mireille Mathieu, the ambassadress of lower middle-class France.

Undoubtedly, Jean-Paul Goude had captured the very essence of our fake, ephemeral age when, using the tools of high technology and sales promotion, he poured into the Champs-Elysées all the 'tribes' of the world and marched them down to Place de la Concorde to the cacophonic sounds of bagpipes, tam-tams and electric guitars. He named this multiracial, multicultural, multi-tudinous, sterilised 'brave new world' of universal brotherhood '*La fête des tribus planétaires*'. More to the point, one journalist, Ph. Noisette, inspired by Benetton's catch word, called it United Colours of Goude!

A less scintillating reality greets the stroller once the footlights are extinguished and the Avenue des Champs-Elysées is restored to its daily routine. Already a generation ago General de Gaulle was aware of this fact when he described it as 'the most beautiful avenue in the world . . . if you disregard the buildings that line it' – banks, insurance and airline companies, cinema halls, and a growing number of American fast food restaurants . . . which de Gaulle was fortunate enough not to live to see! Its heavy traffic exuding gas fumes, its littered pavements and unkempt crowds are barely reminiscent of the aristocratic promenade originally laid out here by Le Nôtre in 1670.

Enclosing medieval Paris to the west, the Louvre had originally been erected as the westernmost defence tower of the city walls. Hence, the royal palace that grew out of it bordered Paris to the west, which meant that any extension of the palace or of its grounds would inevitably follow the same westward direction. Catherine de Medici, the wife of Henri II, had started the process when she bequeathed to posterity the palace and gardens of the Tuileries. But it was Marie de Medici, the wife of Henri IV, who first crossed over the borderline into the future 8th arrondisse-ment – then largely covered with marshes (remnants of prehistoric days when the area was entirely submerged by water), and other-wise interspersed with kitchen gardens and poor men's hovels. Here she laid out a promenade for her husband as an extension of the grand axis of the Tuileries gardens along the Seine. Beyond wifely concern for the King's well-being, the spiteful arrogant Florentine Queen meant the Cours-la-Reine to outdo the beaut-iful gardens opened on the opposite bank of the river by the repudiated Queen Margot.

A further development occurred in 1670, when Colbert ordered Le Nôtre to 'have avenues of trees planted behind the Tuileries as far as the hill of Chaillot (today's Place Charles de Gaulle-Etoile)'. However, it was mainly the lower stretch of the promenade, up to the present Rond-Point-des-Champs-Elysées, that was designed by Le Nôtre and turned into a beautiful landscaped garden; the rest of the promenade was merely lined with trees. The artery gained prestige in the 18th century, as townhouses were built along the parallel Faubourg Saint-Honoré with gardens overlooking the Champs-Elysées. At the same time it became the shortest route to the aristocratic Abbey of Longchamps, the gathering place of the nobility during Holy Week, which fact gave it a further boost.

After 1789 revolutionary Paris followed suit; having planted its guillotine in the adjoining Place de la Révolution (Concorde), the rejoicing mob would overflow into the Champs-Elysées after each sinister spectacle. From time to time festivities were organised for their sake. Napoleon was quick to follow up on this: a banquet for as many as 10,000 people was offered on the Champs-Elysées by the City of Paris in 1807, in honour of Napoleon's victory at Tilsit. On ordinary days the people would frequent its places of pleasure or just stroll about. On summer days Robespierre could be seen here in the company of some friends . . . and his dog, Brunt; he would come over from his nearby home on rue Saint-Honoré.

At night, however, it was an unsafe place and remained so well into the 19th century – a dark stretch where rogues and ruffians could operate unhampered. One of their victims was Philippe Lebon, the inventor of gas light, who had, ironically, devoted his life to combating the hazards of dark streets; on the night of Napoleon's coronation he was found murdered on the Champs-Elysées. Despite such hazards, this being a rare stretch of greenery in the capital, it was bound to become a favourite promenade and a place of pleasure, and exerted an irresistible appeal to the world of fashion. And indeed, except for the short period of 1814/5, when, after Napoleon's defeat the allied forces occupied Paris, pitched camp on the Champs-Elysées and laid it waste, every new regime played its part and helped to turn the Champs-Elysées into the sumptuous, world-renowned thoroughfare of the City of Light. By 1840 it was totally remodelled by Hittorff: gone were the shady dives; 1,200 gas candelabras now lighted the avenue by night, fountains ornamented its squares and elegant establishments – the Panorama, the Cirque d'Eté – provided novelty to the pleasure-seeking crowds. And yet, only under Napoleon III did the Champs-Elysées become a respectable place after dark.

No one was more determined to endow Paris with lovely gardens than Napoleon III who, during his exile in London had been so impressed by its parks. He commissioned Adolphe Alphand to design gardens which would emulate those of the British capital and the results came up to expectations – judging by the legacy of the Impressionist painters and by Alphand's concept of landscaping: 'A garden is a melody of forms and colours.' However, beyond aesthetics and ecological motivations Napoleon III was an astute politician and used town planning as a tool against social unrest: having reshaped the street network of Paris partly for the sake of modernisation, but largely to repress street riots, he meanwhile used the opportunity to push the evicted proletarian population to the periphery, thus 'cleaning' the city of potential agitators.

Likewise, by allocating recreation grounds to the population of Paris, he hoped to take the steam out of the opposition. Hence the lower part of the Champs-Elysées became a pleasure ground where pretty pavilions – theatres, circuses, cafés-concert – alternated with the wooden horses of roundabouts, and the real horses of riding schools and coaches, and with puppeteers and other street performers who awaited the crowds in the open fragrant air.

This was the Champs-Elysées of Marcel Proust's younger days, where he would play with his childhood sweetheart, Swann's daughter Gilberte. A district cherished by Jean Cocteau who remembered its 'Punch and Judy shows, roundabouts, hoop-la, goats, waffles, barley-sugar and jug of liquorice water'. He also remembered its theatres and, notably, that occasion at the Bouffes Parisiens d'Eté, when Cosima Wagner was sitting in a neighbouring box at Offenbach's *Belle Hélène*, weeping at the March of the Kings. And, of course, the magical Palais de Glace or Palace of mirages with all those mirrors! its full-sized orchestra covered with white powder and playing España! Come 5 o'clock exit school children and enter ladies of fashion – *grandes-cocottes* and *demi-castors:* bristling gowns, floating airs of tzigane violins and overflowing champagne. 'This district clung to the skin of my soul,' he concluded.

Pretty jewel-like pavilions are still scattered in the gardens of the lower Champs-Elysées although they are but a pale reminder of a festive past of perpetual rejoicing. Converted predominantly into gourmet restaurants which rank among the top establishments in the capital, they have become ivory towers shut off from the gardens and by no means an integral part of them: Ledoyen which was first opened in 1770 and included Robespierre and Bonaparte among its habitués; Laurent, once the renowned Café du Cirque, l'Elysée-Lenôtre, once the prestigious Petit Paillard. Le Marigny theatre, once Offenbach's Bouffes, and Le Rond-Point theatre, which occupies the premises of Le Palais de Glace, can barely be a match to their predecessors. Nor can l'Espace Cardin on the site of the illustrious Ambassadeurs or Pavillon Gabriel on the site of the no less illustrious Alcazar d'Eté recreate the atmosphere of Gay Paris, fragrant with spring and summer hues by day, shimmering with thousands of lights by night: '*L'effet le plus agréable qu'il soit donné de voir,*' according to the *Revue de l'Art,* 'a linear *féerie*' which, according to one guide-book, extended all the way from Place de la Concorde to the heart of the Bois de Boulogne.

Crowning it all, the now extinct Jardin Mabille on today's Avenue Montaigne, the most famous *bal parisien* of the time, whose pools shimmered with the reflection of as many as 3,000 lights: '. . . an enchantment that goes beyond anything you could imagine on a single acre of land,' Balzac wrote to Countess Madame Hanska in 1847.

The central axis was the domain of horse carriages: running between Place de la Concorde and the Arc de Triomphe they carried the *beau-monde* up and down the Avenue, and into the Bois de Boulogne beyond: 'The great avenue was like a river carrying on its current the bobbing manes of horses and the clothes and heads of men and women,' we are told by Flaubert in *L'Education sentimentale.* An exquisite sight, especially during the Longchamp races. On those three yearly occasions which took place in April, June and September, respectable middle-class Parisians, seated on rows of chairs disposed along the Champs-Elysées, could watch the world of fashion parade by on their way to the racetracks of Longchamp. Longchamp had lost its abbey in the anticlerical turmoil of the Revolution, but it remained the stronghold of the upper classes who, with a stroke of the hand converted the grounds of the aforesaid house of God to an equestrian shrine to suit its Anglomaniac tastes. Their variegated coaches and their graceful attire provided an entertainment in itself and whetted the deliciously gossipy curiosity of the spectators as they tried to identify the characters aboard and find out who was there and with whom.

The burning of the Palace of the Tuileries by the *Communards* in May 1871 struck the political death blow to the 1st arrondissement and heralded, by the same token, the emergence of the 8th, its natural extension. The ruling classes had already chosen it as their residential quarters since the end of the reign of Louis XIV. While some of the independent nobility, who had stubbornly stuck to the capital, settled in the Faubourg Saint-Germain, others preferred the country road that led westward from the city gate of Saint-Honoré to the village of Roule, and beyond it to the bridge of Neuilly, the only road at the time that ran through the future arrondissement. Soon the Faubourg Saint-Honoré, the continuation of rue Saint-Honoré beyond the city gates (hence Faubourg from 'false borough', suburb), was lined with gemlike townhouses, in the style of the *Régence* and *Louis XV*, the pride of French architecture and a match to those of their sister Faubourg Saint-Germain across the Seine. Standing between courtyards and gardens – *entre cour et jardin* – the latter rolled down to Le Nôtre's recently created promenade of the Champs-Elysées, and added beauty to this new neighbourhood of graceful splendour. None of its palatial mansions could match the Hôtel d'Evreux, first built for Henri-Louis de la Tour d'Auvergne, the third son of the Duc de Bouillon and Comte d'Evreux; no wonder Madame de Pompadour had set her eyes on it.

The courtiers of Versailles had spurned the outrageous intrusion of this scandalous Parisian commoner whose presentation at the court had violated the basic rules of etiquette (hitherto all the King's mistresses had been recruited among the ladies of the court) and whose mother had walked the gardens of Palais-Royal, to say the least; an admirable mother though, under whose guidance Jeanne Poisson had been polished up in the city's most prestigious schools, namely its literary *salons* and the great financiers' homes, and turned into an accomplished highly sophisticated, refined and artistic Marquise, a Parisian to her fingertips. Having acquired the Hôtel d'Evreux in 1753, it became her private Parisian residence, which she used lavishly whenever she could stay away from

Versailles. A friend of men of letters and philosophers, a patron of the arts, a pace-setter of fashion and a lover of proliferous luxury (her annual budget for finery alone amounted to 17,500 pounds as against 2,000 pounds spent by the most extravagant of her female compatriots), she organised stunning receptions in her Parisian residence which contributed to putting the future 8th arrondissement on the map. Fit for royalty, the residence was bequeathed to the crown upon her death in 1764; after having changed hands a couple of times, it inevitably became the property of the Republic.

However, only under the Second Republic did it become the presidential residence, and it is significant that Louis-Bonaparte deserted it for the aristocratic Palais des Tuileries after his 1851 successful coup. But his was the last attempt at restoring a monarchical regime in France and in 1873 the victorious Third Republic assigned President Mac-Mahon to the Palais de l'Elysée (l'Hôtel d'Evreux), since when it has been the home of all France's presidents. In 1883 the blackened skeleton of the Tuileries was razed to the ground, which marked the final annihilation of the monarchy and, with it, the irreversible shift of the centre of gravity of Paris from the 1st to the 8th arrondissement.

Roughly four decades after Charles Worth had invented *haute couture* in the 1st arrondissement to cater to the Empress Eugénie and her court at the Tuileries, and Cartier had set out to adorn them with gems and jewels, Paul Poiret, the son of a small-time cloth merchant and native of Les Halles, the lifeblood of the 1st arrondissement, was to carry *haute couture* west to the 8th. After an unhappy period of apprenticeship with Worths – by then the descendants of Charles – and a happy one with Doucet, he opened his own business in 1904 in a beautiful *hôtel particulier* on Avenue d'Antin (now Franklin Roosevelt). Thanks to Doucet, who recommended the celebrated actress and fashion leader, Réjane, to patronise his revolutionary designs, Paul Poiret was catapulted to soaring success; all the more so since he captured and embodied the new spirit of the day, a spirit of liberty which he rendered by freeing women of age-old armours of corsets and layers of underclothes, getting them ready for bicycle rides in the Bois de Boulogne and for swimming in the coastline resorts of Normandy

– a new spirit that suited his client Isadora Duncan, who likewise broke loose from traditions as she moved about barefoot on the stage.

In 1909 Diaghilev arrived in Paris from St Petersburg with the *Ballets Russes* and swept Tout-Paris off its feet. It was not so much the exoticism of the Orient that dazzled Paris – after all Delacroix, Baudelaire, Rimbaud ... and the Universal Expositions had rendered it all familiar, not to mention the long-established craze for *chinoiserie* and other *japonaiserie*. It was the new form of aggressively sensual ballet as rendered by Nijinsky, the new avant-garde music provided by Stravinsky and members of the *Groupe des Six*, the new brightly-coloured sets provided by such *Fauve* painters as Derain and Matisse or by Picasso and Braque that captivated Paris.

Filled with enthusiasm for this explosive, 'barbarian' expression of modernity which electrified the Théâtre des Champs-Elysées on Avenue Montaigne, just a few blocks away from his home, Poiret set about to create a new oriental line of turbans, aigrettes and harem pants and, overall, giving preference to brilliantly colourful designs, as against Worth's subdued, reassuring shades. Poiret always refused to acknowledge the impact of the *Ballets Russes* on his designs and it is true that even back in his teens, when apprenticed to an umbrella maker, he had stolen scraps of silk to make oriental dresses for dolls. There is no doubt that he was a revolutionary designer and, as such, his invention of the hobble skirt in 1909, caused an indignant outcry on the part of the Pope! By the same token, it guaranteed Poiret world renown. Although but a passing fad, the hobble skirt heralded the modern concept of fashion as being ephemeral by definition and of changing fads as being the very essence and foundation of the consumer society. Likewise, in 1911 this precursor of modernity was the first *couturier* to launch his own scent, an initiative followed by all houses, without which none could survive today.

The Great War, but especially Coco Chanel, were his undoing, who, ironically, beat Poiret on his own ground by carrying his ideas one step further. From an even humbler and obscure background (she had been brought up in an orphanage), this highly talented and highly ambitious woman (she stopped at little, had a German lover during the Occupation and mixed with other

German officers) turned her client from object to subject: dressing a woman was no longer about making her look desirable to men, but about making her feel comfortable. The genius of Chanel was to have achieved both! her secret – an impeccably simple line combining ageless classicism and modernity, designs which demanded the highest quality of fabric, execution and finish and left very little room for the superfluous. Even elaborate make-up and hair-styles were done away with and her own short crop was followed by tens of thousands.

Paul Poiret ended up a pauper, Chanel was forgiven. Both were gifted upstarts like Jeanne Lanvin, a messenger girl working for a milliner who began by making dresses for her beloved little daughter, the future Princesse de Polignac. The same story goes for the immortal Madeleine Vionnet who had introduced into *couture* the bias cut. Vionnet was born in the northern working-class suburb of Aubervilliers and went into apprenticeship at age 12. However, she waited for 24 years before opening her own establishment, after having patiently learnt her art in different houses, which does honour to her professionalism and shows something of the old spirit. There was Jean Patou who dressed Mary Pickford and Suzanne Lenglen, there was Jacques Fath who dressed Rita Hayworth; more recently Hubert Givenchy and his unforgettable friend, Audrey Hepburn and today Yves Saint-Laurent who still dresses Catherine Deneuve.

Foreign designers have also flocked to the 8th arrondissement, for nowhere in the world is to be found the tradition and quality of workmanship that has been handed down in Paris for generations. Among them was London-born Irishman, Molyneux who opened his house in 1919 and enjoyed the patronage of the British Embassy. Offering a distinguished clientele a taste of British understatement at its best, he closed down his house in 1950 (having lost one eye in the Great War, his remaining eye was in danger), but tried to make a come back in the 1960s. A sad initiative: Paris had by then followed in the footsteps of London with its mini-skirts, crudeness and all things 'young'.

There was also the Spanish Balenciaga, considered by some the greatest designer of the century. Recreating the Spanish sense of dignity which is to be found in Goya and Velasquez's paintings, he wanted his designs to have a structural body and liked to use fabrics that had weight, such as gazar silk. The Spanish influence was to be found in the colours he used, not unlike those used by Picasso, Miro or Zurbaran. When he closed down in 1968 his comment was: 'It's a dog's life', to be taken, probably, with a pinch of salt. For not only did he create the most elegant designs, but also secured the future of *haute couture* by training such talents as Givenchy, Ungaro and Courrège.

It is in his humble home in Tunisia, that as a little boy Azzedine Alaïa discovered Balenciaga and *haute couture* while glancing through fashion magazines, an encounter that determined his own future career. The story concerning Balenciaga's own calling is even more extraordinary. It is said that one day the young Cristobal Balenciaga, of humble origin too, crossed paths with the Marquesa de Casa Torres. Stunned by the beauty of her dress, which the Marquesa had noticed, she allowed him to copy it. The story goes that she even sent him to Paris to meet Drécoll, the designer of that dress.

When Japan opened her gates to the West, Paris was her focal destination in matters concerning fashion. Disregarding her middle-class father's wish to see her become a surgeon, Hanae Mori became the pioneer of Japanese *haute couture*. Back in the 1950s she began by making costumes for some of Japan's greatest film directors – Oshima, Shindo, Ozu. . . But she dreamt of Paris and of meeting Chanel, and was eventually the first Asian to visit Chanel's house. Chanel offered her a tweed suit with orange trimmings to honour the representative of the land of the Rising Sun. Only in 1977 did she set up shop on the awe-inspiring Avenue Montaigne though, not before having made her début in New York. Today she presides over a worldwide empire – 67 shops in Japan, 52 licences abroad . . . but still takes pride in creating costumes such as the famous kimono of Madame Butterfly for the Scala of Milan.

The house of Hermès goes back to 1837. The original Hermès, Thierry, was a saddler, which accounts for the horsy theme of many of their celebrated scarves. Twice a year the illustrious house on Faubourg Saint-Honoré offers multitudes of its reject scarves at a discount price, causing endless queues on the street and unbelievable havoc within: respectable middle-class women can be seen hanging on stubbornly to their favourite scarves or grabbing savagely coveted ones from unwary neighbours whose only helpless reprisal is a hysterical torrent of abuse.

Before the Revolution the *Ancien Régime* had no use for *haute couture*. There were no dictatorial upstarts in those days to dictate to women how to dress in the court – fashion was made by the court and for the court. There were no fashion shows, no catwalks, no models in the court – the courtiers were their own models and spectators at once, the ballroom their catwalk. But with the advent of plutocracy *haute couture* came into its own in its new stronghold, the 8th arrondissement. The dwellings of these new plutocrats were those solid opulent buildings extending along Haussmann's newly opened tree-lined avenues in the *beaux quartiers*, equipped with more modern conveniences than any of your aristocratic *hôtels* from pre-revolutionary days – some even boasted the installation of hydraulic lifts! The wealthier members of this society, those who had amassed stupendous fortunes of solid, palpable cash in the real-estate speculation due to Haussmann's gigantic works and on the stock exchange, built themselves *hôtels particuliers*, namely around the newly created Parc de Monceau.

Constructed in a true Napoleon III style, which basically implied no style at all but a hybrid display of opulence, they abounded in heavy hangings, Venetian mirrors and gilding. Such is the *hôtel* of the wealthy speculator Monsieur Saccard, Zola's hero in *La Curée*, significantly situated on rue de Monceau. As a matter of fact, real-estate speculation had already begun in the early 19th century to which bears witness the neighbourhood of Europe, on the north-eastern edge of the arrondissement, which sprang up through the initiative of speculative developers to the profit of share holders. Streets bearing the names of European cities were to radiate from Place de l'Europe in what was meant to be an elegant neighbourhood, but the construction of the Saint-Lazare railway station on its southern fringe reversed its destiny. Only the establishment of the Paris Music Conservatory on rue de Madrid salvaged the neighbourhood, turning it into the stronghold of the string dealers of the capital, among them world-renowned names such as Etienne Vatelot. (In 1990, the Conservatory moved to the Villette neighbourhood in the 19th arrondissement and the premises are now used by the less prestigious Regional Conservatory).

It was Haussmann's transformation of Paris that made possible the accumulation of wealth on such a large scale. In Zola's *La Curée* a *tableau* is being staged in Monsieur Saccard's *hôtel particulier*. Gold coins are scattered around, as befitting its title 'The Triumph of Plutus'. The symbol of Monsieur Saccard's *hôtel* is the huge, overpowering dining table around which gathers this profit-seeking society devoted to earthly perishable goods, and whose favourite occupation is eating. And fornication.

Many members of the fair sex were quick to get the idea – actresses, courtesans, *grandes cocottes* and other kept women of obscure descent, all shades of *horizontales* who looked down unabashed on your ordinary street walker. Emulating the likes of the Pompadour, some even ended up, like herself, as respectable Marquises! Why not? After all, since the reign of Napoleon titles had also become consumer goods! Some presided over weekly *salons* similarly to their illustrious predecessors.

There were others who had respectability from the start, having been born into cultivated bourgeois families such as Geneviève Straus, the daughter of an *Académicien*, the famous composer of *La Juive*, Fromental Halévy, and the widow of his student Georges Bizet. Remarried to the fabulously rich Emile Straus, her prestigious *salon* on the corner of the recently opened Avenue de Messine and Boulevard Haussmann was the stronghold of illustrious members of the literary and artistic world – the inseparable Ludovic Halévy and Meilhac, Degas, Maupassant (hopelessly in love with her) . . . and her close friend Marcel Proust who met in her home the assiduous Charles Haas, known to Proust's readers as the celebrated Swann. Even members of the old, aristocratic Faubourg Saint-Germain did not spurn her *salon* despite her Jewish origins, and would deign cross the river to attend her gatherings. It seemed that Plutus had eradicated all previous barriers; but the Dreyfus Affair was to prove otherwise.

Although Plutus was the great healer of France's bruises, the humiliating defeat to the Prussians and the amputation of Alsace-Lorraine were still an open wound. Having crushed any vague hope of liberation that the oppressed people of Paris had nurtured since the collapse of the *Ancien Régime*, having been born out of the ashes of tens of thousands of slaughtered *Communards*, the Third Republic could only rely on exacerbated patriotism as a unifying semblance of credibility. Both Dreyfus and his wife were the affluent products of the Plutocratic Third Republic and as such settled, naturally, in its stronghold of the 8th – at 24 rue François Ier. Pathetically and tragically Alfred Dreyfus shared the Republic's patriotic fervour, yearning to belong to the national community, which was denied him by the likes of Drumont: 'As a Jew and as a German he detests the French,' the latter wrote in *La Libre Parole.*

Geneviève Straus's *salon* did not escape the Affair unscathed; like the rest of society her *salon* included supporters of both camps and she lost the friendship of such *anti-Dreyfusards* as Jules Lemaître. However, with the help of Joseph Reinach, Alfred Dreyfus's staunchest defender and her own close friend, her home became the stronghold of the *Dreyfusards* and it was here that her friends, from Marcel Proust to Halévy, organised the first petition to l'*Aurore.* Geneviève did not stop at that and even succeeded in persuading Waldeck-Rousseau to appoint the *Dreyfusard*, Gallifet, minister of war.

But the Third Republic had better reasons to close the Affair once and for all. Coming up in 1900, the Universal Exposition was seriously threatened by growing anti-French feelings abroad. If every Frenchman secretly dreamt of *revenche* over Germany in the battlefield, the government was aware of the economic profit to be drawn from the fair, not to mention the sheer thrill of self-aggrandisement.

Sprawling between the gardens of the Champs-Elysées and the Seine, the gigantic Grand Palais took three years to build and cost as much as 25 million gold francs! With its modest counter-part Le Petit Palais, it was built to the glory of art and, like Moloch, swallowed everything – from the traditional *pompiers** to the *Fauves.* . . And in between, it housed the autumn car show – an elegant occasion in those early days of the automobile – and the spring horse races. Situated in an arrondissement open to the future, it experimented in everything as it still does. At present even bits of the University of Paris have taken up residence here, for lack of space elsewhere.

* Uncreative academic painters in the second half of the 19th century

Today, nearly a century later, as the veteran pedestrian makes his way up the Champs-Elysées, upset by the crude sight, bemoaning bygone days, he may be reminded that the seeds of this age of impatient greed had been sown way back in 1793, several hundred metres behind him, when Louis XVI and Marie-Antoinette had sacrificed their heads to Modernity on the Place de la Concorde, the gateway to the 8th arrondissement. Meanwhile Paris is continuing its inexorable westward move: ahead, the compound of high-rises of La Défense obstructs the horizon beyond the Arc de Triomphe, heralding the take over by the world of technocrats. Few will remember the time when the Arc de Triomphe stood majestically on top of the hill of Chaillot against the open horizon, against the timeless infinite, against the halo of the setting sun, whose reclining rays streamed in golden splendour underneath its arch – a man-made cityscape of divine inspiration.

WHERE TO WALK

FROM PLACE DE LA CONCORDE
TO THE ARC DE TRIOMPHE

It is from Place de la Concorde that the Champs-Elysées should first be seen, and seen once more after dark – a bewitching vision of dazzling splendour, justifiably the highlight of any 'Paris by Night' tour.

When **PLACE DE LA CONCORDE** was laid out in 1757 as a site for Bouchardon's statue of Louis XV, *Le Bien Aimé*, it was called Place Louis XV. The beautiful statue was commissioned in 1748 to mark the King's miraculous recovery from the pox, which, according to the Church, had been inflicted on the monarch as a divine retribution for his scandalous love life.

Once completed the statue needed a suitable site, which was not easily to be found in a congested city. It was decided therefore to lay out a new square for its display, to be designed by the prestigious architect, Gabriel. The uninhabited stretch of land lying west of the Tuileries, the natural geographic extension of the Louvre, was the only conceivable site for such a project. His Majesty was

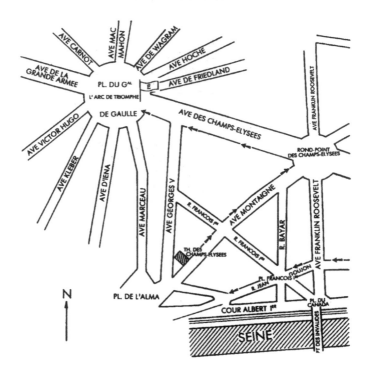

portrayed seated on a horse and dressed as a Roman emperor, his head adorned with a laurel wreath as befitted the king who had defeated the English and the Dutch at Fontenoy, in Belgium, in 1745. (As a matter of fact, the credit should have gone to the Maréchal de Saxe, Louis XV having merely put in an appearance on the battlefield.) The King's face expressed the kindness and clemency he was loved for by his people, while on the pedestal four bronze figures, sculpted by Pigalle, embodied his virtues: Force, Justice, Prudence and Peace. However, by the time the square was inaugurated on 20 June 1763, Louis XV had long ceased to be the *Bien Aimé* and had instead become the unpopular king who had dragged France into a seven-year war that ended with the loss of her Indian and Canadian possessions. Indeed, a couple of days after the inauguration of the statue and square a placard was tied round the horse's neck:

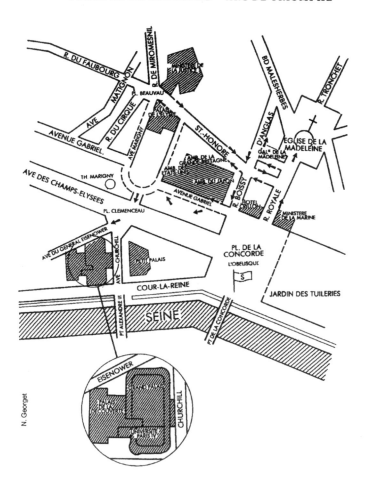

N. Georget

Oh! la belle statue! Oh, le beau piédestal!
Les Vertus sont à pied, le Vice est à cheval.

Oh, hail to the bonny statue, the pedestal fair and bright,
Virtue sits at its feet, Vice sits astride.

On the northern side of the square, on either side of rue Royale,
Gabriel built the twin palaces that frame the church of the Made-
leine in the background. The Ministry of the Marine, then the
Crown's storehouse, was on the eastern side. To the west was the

superb **Hôtel de Crillon**, named after the Duc de Crillon, in whose descendants' hands it remained until 1907. Both have splendid interiors but the Ministry, naturally, is closed to visitors except on special occasions. With its breathtaking view of the Place de la Concorde and beyond, the Crillon is possibly the most desirable hotel in Paris and has hosted the most privileged and celebrated of visitors.

With the American Embassy located next door, at 2 Avenue Gabriel, it became a magnet for wealthy American visitors who appreciated, as they still do, the sweeping urban landscape of a square described by Fitzgerald as 'one of the predestined centres of the world'. Fitzgerald loved the bar, where he used to meet Hemingway for drinks. Sadly, it was done away with in the mid-1980s to make room for the restaurant L'Obélisque. Owing to its exceptional location, the Crillon also served as a setting for some momentous historic events, such as the signing of the Treaty of Friendship and Trade between France and the newly independent 13 colonies of the United States, the respective signatories being Louis XVI for France and Benjamin Franklin for the United States.

During World War I the hotel was requisitioned and served as British, then American headquarters. All the preparatory sessions that led to the Versailles Treaty in 1919 and the meeting at which the first agreement of the Covenant of the League of Nations was signed were held in the hotel's sumptuous Salon des Aigles. During all this time President Woodrow Wilson occupied one of its suites. The Germans too picked out the Crillon as their headquarters during the Occupation, followed in 1944 by General Eisenhower, who made it the Supreme Headquarters for the Allied Expeditionary Force, after Paris had been liberated. Some of the fiercest fighting of the liberation had indeed taken place right in front of the hotel. With peace restored, the Crillon became the Paris *pied-à-terre* of such American celebrities as Orson Welles, Gregory Peck and Jackie Kennedy.

It was in 1790 that the square assumed its present aspect and that sculptor Cousteau's horses (*les chevaux de Marly*) were placed at the entrance to the Champs-Elysées as suggested by the painter David. The square was renamed Place de la Révolution, the equestrian statue of Louis XV was sent to the foundry and the stones recovered from the demolished Bastille fortress came in handy for the construction of the bridge of La Concorde. But the two matching façades of the church of the Madeleine and of the National Assembly had yet to face each other on either side of the square. It was Napoleon, a lover of both Greek architecture and grandiose vistas, who had the brilliant idea of adding a neo-classical façade to the 18th-century Palais de Bourbon, across the bridge of Concorde to match the style of the Madeleine.

With the bridge running on the axis of rue Royale, he created a near-perfect symmetry from the centre of the square, in harmony with Gabriel's palaces, and opened an additional breathtaking vista, perpendicular to that of the Champs-Elysées. However, the Obelisk of Luxor that marks the centre was erected only in 1836, a technical feat fraught with danger, of which Philippe Lebas, the engineer in charge of the operation, was fully aware. 'On 25 October, already in the morning, more than two hundred spectators scattered on Place de la Concorde, on the terrace of the Tuileries, on the Avenue des Champs-Elysées, waiting to attend the last act of a drama which might not be devoid of a terrible incident; for a misunderstood order, a badly secured cable, a bent bolt . . . would have caused a dreadful catastrophe: the shattered obelisk, the loss of millions, the hundred or so workmen crushed inevitably by the collapse of the rig. I confess I could not think, without some sort of anxiety, of the deep responsibility that weighed upon me.'

The Obelisk was donated to Charles X in 1829 by Mohammed Ali, Viceroy of Egypt, but, by the time it reached Paris in 1833, Louis-Philippe had replaced him on the throne. Later the Baron Haussmann wanted to remove it and restore the square to its original aspect, but for once the wilful Baron did not have his way and today this most ancient monument of Paris, with its 13th-century BC hieroglyphics celebrating Ramses II, is the square's most famous landmark. The two impressive fountains, instead of the four originally planned, are the work of Hittorff who was inspired by the fountains of Saint Peter's Square in Rome and were likewise erected during the July Monarchy.

Place de la Concorde had not been completed on 30 June 1770, when the introverted Dauphin and future Louis XVI came here to mark his debut in public life on the occasion of his marriage to

Marie-Antoinette. The high and lowly poured into the square from rue Royale, then its only access, the 'high' in their carriages, the 'lowly' on foot and rather tipsy, the fountains of Paris having been filled with wine to mark the celebration. The day, however, ended tragically, when the 'Temple de l'Hymen' ('the Temple of Marriage'), put up in honour of the newly-wedded couple, was set ablaze accidentally by the fireworks which had been meant as the highlight of the celebration. One hundred and thirty-three people perished either in the fire or trampled by the panic-stricken crowds, an ominous start for the career of a most unfortunate heir to the throne. And it was in this same square, on 21 January 1793, that Louis XVI made his final exit, followed in October by his wife.

By that time the square had been renamed Place de la Révolution and a colossal statue of Liberty in a red bonnet, a spear in her hand, replaced Louis XV on the pedestal, a silent witness of the bloody activities of the guillotine. Hitherto erected in the courtyard of the Carrousel, the guillotine made its first appearance on Place de la Révolution in November 1792. Its victims on that first occasion were common criminals who had broken into what had become the nation's storehouse and stolen many of the crown jewels.

The guillotine was then erected in front of the storehouse, to set an example at the scene of the crime, after which it was not to be seen again until the terrible morning of 21 January 1793, when it was to perform the terrible act of regicide. This time it was moved for the purpose to a site only a dozen metres away from the statue of Liberty, which was perhaps intended to legitimise what was in fact an ignominious crime. The murder may have even been a personal vendetta, for at the head of the drummers who accompanied the King to his death, was an illegitimate son of Louis XV and uncle of Louis XVI, the dancer Morphise. . . On a Monday morning at 10.22 the bloody act was carried out, under duress, by the public executioner Monsieur Sanson, a loyal subject of his Majesty who retired soon after this traumatic event. Some nine months later, on 16 October, his son Henri was ordered to execute his Queen.

Madame Roland, a fervent *Girondin**, was not fooled by the ideological bankruptcy of the Revolution. When her turn came to mount the scaffold in 1793 she turned towards the statue and called

* Member of the *Gironde* party (1791–3), who advocated moderate republican principles.

out, 'Liberty, Liberty! What crimes are committed in your name!' Her husband, the Minister of the Interior for the past year, took his own life on hearing of her execution.

By then the guillotine had become a permanent fixture on Place de la Révolution, halfway between the statue and the entrance to the Tuileries Gardens. It remained there from 11 May 1793 to 9 June 1794, when it was transferred to the Bastille, and was brought back on 28 July 1794 (10 Thermidor, year II in the Revolutionary calendar), for the execution of the executioners – Robespierre, Saint-Just and fellow *Montagnards**, the final act in this episode of terror. 1,119 people were guillotined at Place de la Révolution, to the wild cheers of gloating *tricoteuses*, as against 1,306 at Place du Trône Renversé (now Nation) and 73 at the Bastille. Among the victims were Madame du Barry, Louis XV's last mistress, Danton, Charlotte Corday and Louis-Philippe d'Orléans, Duc de Chartres, the King's cousin turned Republican and consequently renamed Philippe Egalité. He was a much richer man than the King and it was rumoured that, behind his egalitarian convictions, he nurtured covert hopes of recovering the reins of government for himself. When the Republic got rid of him in his turn, he walked to his fate with courage and dignity.

After the carnage, the satiated 'good people of Paris' were ready for social truce and to follow an unknown Corsican towards greater destinies abroad. Accordingly the blood-stains were wiped out and the square renamed Place de la Concorde, but the sinister horror hovered for a while, and when Chateaubriand returned from his exile in England it still 'had the shabby melancholy, the deserted air of an old amphitheatre.' In all logic it retrieved its initial name, Place Louis XV, with the restoration of the Bourbon dynasty in 1815, and just as logically was renamed Place de la Concorde with the accession to the throne of Louis-Philippe of the rivalling Orléans branch of the family, the son of Philippe Egalité and guardian of the new bourgeois order.

Some 150 years later Place de la Concorde was again the scene of human fickleness. On 25 August 1944 a surge of Parisians here acclaimed General de Gaulle, who was coming down the Champs-Elysées from the Arc de Triomphe, thus effacing four

---

* Members of the Radical Party, also known as *Jacobins* because they gathered in the premises of the Jacobin Friars.

years of humiliation that had been punctuated by the daily march of a company of the Wehrmacht down the Champs-Elysées to Place de la Concorde. Only four months earlier, on 20 April 1944, another surge of Parisians (or was it the same?) had cheered Maréchal Pétain.

In the last few decades Place de la Concorde has witnessed a new form of belligerency, in the shape of Parisian motorists using it to let off steam. You will therefore enjoy the relative peace of the gardens of the Champs-Elysées on either side of the avenue, all the way up to the Rond-Point-des-Champs-Elysées. Try to arrive in the early morning, before the hassle and bustle, so as to recapture the light and atmosphere you may remember from some Impressionist paintings. But first turn into rue Royale for a detour to the church of the Madeleine and thereabouts.

Gabriel was commissioned to build the façades of the new RUE ROYALE at the same time as the square and he himself lived in the *hôtel* at no. 8, next door to Madame de Staël, the daughter of the Finance Minister Necker, who lived at no. 6. Rue Royale was opened along the site of the city walls built by Louis XIII and, thanks to Gabriel's talent, became one of the most beautiful streets in Paris, attracting many prominent residents. Among them was Monsieur Suard at no. 13, the Royal Censor notorious for banning Beaumarchais's *Marriage of Figaro*.

It was mainly during the Belle Epoque and after World War I that the fashionable set flocked to rue Royale, where their favourite haunt was **Maxime's**, still standing at no. 1 (and now also occupying the neighbouring building). In 1891, Maxime Gaillard, who was working in a bar further down the street, bought an ice-cream parlour here on the verge of bankruptcy. The previous year the establishment had been ransacked by infuriated Parisians, its owner having taken it into his head to deck his shop window with a German flag – and on 14 July, of all days! Maxime's ownership did not last long, nor did his successor's. It was Max Lebaudy, a sugar manufacturer, who launched it into international fame, helped by the visits of such illustrious figures as the Prince of Wales, and also by that apostrophe and 's' clinging to the name of the now forgotten Maxime Gaillard, a little appendage imported from across the Channel, the ultimate chic that made all the difference. Today

Maxime's has preserved both its 1900 setting and its name but the aura is gone, not through any fault of its own but through the changing of times. As part of the eating and entertainment industry of Pierre Cardin, which has tentacles in New York and Beijing, how could it be otherwise? The dilapidated state of Gabriel's façades along the noisy, traffic-ridden rue Royale is proof of the pollution that has largely driven the privileged away from the centres of big cities.

Across the street, at no. 10, the flower shop **Lachaume** has also stuck out – since 1845! – resisting both car fumes and the changing times. Its flowers still diffuse the wonderful fragrance that so enchanted Marcel Proust, an habitué of rue Royale. **Christofle** moved to no. 9 rue Royale only before World War I but his career went back to the early reign of Louis-Philippe and during the Second Empire he became purveyor to the court of Napoleon III. **Lalique**, his next-door neighbour at no. 11, on the other hand, moved here from rue de la Paix only in 1936, enchanting passers-by with his extraordinary glass wares (don't hesitate to visit the premises). Although the Art Nouveau jewellery he created during the 1890s brought him great renown and wealth, he gradually turned to glassmaking instead. He first made scent bottles, notably the one for the *Libellule* (Dragonfly) still reminiscent of his Art Nouveau jewellery but already heralding Art Deco. Another scent bottle was *L'Oiseau de Feu* (*The Firebird*), a stunning masterpiece inspired by Stravinsky's famous ballet, which Diaghilev's *Ballets Russes* created in 1910. Lalique's work was the highlight of the 1925 Decorative Arts Exhibition, alongside that of Brand (wrought iron) and Ruhlman (furniture). His sculpted glass panels were inserted into the fabulous metal framework Brand had made for the main gate in front of the Grand Palais and the obelisk-shaped glass fountain he created for the Esplanade des Invalides – magically luminous by night – was the jewel in the crown.

The **Brasserie Weber** at no. 21 closed down only in 1961. Before World War I the foremost literati, journalists and actors would crowd on to its leather benches after the show, among them Marcel Proust, then a young chronicler for *Le Figaro*, 'wrapped up in summer as well as in winter in an enormous cardigan,' as Léon Daudet recorded. Across the street, at no. 16, **Ladurée**, still in the hands of the founding family, has preserved its velvety, padded atmosphere and thus numbers among its clientele several genteel, elderly ladies, who come here for afternoon tea, served in delicate, flowery bone china and accompanied by home-made macaroons and dainty sandwiches. At no. 27 stood the no less prestigious Larue, while **Lucas Carton**, which opened back in 1880 at no. 26 Place de la Madeleine, on the corner of Boulevard Malesherbes, is still one of the most highly rated restaurants in Paris. The turn-of-the-century style of its façade is matched by an extraordinary period decoration within, where wrought iron and wood have been used in the best of taste.

At the end of the street, the **church of the Madeleine** was built by Napoleon in a neo-classical style that matches the façade he ingeniously contrived for the Palais Bourbon, at the other end of the vista. The flower market on the eastern side of the church, on the busy, noisy **PLACE DE LA MADELEINE**, takes us back to the days of leisurely shopping at the famous food shop **Fauchon** at no. 9, or of savouring deliciously fresh oysters or other gastronomic dishes at **Prunier** still going strong at no. 9 rue Duphot, off the square. The celebrated **Durand**, at no. 2 Place de la Madeleine, frequented by artists, literati and politicians, was where Zola wrote *J'accuse*. It was opened back in 1830 but was replaced by Thomas Cook early in the 20th century, when the Madeleine was a centre of British tourism and one of the five or six landmarks of Paris featured on the picture postcard one would send back home.

A primitive chapel stood in the area already in the early Middle Ages, catering to the little borough of Ville l'Evêque, called after the Bishop of Paris who owned roughly all the territory of the present 8th arrondissement. The first precise information concerning a church dedicated to Madeleine dates from 1238. It stood on the site of the present no. 8 Boulevard Malesherbes and faced east, towards Jerusalem, according to tradition. Reconstructed several times in the course of its history, it became a parish church in 1636, by which time it was decided to rebuild it. In 1660 the Grande Mademoiselle, Duchesse de Montpensier and daughter of François, Duc de Guise, came to lay the cornerstone of the new church, but with the rapid growth of the Faubourg Saint-Honoré, by the next century there was a need for a more glamorous church, a project which took shape with the opening of the Place Louis XV in 1763, since 'the monument would serve as a pleasant ending to rue Royale.' For aesthetic reasons, however, the altar was directed to the north so that the front of the church would face the square and rue Royale, lying to the south.

The church was meant to have the shape of a Greek cross, topped by a dome, but work came to a halt with the outbreak of the Revolution, when the old church on the present Boulevard Malesherbes was torn down. A suitable use was sought by Napoleon for the new monument: the Banque de France, the stock exchange, the Tribunal du Commerce, the Imperial Library or an opera house were the options he toyed with before finally opting for a more uplifting function, the glorification of the Grande Armée. In 1802 he proclaimed the monument a 'Temple à la Gloire'. 'I mean a monument such as there is in Athens and does not exist in Paris,' he wrote.

A contest was organised and the winner, Vignon, was entrusted with the scheme. A few years later Napoleon endowed Paris with a second neo-classical monument, the stock exchange. With the collapse of the Empire the monument was restored to its original Christian function but was not altered. It is therefore the only church in Paris lacking both a bell-tower and a cross. Despite its austere architecture and generally uninspiring interior, Tout-Paris called it its own from the start and still likes to celebrate its weddings and funerals here. Thousands gathered to pay their last respects to Josephine Baker in 1975, to the Corsican singer Tino Rossi in 1983, and in 1992 to Marlene Dietrich, before her remains were flown back to her birthplace, Berlin. In 1849 Mozart's *Requiem* was performed here on the occasion of Chopin's funeral and in 1887 Gabriel Fauré's *Requiem* was premiered here, though in its still unfinished state. The complete work was performed here for his own funeral in 1924.

Cross over Place de la Madeleine to the west, on the southern corner of Boulevard Malesherbes. Next to Lucas Carton is the **Galerie de la Madeleine**, which, like other arcades in central Paris, was opened in the 19th century to allow for a pleasant stroll among attractive shops on rainy days. Retrace your steps into rue Royale and turn right at no. 25 into the **Village Royal**, an elegant alley lined with fashionable shops and cafés, leading to rue Boissy-d'Anglas.

Turn right into RUE BOISSY-D'ANGLAS, once the haunt of Jean Cocteau and his 'clan', Erik Satie and the *Groupe des Six* (Poulenc, Auric, Durey, Honegger, Milhaud, Germaine Tailleferre), to whom he acted as patron. Indeed, at no. 28 was the celebrated **Boeuf sur le Toît**, whose odd name was borrowed from an article published in 1919 in *Littérature* entitled *Le Boeuf sur le Toît (Samba carnavalesque)*, which enthusiastically described the Carnival of Rio and was signed Jacarémirim. It mentioned the meeting during the Carnival between the author and Darius Milhaud, who turned out to be one and the same person. The exotic pseudonym was taken from the Brazilian Indian language and means 'crocodile'. *Le Boeuf sur le Toît (O Boi No Telhado)* was the name of the samba that had so impressed Milhaud: 'I adore Brazil. How full of life and fantasy this music is.' He was so inspired by its lively rhythms, their repetitive monotony, the contrasting colours of the blue dresses of the dancers against their dark bodies that he intended to write a ballet by the same name. Instead, it ended as a score for a pantomime with a story by Cocteau, who, however, set it in a bar in the United States rather than South America, the only concession to the Carnival being the grotesque negro masks. As Cocteau put it, 'It is an American farce, written by a Parisian who has never been in America.'

It opened in February 1920 for four performances only, at the Comédie des Champs-Elysées theatre, a 400-seat hall above the celebrated theatre of the Avenue Montaigne (described below). The premiere was a big social affair and included the Shah of Iran and his suite among the audience. Both public and critics loved it, but not so Milhaud himself who was unhappy with the way his original intention to produce a divertissement celebrating the Carnival had been distorted. So remote was the work from Brazil that when it was later produced at the Coliseum in London it was renamed *The Nothing-Doing Bar*.

On the night of 10 January 1922 the Brazilian samba in its French translation, *Le Boeuf sur le Toît*, became the name of a new bar on rue Boissy-d'Anglas. Its owner, Louis Moysès, moved to these larger premises from the less convenient location on rue Duphot, where he had a bar called le Gaïa. From the start Le Boeuf attracted the artist community, as it was located strategically halfway between Montmartre and Montparnasse. Moysès had obtained permission from Milhaud and Cocteau to name the establishment after their work and, of course, the 'clan' and everyone else was present at the opening. It became a sensation right away, rivalling Maxime's and the Moulin-Rouge, one of the 'musts' of Paris, of which Cocteau later said: 'The Boeuf became not a bar at all but a kind of club, the meeting-place of all the best people in Paris, from all spheres of life . . . the prettiest women, poets, musicians, businessmen, publishers – everybody met everybody at the Boeuf.'

But it is with the *Groupe des Six* that the name is first and foremost associated. Their spokesman was Jean Cocteau, about whom malevolent Dadaist tongues had spread the rumour that he had actually become the bar manager! In short, this was the mecca of Tout-Paris as Léon-Paul Fargue observed, 'The Tout-Paris who cannot keep in one place, who are bored, who change their grocery shop ten times in one evening to escape something they will never escape, barged into the 'Boeuf' regularly and never moved out again. . . Marcel Proust often ventured in, amused and pleasant.' When a couple of years later Moysès's sister took the Boeuf to rue du Colisée off the Champs-Elysées, it became just another Parisian café. Nothing has survived on rue Boissy-d'Anglas to remind us of its short-lived glory. No. 28 rue Boissy-d'Anglas is now an optician's.

Some two and the half centuries earlier, in 1687, the musician Lully died next door, on the site of no. 30. While conducting a concert, he hurt his foot with his baton as he was beating the rhythm on the floor, then the customary way of marking time. The wound became gangrenous and proved fatal. Some say that it is because of this accident that the old way of conducting was abandoned in favour of the present method.

You will now reach the fashionable FAUBOURG SAINT-HONORÉ, heralded by the house of Hermès on the right-hand side corner. The street is a window-shopper's paradise, lined with the ready-to-wear goods of such prestigious *haute couture* houses as Yves St-Laurent, Lanvin, Louis Féraud and Christian Lacroix. This is also the old road that once led to the village of Roule, as can be perceived, here and there, from the odd rustic house that has survived, though most of the houses display elegant 18th-century architecture, reminders of the splendid past of the Faubourg Saint-

Honoré. The first few buildings of the street, which starts at rue Royale to the left of rue Boissy-d'Anglas, were burnt down by the Commune in 1871, but from no. 5 on there are many fine buildings.

Turn left if you wish to explore the beginning of the street. No. 5 was home to the fashion house Henri à la Pensée, founded here back in 1809 and for many generations a symbol of Parisian chic. It is no accident that there is no no. 13: Felix's hairdressing establishment chose to be no. 15 so as not to vex the highly superstitious Empress Eugénie, who was their most illustrious client. Notice the elegant mansion at no. 14, decorated with beautiful wrought iron. From 1811 to 1835 it housed the town-hall of what used to be the 1st arrondissement (the old salle des fêtes can still be seen inside). Jeanne Lanvin's house still stands at no. 22, next door to Hermès at no. 24, founded by Thierry Hermès as a saddling house in 1837. The **British Embassy** is at no. 39. This is how Nancy Mitford describes it in Don't Tell Alfred through the eyes of the British Ambassador's wife, when she first arrives from the Gare du Nord in the 1950s: 'the large, beautiful, honey-coloured house, in its quiet courtyard, seemed a haven of delight.'

The mansion, which is indeed beautiful, was built in 1720 for Paul-François Béthune-Charost and is therefore known as **l'Hôtel de Charost**. In 1803 it became the property of Napoleon's sister, Pauline Borghèse, who, owing to the unfortunate turn taken by her brother's ventures, had to sell it in 1814, ironically, to the British government, whose representative, equally ironically, was Napoleon's arch enemy, the Duke of Wellington! Among the Embassy's honoured guests can be mentioned the Emperor of Austria, Queen Victoria and Edward VII. Somerset Maugham was born here in 1874, one of several babies delivered in a wing of the Embassy which was turned into a maternity ward after France's defeat by the Prussians. This was to enable British subjects born on French territory to evade conscription in the French army as was required by a new bill.

You will now approach **PLACE BEAUVAU** with the Ministry of the Interior on your right and the main entrance to the residence of the President of the Republic to your left, the **Palais de l'Elysée**, once the Paris pied-à-terre of the Pompadour. The Pompadour left it to the Royal family, who used it as a furniture storehouse for a while. Eventually Louis XVI sold it to his cousin, the Duchesse de Bourbon, who emigrated to England during the Revolution. The abandoned mansion fell into the hands of an impresario who turned it into an amusement park. As this did not bring in much business, his enterprising daughter decided to set up stalls and booths in the gardens instead and divided the house into apartments which she let out. This is how a little boy by the name of Alfred de Vigny, later to become one of France's great romantic poets, came to grow up in the Palais de l'Elysée. He described his childhood there in his *Memoirs*. Napoleon recovered it for the use of his family and eventually it became the residence of the President of the French Republic, Louis-Napoleon Bonaparte, his nephew. But he was not to remain here for long. On the night of 1 December 1851, while numerous guests were assembled in the magnificent halls, he retired discreetly to his cabinet, where he joined his fellow conspirators with whom he had planned a coup for the following day. 15,000 opponents were arrested and deported overseas. On 20 December he moved from the Republican abode of the Elysée to the royal abode of the Tuileries Palace, a more suitable environment for the future Emperor Napoleon III, which he was to become in 1852. It was only with the advent of the Third Republic, after the unsettled times of the Prussian War and the *Commune*, that the Palais de l'Elysée became the permanent residence of the President of the French Republic.

Retrace your steps to Place de la Concorde by way of rue Boissy d'Anglas and turn right into the leafy **AVENUE GABRIEL**, a lovely walk as it runs between the gardens of the mansions of Faubourg Saint-Honoré and those of the Champs-Elysées, strewn with clumps of flowers and elegant pavilions. This was the playground of the young Proust, who is honoured with a path marked by a plaque, Allée Marcel Proust, just before the pavilion l'Espace Cardin, at no. 1 Avenue Gabriel. Pierre Cardin's establishment houses both a restaurant and a theatre but is, unavoidably, a pale shadow of the celebrated Ambassadeurs which stood on this site until 1929. On a warm summer night its open-air café, illuminated by beckoning lights against the background of slender trees, was enlivened by variety shows and music, attended by Paris's scintillating *beau monde*. Its rivals, l'Alcazar d'Eté, the first 'singing café' or *café-concert* in France, and l'Horloge have disappeared without leaving any trace. Today the premises of Pavillon Gabriel next to Espace Cardin are used for television programmes. Every now and then a man in grey suit and tie is seen stepping in or out, attaché case in hand. The days of Gay Paris, when Mistinguett and Maurice Chevalier performed at the Alcazar are light years away.

The charmingly pompous pavilion next door stands as a happy reminder of those days. Surmounted by a conpicuous *fin de siècle* dome and topped by an equally conspicuous Cupid shooting his arrow against the sky, this eclectic piece of architecture, a mishmash of all possible 'neo' styles, was once Le Petit-Paillard, a place of ribald pleasures, as indicated by its name (*paillard* means 'wanton'). It was built for the 1900 Exhibition and all the crowned heads of Europe honoured it with their presence, among them Alphonso of Spain and the future Edward VII. Today it is yet another excellent pricey restaurant, l'Elysée-Lenôtre. As you meander through the pretty lawns and shrubberies, you may picture young Proust playing hide-and-seek with his sweetheart, the red-haired, freckled Gilberte.

Champs-Elysées: châlet de nécessité

In the afternoons and all day Thursdays, when schools were closed, the gardens were frequented by the children of the upper and the upper middle classes. Sometimes young Marcel would discuss literature or recite his favourite poets – notably Leconte de Lisle – on the gravel-walk of the Alcazar, while others played the game of prisoner's base. Although the Alcazar is gone, the '*chalet de nécessité*' (public conveniences), described by Proust, is still standing (along the Avenue des Champs-Elysées level with Pavillon Gabriel). Proust the narrator reports that his grandmother once had a stroke in this 'little rustic theatre', a place run by a proud, fastidious woman whom he nicknamed the Marquise, even though she depended on tips for her living. Her counterpart today, known as *Dame Pipi*, no longer depends on the whims of clients such as the narrator's grandmother, but charges admission at a fixed price and closes down at lunch-time. But the dignified cast-iron structure has remained intact and has preserved its mahogany cabin doors with their brass handles and its plain, unpretentious white tiles.

Only one carousel was there on our last visit, a gaudy product of the plastic age and a sad substitute for those period pieces, first introduced in 1777, with their proud, galloping, wooden horses, which delighted young Cocteau. Some wooden booths still stand under the chestnut trees but they sell hot dogs, hamburgers and Coca Cola, rather than the gingerbread, barley sugar, and lemonade Jean Cocteau remembered from his childhood. At least the toy drums and windmills have survived. So has the old Punch and Judy theatre by Avenue Matignon, a picturesque structure still bearing the sign VRAI GUIGNOLET, where the rudimentary traditions of Guignol have been preserved since 1818 – a magical place filled with the innocent cries of children.

Before you reach Avenue de Marigny, running at right angles through the gardens, you will notice the spectacular wrought-iron gate of the gardens of the **Palais de l'Elysée** and may also notice that they encroach on the gardens of the Champs-Elysée. Madame de Pompadour, the one-time landlady of the place, had natural priority over the public gardens that lay outside and saw no harm in expanding her own territory at their expense. She would have taken more had there not been a general outcry, nor did she have any qualms about asking her brother, the Marquis de Marigny who was in charge of the Champs-Elysées, to chop down the trees on the other side of the avenue so as to clear the view from her palace to the Seine and the Invalides! This did not enhance her popularity, already damaged by her extravagance. The curtains alone for the numerous windows were estimated at 5,000 louis each. By the time she was through with this game of interior decoration, it was a genuine palace, worthy of her royal companion, stamped with the coat of arms of his family and enlaced L's everywhere. And yet she hardly ever slept here. Instead she used it for splendid balls and receptions. In his *Paris-Guide* Ferdinand de Lasteyrie tells of one occasion when a flock of sheep, bedecked in pretty pink and green ribbons, was brought into the mirrored hall to create a pastoral atmosphere (*bergerie*), much in vogue among France's decadent aristocracy, as Watteau's paintings attest. The guests were enchanted by the exquisite sight. The frightened sheep, however, failed to get the point and tried to escape. A gilt-horned ram, mistaking his own reflection in the mirror for a rival, charged right in and ransacked the entire place. Retreating to the other end of the hall, the hitherto delighted ladies now turned to shrieking and swooning, while their cavaliers roared with laughter.

In June 1763 the inauguration of the statue of Louis XV in the new square was accompanied by a magnificent display of fireworks, which the Pompadour watched together with her brother Marigny from one of the 19 red linen tents put up in front of the Palais de Bourbon for the occasion. Each was lined with scarlet damask and lit by a beautiful chandelier. After this the Marquise put on an even finer display of fireworks at her own dwelling of the Elysée. This was her last appearance in public: the following year she was dead. The laced L's for Louis have long disappeared and today a proud Republican cock crowns the regal gate.

The **Théâtre de Marigny,** across **Avenue de Marigny,** is one of the better-known theatres of Paris and often boasts top of the bill names. Hittorff's historical Bouffes Parisiens d'Eté, which Offenbach himself directed for five years, stood here until 1883, when it was replaced by Charles Garnier with the present building; it remains the oldest theatre in the area. Offenbach took over the previous theatre in 1855, foreseeing its certain success at the time of

Champs-Elysées: Fontaine des Quatre Saisons

the Universal Exposition, largely to be held at the Palais de l'Industrie across the avenue. When his five-year lease expired, the theatre was taken over by Deburau, the son of the famous mime from the Théâtre des Funambules on the Boulevard du Temple, more generally known through Jean-Louis Barrault's impersonation in *Les Enfants du Paradis*. Rue du Cirque north of the Théâtre de Marigny commemorates Franconi's beautiful Cirque d'Eté, which was much in vogue during the Second Empire, but by the end of the century it could no longer fill its 1,800 seats. Its lovely winter counterpart has survived in the 11th arrondissement. Beyond rue du Cirque stands the peach-coloured **Laurent**, where you can be sure of an unforgettable, expensive meal in an unfussy, pleasantly conservative setting. Outside the Laurent, Hifforff's Fountain of the Four Seasons will bring a smile to your face. Four adorable, chubby children represent the four seasons – children of nature, full of grace. Adorned with a wreath of flowers, Spring holds a pair of turtle doves in her graceful hands, Summer a sheaf of wheat and a sickle, Autumn a bunch of grapes, while Winter is covered in a blanket. All four support the fountain whose trickling water contributes to the pleasure of an outdoor meal at the Laurent, provided no motorcycle zooms by.

Next to the Laurent, along the Avenues MATIGNON and Gabriel, the open-air stamp market is held on Thursday, Saturday and Sunday mornings. Avenue Matignon should also be explored for the sake of its world-famous art galleries, notably Artcurial at no. 9.

Across the AVENUE DES CHAMPS ELYSÉES, the sprawling structure of the Grand Palais was completed in 1900 in time for the Universal Exposition, together with the Petit Palais which faces it on the other side of the Avenue Winston Churchill. An even more colossal structure, the Palais de l'Industrie, stood previously on their site and stretched parallel to the river. Set up for the 1855 fair, it was 200 metres long, 47 wide and 35 high. Since 'Perfidious Albion' had made so much ado about its glamorous Crystal Palace in 1851, on the occasion of the first World Fair, the French simply had to go one better. The Palais de l'Industrie had two storeys, 408 windows and was surmounted by a glass roof. At its entrance (approximately where the main entrance to the Grand Palais's temporary exhibitions is now, on Avenue du Général Eisenhower) was erected a pompous gate, topped with a bombastic, allegorical France, crowning the figures of Industry and Art. How gratifying to see Queen Victoria pass under such an emblem when she came to visit it! For the next four decades most official exhibitions took place here, including the famous salons, hermetically sealed to the Impressionists. The latter were instead condescendingly allocated small premises near by, where they could organise their Salon des Réfusés.

By the end of the century, the Palais de l'Industrie had become obsolete and two structures replaced it for the 1900 Exhibition, the Grand and the Petit Palais, the work of Charles Girault. They faced each other on either side of a new artery, Avenue Nicolas II, which was extended by a grand new bridge, Pont Alexander III, worthy of the ambitions of the Third Republic. Thus the recent and everlasting friendship between France and Russia was sealed and Paris could take pride in yet another stunning vista across the river, this time all the way from the Rond-Point-des Champs-Elysées to the Invalides.

On 14 April the first visitors entered the main gate to the exhibition, on Cours-la-Reine behind the Petit Palais. This gate too was surmounted by an allegorical figure, this time of La Parisienne, in a dress designed by Paquin. Fifty-one million visitors came to this playground between 14 April and 12 November. Sadly, nothing was preserved of the gate after the show had ended on 12 November, not even Paquin's dress.

Less ephemeral were two artistic events which took place at the Grand Palais – the Centennale, which, at long last, confirmed the success of the Impressionists, and the Décennale Internationale des Beaux Arts. From then on, the Grand Palais became the home of young artists, where they were given a chance to exhibit in its *salons*. Thus in 1905 there emerged a scandalous new group, nicknamed *Les Fauves* ('wild animals'), who splashed their canvases with bright colours. Little did the prim and proper critics of the time suspect that less than 100 years later a retrospective exhibition of Matisse in New York and Paris would break all the attendance records. In 1906 Gauguin's works were revealed here to the public and in 1907 Cézanne's. And it was in the Salon des Indépendants that shocked visitors were first confronted with a grotesque concept labelled Cubism, spearheaded by an unknown Spaniard named Pablo Picasso. Today the FIAC (Foire Internationale d'Art Contemporain) is held here every autumn, but times have changed and neither Paris nor the modern age can match the exceptional density of creative genius that flowered under the Third Republic. Other cultural events take place here: the antique fair, the book fair, the stamp fair . . . as well as major retrospective exhibitions, which draw huge crowds, and correspondingly long queues. In 1901 the Petit Palais was used for the first automobile show, while in 1908 the Grand Palais exhibited the achievements of aeronautics. Since 1937 part of the southern section of the Grand Palais has been used as a science museum, Le Palais de la Découverte, which also houses a planetarium.

The Grand Palais also houses some language departments of the University of Paris, known as Sorbonne IV. Against all human considerations the future linguists have been exiled from the Latin Quarter to this expensive, deserted environment, totally unsuitable for student social life, for the mere reason that the gigantic structure had vacant space in its southern wing; but then, the social aspect of academic life has never been a priority in the French educational system. The entrance to their department is from the deserted Cours-la-Reine, once the promenade of Henri IV, today a busy, albeit leafy, throughway along the Seine. During the Second Empire the celebrated Concert Musard was situated here, close to the present Avenue Franklin-Roosevelt, the most fashionable open-air establishment in the Champs-Elysées gardens, *de rigueur* for all true *Parisiennes* of fashion on Friday night. Monsieur Musard, the owner of the establishment, was the son of a famous musician and conductor, and his wife, the beautiful Madame Musard, found great favour in the eyes of Napoleon III, which served further to enhance the establishment's reputation.

When it first opened, Le Petit Palais housed a retrospective collection of French art. Today the building belongs to the City of Paris, which keeps and displays its own collections here. Temporary exhibitions are organised here too, but usually of less fashionable or publicised artists or aspects of art, which makes for a more pleasant experience for the visitor.

Behind the Petit Palais, the pretty pavilion of the remodelled Ledoyen is the offspring of the oldest restaurant in the gardens of the Champs-Elysées, frequented in the 18th century by Saint-Just and Robespierre. The last time they dined there was on 26 July 1734, two days before their execution. The establishment began in 1779 as a humble, country inn, Au Dauphin, a white building with green shutters, surrounded by a trellis fence, near the site of the future Ambassadeurs. On 4 August 1791 Michel Ledoyen rented the inn from Citizen Desmazure, hence its new name, but it was not until 1848 that it was transferred to its present location. Once more Hittorff was called on to design the new pavilion, which Maupassant described as 'one of the most pleasing cafés in Paris.' In 1988 it was taken over by a show-biz star, Régine, but she too has since left and today's Ledoyen takes pride in the talent of an excellent woman chef, Ghislaine Arabian.

Retrace your steps and cross over Avenue Winston Churchill. Continue on AVENUE DU GÉNÉRAL EISENHOWER along the northern side of the Grand Palais. On your right is the Théâtre

Renaud-Barrault, also known as the Théâtre du Rond-Point, the last of the old pavilions to survive, originally a Panorama built in 1860 by the up-and-coming Davioud, to replace Hittorff's earlier Panorama. This form of entertainment, introduced by the Englishman Robert Barker, transported the spectator to faraway lands, but the vogue was soon to die out. In line with new tastes, it became the ice-rink of people of fashion, where young Cocteau liked to come. More recently it became the home of a theatre company run by the illustrious Jean-Louis Barrault and Madeleine Renaud.

After the 1968 *événements* Jean-Louis Barrault was banished from the Odéon theatre on the Left Bank for his active sympathy towards the students. He was granted some premises in the old railway station of Orsay, where he built an attractive, modern theatre for his new company. When works began on the new Musée d'Orsay, the company was once again asked to pack up. The indoor structure of Théâtre d'Orsay was dismantled and put up again in Davioud's Palais de Glace.

The excellent Sunday morning chamber music concerts and the vitality of the great couple Renaud-Barrault made the Théâtre du Rond-Point a place of genuine culture and atmosphere in the best sense of the word. However, the old couple spent the last years of their lives withdrawn into a lonely, forsaken shell, hardly ever mentioned by Parisians, who gave a brief nod of respect in their direction when they eventually passed away, first Jean-Louis Barrault in 1994, then, a few months later, Madeleine Renaud. Because of the growing success of the Sunday morning concerts, space became short and the theatre was moved to the neighbouring Théâtre des Champs-Elysées. At present the melancholy Théâtre du Rond-Point is in need of a new coat of paint, and its food no longer warrants a Sunday lunch under the chestnut trees.

Cross over Avenue Franklin Roosevelt and continue into RUE JEAN GOUJON. Ahead is the attractive PLACE FRANÇOIS I with Davioud's graceful fountain. You may wonder why François I and his sculptor Jean Goujon should be celebrated in these remote parts, way out of Paris in the 16th century. As a matter of fact this is the result of a hoax. Colonel Brack and his friend the architect

Constantin had set up a building company in the early 19th century in order to develop the area lying between the present Avenues Franklin Roosevelt and Montaigne. In order to impress his mistress, the celebrated actress Mademoiselle Mars, Colonel Brack had a Renaissance façade brought over, stone by stone, from the town of Moret and put up by Constantin as a cladding for the house he was just finishing on the corner of Cours Albert I and rue Bayard. The doors of the façade being carved with salamanders, the King's emblem, the façade was assumed, without any further investigation, to be that of the house the King had built for the Duchesse d'Etampes. And because it was so beautifully sculpted, it was likewise assumed to be the work of the King's sculptor Jean Goujon. In fact, the house had belonged to a bourgeois by the name of Chabouillé and had no connection with either François I or with the sculptor. But the names of the streets have remained.

Continue along rue Jean Goujon. At no. 15, on your left, the Armenian church was built in 1903 on part of the site of the Bazar de la Charité which burnt down on 4 May 1897, the day after its opening. 135 people perished in the fire, among them the Duchesse d'Alençon, sister of the Austrian Empress. The monumental, richly ornate church of **Notre-Dame-de-Consolation** at no. 23, built in memory of the victims, bears witness to their aristocratic extraction.

Ahead is the elegant **AVENUE MONTAIGNE**, known as l'Allée des Veuves in the 19th century because it was frequented by merry widows of ill repute. Today, with the perpetual westward shift of Paris, it is an artery of great wealth, where the Plaza Athénée, one of Paris's luxury hotels, is located. Outsiders are welcome to the hotel's Sunday brunches and teas. The avenue has gradually taken over from Faubourg Saint-Honoré as the backbone of *haute couture*; all the more so as it is situated in a more spacious, less polluted neighbourhood, unquestionably more appealing for a leisurely window-shopping spree. In recent years most of the big names have opened shop here or in neighbouring streets. These are worth discovering for yourself, but note also the Carré d'Or, the jewellers' compound at 10 Avenue Georges V. Try also the section of rue François I between these two avenues and the side streets where several luxury food and wine shops are also located, catering to a wealthy local clientele.

At no. 13 stands the historical **Théâtre des Champs-Elysées**, the artistic highlight of the arrondissement, the home of the most memorable ballet creations of the 20th century, and also the scene of one of the century's most notorious '*scandales*'. The brash, brand-new Théâtre des Champs-Elysées, built of reinforced concrete by Astruc with decorations by Bourdelle, Maurice Denis and Vuillard, was inaugurated on 29 May 1913, with the opening of the eighth Parisian season of Diaghilev's *Ballets Russes*.

The programme included the world premiere of Stravinsky's *The Rite of Spring*, conducted by Pierre Monteux and choreographed by Nijinsky. The event was as revolutionary to the world of ballet as Picasso's *Demoiselles d'Avignon* had been to plastic art six years earlier – and as shocking to Parisians. 'The ballet splashed Tout-Paris with colours,' wrote Cocteau. Paris had already been scandalised a year earlier, when Debussy's *Le Prélude à l'après-midi d'un faune* (*Prelude to the Afternoon of a Faun*) had been performed at the Théâtre du Châtelet, with Nijinsky, looking '*plus nu que nu*' ('more nude than nude') in the spotted, skin-tight leotard designed for him by Bakst and with a bunch of grapes attached over his genitals, moving suggestively over the nymph's scarf. Gaston Calmette of *Le Figaro* spoke of 'a body deliberately contrived to be bestial – hideous when seen from the front, and still more hideous in profile.' The '*scandale*' saved the season . . . as Diaghilev shrewdly knew it would.

With the same calculating foresight, Diaghilev gathered a claque for the historic premiere of *The Rite of Spring*. Things went wrong from the beginning that night: mocking remarks and laughter were heard even as the orchestra struck up the first notes of the introduction. They carried on when the curtain rose, at which point the claque protested vehemently and before anyone knew it the din was such that nobody could hear the music, not even the dancers. '*Taisez-vous, garces du XVIème!*' ('Keep quiet, tarts of the 16th'), someone yelled. '*Ta gueule!*' ('Shut your trap!'), someone else retorted. Ravel was called '*Sale Juif!*' ('dirty Jew') and one elegant lady was seen slapping her whistling neighbour.

The abuse and the catcalling came as much from among the ostrich plumes, aigrettes, strings of pearls, tulle and tailcoats in the boxes and the stalls, as from the people in their sloppy everyday clothes up in the gods. Good grounds for a riot. . . Brandishing her fan, the indignant old Comtesse de Portalès stood in her box, red in the face, shouting,'This is the first time in sixty years that anyone has dared to make fun of me!' Standing on a chair in the wings, the desperate Nijinsky stamped and shouted out the beat for the dancers. Only Monteux, at the head of the orchestra, remained 'impassive and as thick-skinned as a crocodile.'

Needless to say, the critics had a field-day, 'Imagine people sporting the most gaudy colours, pointed caps and bathrobes, animal skins or purple tunics, gesticulating as though possessed, repeating the same movement a hundred times in a row: stamping, stamping, stamping away. . .'

If Stravinski was spared, in deference to his past successes, Nijinsky was torn apart and labelled *'ce primaire exaspéré'*. 'A ballet master totally devoid of general ideas and basic common sense,' wrote Léon Vallas, the future biographer of Debussy, going on to condemn 'the essential stupidity of a dance reduced to spasmodic movements.' Reacting as they had to daring new concepts in painting, the audience too were baffled by the 'stamping' and 'trampling', by what seemed to them 'the negation, the destruction of art and of style in the dance,' as Pierre Lalo put it. Moreover, they were affronted by the unbelievable fact that they were being presented with a ballet performance without a story. Jean Cocteau, however, immediately hailed *The Rite of Spring* as the 9th Symphony of the 20th century. *'Quelle bombe! Quel chef-d'oeuvre!'* Diaghilev, asked about his feelings the next day, as he was reciting Pushkin in the Bois de Boulogne, is said to have replied dryly, 'Exactly what I wanted.'

A minor *scandale*, but a *scandale* nonetheless, was provoked by Erik Satie's *Parade* in 1917. Nijinsky had been rejected and replaced by a new choreographer, Diaghilev's new companion, Léonide Massine. The sets too were made by a new collaborator, to wit Pablo Picasso. By now *The Rite of Spring* was universally acccepted, certainly in its orchestral concert version. However, the disruption of the war years had a damaging effect on the company, which was in desperate need of regeneration. It was Diaghilev's intuitive initiative in bringing together Stravinsky and Picasso that achieved this. With the staging of *Pulcinella* he carried his troupe into the Roaring Twenties and on to the planks of the Théâtre des Champs-Elysées, Serge Lifar shortly coming in to take the place of Nijinsky.

In the 1920s too an up-and-coming designer by the name of Coco Chanel entered the picture. She made the costumes for *Le Train Bleu*, another of Cocteau's concoctions, with music by Darius Milhaud and sets and curtain by Picasso. Groping with new concepts such as abstraction and dissonance since the beginning of the century, western civilisation could no longer ignore the signals sent out from other, sometimes far distant cultures, as Milhaud's experience in Brazil exemplified.

While Gauguin had explored the islands of Tahiti and Picasso had emulated *Art Nègre*, jazz and the music and dance of Black America were making their way into Paris. The *Revue Nègre*, which opened the season at the Théâtre des Champs-Elysées on 2 October 1925, with Josephine Baker in the lead, hit Paris with a new culture shock. For Josephine Baker was a living Gauguin, an animated sculpture of *Art Nègre*, a daughter of the jungle who brought to the stage the beauty of African art, who gave life to Cubism as she danced frantically to the novel sound of jazz, glorifying the primitive rhythms of pristine days just as Nijinsky had tried to do in *The Rite of Spring* – the difference being that eroticism worked in Josephine Baker's favour. At the same time, the International Art Deco Exhibition, taking place just around the corner, between the bridges of Alexander III and Alma, was initiating Paris masses in new forms of visual art. Janet Flanner, who watched the *Revue Nègre*, reported how the white males in the audience responded intensely to the magnificent dark body of Josephine Baker, covered in nothing but one pink flamingo feather between her limbs, slithering about on the back of a huge black performer. Naturally she brought the house down, though some outraged spectators stamped out of the theatre in the middle of the performance, slamming the doors behind them calling it a disgrace, an anarchy. 'The most direct assault ever perpetrated against French taste,' wrote the librettist and boulevard playwright De Flers in *Le Figaro*, reflecting the puritanical outlook of the establishment.

Generations of great artists were to honour the Théâtre des Champs-Elysées over the years, among them Chaliapin, Pavlova and Toscanini, and more recently Munch, von Karajan and Solti. Arthur Rubinstein gave his last Paris concert here, entirely devoted to Chopin; so did Jascha Heifetz, in 1970; and in 1980 Nathan Milstein performed here all Bach's solo violin works. The theatre also hosted the Barenboim-Ponnelle Mozart opera festival for several seasons in the 1980s.

Although of late the municipal authorities have shockingly allowed the building to be surmounted by a luxury restaurant, thus ruining its architectural harmony, it still remains a jewel of a theatre, topped by a gorgeous, luminous dome of glass and gilded metal, endowed with excellent acoustics and wonderfully comfortable seats. Why it is not used more often for major performances is incomprehensible. The Comédie des Champs-Elysées next door deserves special mention too, being the first home of Louis Jouvet's troupe, where he gave the historic performances of Jules Romain's *Knock* in 1924.

You will have now reached the **ROND-POINT-DES-CHAMPS-ELYSÉES**, where the Elysian lawns and shrubberies are taken over by commerce. Already in the early 1930s Jannet Flanner described the rash of coloured cinema signs bursting out from the ground floors of the mansions. Today there are few mansions left and the movie houses, in those days surrounded by vast, inviting café terraces, now have fast-food restaurants and cheap clothing shops for company. You may decide to walk up the **AVENUE DES CHAMPS-ELYSÉES** to the Arc de Triomphe or catch a bus to save your feet. Let us just mention a few places of note on the way.

No. 1 was the home of Joseph Oller, the enterprising owner of the Moulin-Rouge and Olympia. No. 15 was the lavish dwelling of the Duc de Morny, a man of extraordinary descent, being at once the son of Queen Hortense, the grandson of Talleyrand and the great-grandson of Louis XV, the intricate product of unbridled amorous licence among France's upper classes.

At no. 25 is the Hôtel de la Païva, a rare example of a courtesan's mansion in the 19th century, which can be visited only by prior arrangement since it now belongs to a private club. The Marquise de la Païva, *née* Thérèse Lachmann, was the leading courtesan of the Second Empire. She was born in Poland to a Jewish family around the year 1818. The family escaped to Russia and soon she married a French tailor, whom she left for a turbulent life abroad – in Constantinople, Paris and London. It was the composer Hertz who introduced her to Parisian society. Having married him, she proceeded to ruin him and when he died was free to marry the

Portuguese Franco Aranjo, Marquis de la Païva. Equipped with a title, she formed a liaison with the Count Henckel of Denmark, a cousin of Bismarck and a multimillionaire, who built for her the present *hôtel*, a place of appallingly extravagant taste, befitting a parvenue, which the Parisian literati did not mind – Taine, Renan, Sainte-Beuve, Théophile Gautier, Edmond Goncourt – were happy to come to her magnificent receptions, although this did not prevent Goncourt from tearing apart both hostess and house in his *Journal*. After the 1870 war, Henckel became the governor of Alsace-Lorraine and the Païva had to leave Paris a few years later. By the time she died in 1884 she had also acquired the reputation of being a spy. Meanwhile her poor ex-husband, the Marquis de la Païva, is said to have shot himself in 1871, after an elegant meal at the celebrated Maison Dorée, on the Boulevard des Italiens. His wife had just obtained from Rome the annulment of their marriage, so as to marry Henckel.

Another celebrated courtesan, Cora Pearl, lived for a while on the site of the present no. 29. Roughly on the site of the present rue de Marignan was situated the splendid Jardin d'Hiver, a glass-and-iron construction which housed an enchanting, all-year weatherproof garden. Fountains, exotic flowers and music made it a most sought-after place. The painter Delacroix commented on his outing there in the evening of 21 February 1852: 'I was enchanted by the exotic trees – some of them enormous – lit up by the electrical illuminations; the fountains and sound of splashing water made it perfectly delightful. Two swans were swimming about in one of the basins among the water-plants beneath the spray of a fountain forty or fifty feet high.' Delacroix was amused by 'the vulgar orchestra, the dashing bowing of the fiddlers, the drums and cornets, and the zest of the little shop-assistants fluttering about in their fine clothes.' The orchestra was often conducted by the son of the celebrated musician Musard, and it was here that the Belgian Antoine Sax launched an instrument he had himself invented, first known as the saxhorn, and in the 20th century, the indispensable saxophone.

At no. 44 across the avenue, the **Colisée** is one rare café to have preserved its terraces from the 1930s. Prices here match its celebrity. On this same side of the avenue the **Claridge** at no. 74/76, once a top-ranking luxury hotel, is just a shadow of its former self, an apartment hotel today, of no particular interest. The famous **Lido**, which still features the kind of 'feathered-flesh' reviews that made Gay Paris world-renowned, occupied no. 78 from 1946 to 1976, when it moved to new premises at 116bis.

At no. 92, on the corner of rue de Berri, was a beautiful 18th-century mansion, built by Chalgrin for the Comtesse de Langeac. Between 1785 and 1789 it was occupied by Thomas Jefferson, the US Ambassador to France. Opposite was the house that then belonged to Santerre, the brother of the famous brewer of Saint-Antoine, the 'King of the Faubourg' who incited its inhabitants to rise against oppression and topple the *Ancien Régime*. This Santerre, Jean-François, emulated his brother and opened a brewery on this site but went bankrupt in 1806. The presence of old houses in these remote parts is explained by the fact that rue de Berri already existed in the 17th century; it was a country lane running along the domain of the Oratoriens of the village of Roule further east.

Across the avenue again, at the corner of the Champs-Elysées and Avenue Georges V, is the red awning of **Le Fouquet's**, the only survivor of a time when relaxing on one of the terraces here equated with gracious living. Opened in 1901, it emulated Maxime's with its own apostrophe and 's', a ticket to a prestigious future. In the 1930s Léon-Paul Fargue said that 'Le Fouquet's was one of those places that could only go out of fashion in the wake of a bombing!' Indeed, this is still the stronghold of show-biz, of Tout-Paris and of Parisian gossip. Here the lists of candidates for the *Césars* (The French oscars) are compiled before the night of the ceremony. After the ceremony France's film stars gather once more at *Le Fouquet's* (pronounced Fouquetz).

At **no. 103**, at the corner of rue de Bassano stands a stunning building in Art Nouveau *nouille* style, complete with cherubs, pillars and garlands. This was once l'Elysée Palace, a luxury hotel of 400 rooms, where the spy, Mata Hari, was arrested on 13 February 1917. **No. 133** houses the Publicis Company, which was founded by the well-known advertising man, Marcel Bleustein-Blanchet, and the company's Drugstore, the first of its kind in Paris, a much more luxurious establishment than its American counterpart. The building replaces the Belle Epoque pompous and festive Astoria which was reduced to ashes in 1972, in a tragic yet spectacular fire. Standing among the crowd, Bleustein-Blanchet watched his creation go up in flames but did not lose heart. The very next day he decided to start again with a new building, made of glass and resolutely modern. The old Astoria was built for Emile Jellinek, a citizen of the Austro-Hungarian Empire. Many celebrities frequented the Astoria, notably the Emperor William II, who in 1914 reserved a large suite with a balcony overlooking the avenue to watch his victorious army marching down the Champs-Elysées, an honour that fell to his heirs some 25 years later. Jellinek was also the representative in France of Daimler automobiles, which he renamed Mercedes after his daughter.

Across the avenue at no. 152 was the *hôtel* of the conductor Musard. Later it belonged to the Comtesse de Loynes, hostess of one of the most illustrious *salons* of the Second Empire and Third Republic. She too started out as a kept woman. Little is known about her obscure, humble extraction, except that she was born poor in Reims in the year 1837. Before long Marie-Anne Detourbey came to be known in Paris as Mademoiselle Jeanne de Tourbey, which sounded much better and more suitable for the higher circles which she was eyeing. She too ruined her lover, in her case the director of the Théâtre de la Porte-Saint-Martin, who relinquished her to Prince Napoleon in favour of certain material advantages. From then on she played hostess to the same elite as the Païva – Renan, Sainte-Beuve, Gautier and Flaubert, said to be her hopeless suitor, a rumour confirmed by the numerous ardent letters he sent her. In 1870 her lover Ernest Baroche, a high civil servant and son of a minister, was killed in the war, leaving her 800,000 francs, a colossal sum for those days, which enabled her to abandon the *demi-monde*, to buy herself a husband – preferably a titled one – and to enter the *monde* with the necessary asset of respectability. She found her prey in Comte Victor Edgar Loynes, and after an ephemeral marriage which ended with his disappearance, perhaps in South America, she became known as the Comtesse de Loynes and opened her doors wide to society from 5 to 7 pm. With the nascent Third Republic her circle included such celebrities as Clemenceau, Porto-Riche, Dumas fils and, not long after, some nationalists, headed by Maurice Barrès, all of them later to be ranged against Dreyfus. Her most cherished visitor was Jules Lemaître, her current lover and 15 years her junior, the one real love of her life. Thanks to her influence he entered the Académie

Française in 1895 and it was through their collaboration that the *League de la Patrie Française*, portent of darker days, was founded. No wonder Léon Daudet, the son of Alphonse and co-founder of *Action Française*, depicted her as the bravest and most praiseworthy of characters: 'She is as delicate as a flower physically . . . she would have braved all the perils, all the demons, for the cause of her country.' Naturally, when the Dreyfus Case unsettled France, this illustrious couple found themselves lined up alongside such people as Drumont, Maurras, Barrès, Déroulède and Léon Daudet and, by the same token, at odds with the likes of Clemenceau and Anatole France. After the victory of the *Dreyfusards*, she continued to be politically militant and helped to promote what was to become *Action Française* some 20 years after her own death, in 1908.

You will have now reached the **Arc de Triomphe** crowning the flattened summit of the hill of Chaillot. There was heated controversy after the death of General de Gaulle as whether to rename this gigantic roundabout after him or leave it as PLACE DE L'ETOILE. His unconditional supporters believed that no lesser a site would do justice to the memory of the man who had been acclaimed here by 2.5 million people as the liberator of Paris and eventually of France, as he himself reported in his *War Memoirs*. But the man in the street was attached to the old name, which was familiar, concise and admirably applicable to its star-like shape with the twelve broad avenues radiating from it. An awkward compromise was reached, by which the two names were combined; to satisfy the Gaullists, Charles de Gaulle was placed first. But in the end the man in the street had the upper hand – 25 years later Parisians stubbornly refer to the Etoile. The innocent tourist asking for Place Charles de Gaulle, may find himself being given instructions to get to the airport.

Seeing the Place for the first time, he may also be overwhelmed by the traffic. Unlike Place de la Concorde and other such open spaces in the capital, the Place de l'Etoile has never been provided with traffic lights. Here one just takes a deep breath and plunges in, praying. Then one zooms round the Arc with everyone else and, eventually, with tremulous palpitations and another little prayer, one tries to whizz out. *Sauve qui peut!* Incidentally, somehow very few collisions actually occur here.

Because of its privileged position on the summit of a hill and on the axis of the Tuileries Palace, this spot naturally drew the attention of rulers and their town-planners, architects and landscape gardeners. One extravagant plan, dating from the time of Louis XV, was to erect a gigantic elephant on the site. A plaster model of the said creature was in fact cast at the Bastille, which Victor Hugo describes in detail in *Les Misérables*, and where the street urchin Gavroche finds shelter. Napoleon, however, preferred to follow Roman traditions and in 1805 entrusted Chalgrin with the task of constructing a monumental Arch in commemoration of his Great Army and its glorious victories. Chalgrin died in 1811 and, with the fall of Napoleon and the ensuing unsettled times, the monument was not completed until 1836, under the instigation of Minister Adolphe Thiers, who commissioned several of the country's most illustrious sculptors – notably Rude, Pradier, Etex and Cortot – to decorate it. A list of 600 generals and of 128 battles was added to the monument.

The Emperor's ashes were brought here in 1840, before being laid under the Dome of the Invalides. The body of the venerated Victor Hugo was also brought here in 1885, before being taken to the Panthéon, where he was buried as the first hero of the Third Republic. From then on many of France's heroes were brought here on their way to eternal rest, notably Gambetta, the Marshals Foch and Joffre and General Leclerc. On 28 January 1921 the remains of an unknown soldier from the Great War were buried under the Arch and on 11 November 1923, Armistice Day, the eternal flame of remembrance was lit on the site, since when it has been rekindled daily by an official delegation. Twice the Prussians and Germans marched here – in 1871 and 1940 – and twice the Allies – in 1919 and 1945. Apart from the symbolic connotation of the Arch, Place Charles de Gaulles-Etoile is a very elegant place, surrounded by the imposing *hôtels* that Hittorff built for it, displaying his exceptional talent.

At the foot of the Arch is a museum which tells its story, but it is the climb to the top that is most to be recommended. You will be rewarded with sweeping views across western Paris – to the east, all the way down to Place de la Concorde and the past, to the west, as far as the Arche de la Défense and the future.

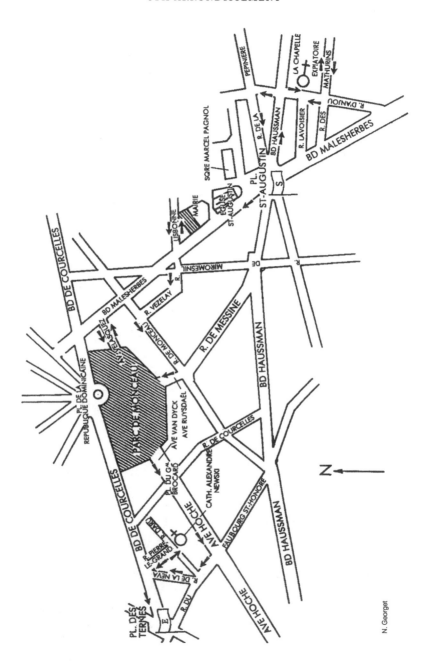

N. Georget

FROM PLACE SAINT-AUGUSTIN
TO PLACE DES TERNES

This walk will begin on PLACE SAINT-AUGUSTIN, so called after its church, on the north-eastern corner of Boulevards Haussmann and Malesherbes. It will take us through what used to be the residential quarters (*les beaux quartiers*) of the triumphant bourgeoisie in the 19th century. At present hardly anyone lives in the solid, opulent buildings which have been turned into offices. Few private families today could afford the cost of the large staff it would take to run such large dwellings or, for that matter, the maintenance of the buildings themselves.

With its population depleted, this is now an uninviting neighbourhood – polluted and traffic-ridden by day, a ghost town by night and at weekends. And there is worse to come: insensitive to the architectural heritage at stake, developers have lately introduced a new scheme which consists of systematically demolishing the interiors of buildings, scooping out gorgeous staircases and wrought-iron works, turning the façades into pathetic, soulless cardboard sets. Nonetheless, this walk is of interest to those who wish to recapture the Paris of the privileged in the late 19th century and will also lead you to Parc de Monceau, one of the loveliest gardens in Paris.

BOULEVARD HAUSSMANN celebrates, as it should, the man who turned Paris upside-down and who, within 17 years, brought it out of its medieval ashes – a brand-new, modern city. At least so it seemed. For behind the new façades most of the side alleys and labyrinths remained untouched until well into the 1950s and even the 1960s. In these parts, however, there was little to tear down, for this was still countryside when Napoleon III came to power in December 1851. And the result was not displeasing, for the monotony of the new blocks of buildings was largely compensated for by the breadth of the arteries, which meant more air and more light, and by the profusion of trees, a luxury formerly unknown. Haussmann acquiesced willingly to the destruction, considering it beneficial, for as he put it, '*J'étais choisi comme un artiste démolisseur*' ('I was chosen as a demolition artist').

Less apparent but just as important was his installation of a new sewage system and water-supply network, both acutely important to a city which had suffered two raging cholera epidemics in the first half of the 19th century. However, although in fact he merely followed the bidding of his employer, the Emperor, and although he did not seek any financial gain and never became wealthy, he was dismissed by the ungrateful Emperor eight months before the latter's downfall because the works that he himself had ordered were too costly. A sad ending for a loyal, principled subject, who died 20 years later in total oblivion, aged 82.

As you walk eastwards on the left-hand side, you will come to no. 102, where a plaque indicating that Proust lived here between 1907 and 1919 confirms that this was the right address for the worldly. Proust settled here soon after the death of his father (1903) and mother (1905), in deep mourning but also freed and ready for the great work of his life, *La Recherche du temps perdu*, which he wrote here with all the intensity of his feverish and bruised body and soul. It was in 1907, the year he moved to Boulevard Haussmann, that he uttered in despair, '*Rien ne dure. Pas même la mort*' ('Nothing lasts. Not even death'). The apartment, however, belonged to his aunt and when she decided to sell it in 1919 he had to move out. He resigned himself to settling temporarily at 44 rue Hamelin in the remote 16th arrondissement, but illness was already getting the better of him and he died there three years later, having been unable to make the move back to the centre.

Cross over and turn right into RUE D'ANJOU, an ancient way that dates from the 16th century and is named after the Duc d'Anjou, the future Henri III, who, it is rumoured, had a love-nest here, where he carried on his illicit homosexual affairs. Some locate the house, 'where the King came with his fairies', on the neighbouring rue de la Pépinière, then the dirt road leading to the village of Roule; that house was still standing in the 18th century.

Since Henri III had been King of Poland briefly, before his accession to the throne of France, the area came to be known as La Petite Pologne, a slummy enclave before Haussmann got to it, with a rubbish dump near by. 'It was the homeland, at tenpence a night, of all the street organ players, of all the monkey tamers, of all the acrobats and of all the chimney sweeps that swarm the streets of the town,' wrote Albéric Second in 1860. The street runs along a little square, the only spot of greenery next to the crowded Boulevard Haussmann and its packed pavements one block away, where the Printemps and Galeries Lafayette department stores are located. In the 18th century this was the parish cemetery of the Madeleine, lying amidst kitchen gardens which were watered by the open-air sewer (*Le Grand-Egout*), that ran all the way from Belleville, through the present Boulevard Haussmann and on to the Seine at Place d'Alma.

Its malodorous smells did not deter privileged families from coming to live on rue d'Anjou and adorning it with elegant *hôtels* all the way from Faubourg Saint-Honoré. The one at no. 51 was occupied by Félix Tournachon, much better known as Nadar, in 1910, when he died there, aged 90. Famous photographer of Belle Epoque Paris, friend of painters and of literati, who had offered the Impressionists his premises on Boulevard des Capucines for their first exhibition in 1874, Nadar was himself a novelist and aeronaut. His famous balloons enabled besieged Paris to communicate with the outside world and ease the Prussian pressure in 1870, and he also served as a model for Ardan in Jules Verne's *Voyage Round the Moon*.

The 18th-century *hôtel* at no. 52 was the home of Destutt de Tracy who, in 1834, made the official announcement of the death of La Fayette, a friend of his father, in the old townhall of the arrondissement, on Faubourg Saint-Honoré. (The Marquis de La Fayette died on 20 May at no. 8, down the street.) The 18th-century philosopher Helvétius owned a property at the present no. 54. No. 59 was the home of the Comte de Chazelles, a wealthy Farmer General who was sent to the guillotine in 1794, a fate he shared with his son-in-law, the famous chemist Lavoisier. Rue Lavoisier on your right was opened through the gardens of his property. It is said that when it was time for Lavoisier to set out for Place de la Révolution he requested a couple of hours' delay so as to finish an experiment, but this was denied him because 'the Republic is in no need of scientists'.

The **cemetery of the Madeleine**, shut off from the countryside by a high wall, was opened in 1721. Some noteworthy figures of the 18th century were brought to rest here and also all the 133 victims who perished in the accidental fire on Place Louis XV (Concorde) during the wedding celebration of Louis XVI and Marie-Antoinette on 30 May 1770. To these were added on 10 August 1792 the bodies of the Swiss Guards who were massacred during the assault on the Tuileries and on 26 August it became the burial-ground of all the decapitated bodies that were brought here from Place de la Révolution, among them King Louis XVI.

His cart followed the itinerary of the present rue Boissy-d'Anglas, then turned left into rue du Faubourg Saint-Honoré and right into rue D'Anjou. The King was granted a coffin and his body was clad in a shirt, grey woollen breeches, grey silk stockings and a white quilted coat. His head was laid between his legs. The coffin was painted with quicklime and buried in a grave over three metres deep and three metres away from the wall along rue d'Anjou. At least he was accorded a modicum of respect and, despite the ungodly times, the vicars of the Madeleine were allowed to preside over the ceremony and recite prayers for the soul of the deceased, according to Roman Catholic rites. 'the Patriot Palloy', a profiteering crook from Faubourg Saint-Antoine, showed less respect for His Majesty and commemorated the event with a new dish, '*tête de cochon farcie*'.

In 1802 Pierre-Louis Ollivier Desclozeaux, resident at no. 48 rue d'Anjou at the time of the Revolution, bought the closed-down cemetery and made it part of his garden. In 1793 he had carefully taken note of the precise spot where the King and Queen had been buried, which was corroborated by his son-in-law, the lawyer Daujou. He then proceeded to plant two weeping willows and several cypress trees around their graves.

When Louis XVIII acceded to the throne in 1815 he set his heart on finding the bodies of Louis XVI and Marie-Antoinette and Desclozeaux pointed out to him the location of the two graves. This was confirmed by a certain Pierre Seveste, the grandson of one of the grave-diggers who had buried the King. For his help Seveste was granted a monopoly over all the suburban theatres, as well as the right to produce plays that were running in Paris at the same time, hitherto forbidden. As for Desclozeaux, he was rewarded with a generous pension, which was extended to his two daughters, and the honorary sash of Saint-Michel. He also received, after much haggling, substantial sums of money for the sale of his house and garden to Louis XVIII a year later (11 January 1816), 100,000 and 60,000 francs respectively. The bodies of the royal couple were exhumed, the Queen on 18 January 1815, the King on the 19th, and transferred to the Basilica of Saint-Denis where France's royalty had been buried since Dagobert I had been laid there in 638. A monument called La Chapelle Expiatoire was erected over the area of the entire cemetery and was inaugurated in 1826. Sadly, in 1862, the cypress trees and weeping willows planted by the faithful Desclozeaus were chopped down − one wonders why.

Today only some politically-minded royalists, on the extreme right, gather at this otherwise deserted spot on special commemoration days, especially on 21 January, the anniversary of Louis XVI's execution, while the shoppers at the nearby Galeries Lafayette, Au Printemps or Marks and Spencer's are totally unaware of the existence of the monument to the defunct French monarchy. If the Revolution proved incapable of fulfilling its ideals, it was however prompt in obliterating from France's collective memory its murderous destruction of the *Ancien Régime*. If you wish to go in, enter through rue des Mathurins, called after the order of the Mathurins who owned a farm here.

Retrace your steps and continue on rue d'Anjou beyond Boulevard Haussmann and turn left on RUE DE LA PÉPINIÈRE, which ran along the royal nursery (*pépinière*) at the time of the nature-loving Louis XVI. At no. 24/26 you will see the imposing buildings of the military barracks (La Caserne de la Pépinière), built by the Maréchal, Duc de Biron in the second half of the 18th century. Before that time local Parisians had been required to provide soldiers with food and lodgings, much to their displeasure, for these ruffianly lodgers would usually turn in totally drunk and often pester the young female members of the household. Setting the soldiers apart and thus sparing the people this nuisance was a judicious move on the part of Biron.

Ahead is PLACE DE SAINT-AUGUSTIN with its Cercle Militaire, part of the same barracks. Today its imposing halls are let out for functions. On your right, beyond rue Laborde, the busy neighbourhood has been graced with another welcome patch of greenery, Square Marcel Pagnol. Nobody seems to question the presence of a statue in honour of the ardent nationalist Paul Déroulède, a notorious anti-Semite at the time of the Dreyfus Case. It must be conceded that most of today's Parisians have never heard of him, but to his own contemporaries he was a galvanising character.

The church of Saint-Augustin is of architectural interest for it was built by Victor Baltard on an iron structure, like his famous pavilions of Les Halles, which explains why, despite its gigantic dimensions, it took only eight years (1860–68) to complete. But whereas the use of iron was applauded on a market-place, it was too revolutionary for a church and Baltard had to cover up or camouflage most of it. However, if you look carefully inside, you will notice the metal pillars and vaults, among other elements. Baltard also succeeded in overcoming the limitations imposed on him by the uneven, cramped space of Place Saint-Augustin and created an illusion of symmetry and a feeling of spaciousness as required in the house of God. An organ recital here can be an uplifting experience.

In front of the church is an equestrian statue of Jeanne d'Arc, one among several scattered in the capital. Today she has become the unfortunate emblem of the National Front, whose members prefer to honour her not here but around her statue on Place des Pyramides, in the 1st arrondissement. Opposite is the Boulevard Malesherbes, which runs all the way from the Madeleine to Parc de Monceau, already laid out in 1800 by Napoleon, again exemplifying his vision and scope. The Boulevard is named after yet another victim of the Revolution, Guillaume de Lamoignon de Malesherbes, a minister of both Louis XV and Louis XVI, who tried to overturn the latter's death sentence.

Walk north along BOULEVARD MALESHERBES. The Mairie of the 8th arrondissement has taken up residence at no. 56 in the Hôtel de Cail, built by Labouret in 1865. Jean-François Cail was born in 1804 to a poor peasant family. Forty years later he was at the head of the French metal industry! His amazing rise to power was achieved because of a rough-and-ready liberalism, but he ruled his workers, once his social equals, with an iron rod. For a better look at the mansion turn into rue de Lisbonne. At no. 6, another *hôtel* bears witness to the past prosperity of the neighbourhood's inhabitants. It was the home of the Martel family, originators of the famous cognac. To judge by the two mansions, they were not quite as wealthy nor as grand as Monsieur Cail.

Retrace your steps and continue on RUE DE LISBONNE. You will come to its junction with rue de Miromesnil. Geneviève Halévy, the daughter of the composer of *La Juive*, and wife of Georges Bizet, later Madame Emile Straus, was living round the corner at **104 rue de Miromesnil**, at the junction of rue de Messine and Boulevard Haussmann, where she held one of the most celebrated *salons* of Belle Epoque Paris. Her large round drawing-room, decorated with paintings by Nattier, de La Tour and Monet and with her own famous portrait by Delaunay, was the gathering-place of an extraordinarily eclectic assembly, whose members ranged from such left-wingers as Léon Blum to reactionary anti-Semites such as Degas. In the wake of the Dreyfus Case, a rift became inevitable. At the instigation of the family's friend and staunch supporter of Dreyfus, Joseph Reinach, the first petition to *l'Aurore* was written here by a group of friends, among them Marcel Proust, one of her close friends. Madame Straus was, as a matter of fact, one of Proust's models for the Duchesse de Guermantes, and it was also at her *salon* that he first met Charles Haas, his model for Swann. Although she moved in circles of assimilated Jews, Madame Straus would not convert to Catholicism. When this was suggested to her before she died in 1925, she is reported to have answered, '*J'ai trop peu de religion pour en changer*' ('I have too little religion to change it'). Her son, Jacques Bizet, was living at no. 72 Boulevard Malesherbes. He was one of the pioneers of small cars, but his cars were snubbed at a time when parking space was not an issue and in the end, broken-hearted, he committed suicide.

Continue along rue de Lisbonne, then turn right into RUE DE VÉZELAY. An opulent 19th-century *hôtel*, embellished by wrought iron, stands at no. 11*bis*, a reminder of past glories, of which much more on rue de Monceau. This was a mere dirt track when it was laid out in the 17th century to connect the villages of Roule and Monceau, but in the latter part of the 19th century the streets around Parc de Monceau became the home of wealthy people. Today this is still an enclave of splendour, exuding an air of self-confident prosperity, unimpaired by modern developments.

Turn left on RUE DE MONCEAU. At no. 63 the **Musée Nissim de Camondo** is a beautiful relatively unknown museum with a gorgeous collection of works of arts disposed in an 18th-century setting, offering the visitor a rare opportunity to recapture the interior of an aristocratic mansion of that time. To achieve this effect, in 1911 the owner, the wealthy banker Moïse de Camondo, simply tore down his *hôtel*, which had been put up in 1866, and replaced it with a lovely copy of an 18th-century *hôtel*. Moïse de Camondo bequeathed the house, the garden and the art collection to the Union des Arts décoratifs, his only condition being that it should be named after his son Nissim, who had been killed in 1917 in the Great War – a generous patriotic act overlooked by Vichy France, which deported to Auschwitz his daughter Béatrice Reinach and her children, his only descendants, who never came back.

Another magnificent dwelling was situated at no. 45/47, the home of the Rothschilds, scandalously torn down to make room for the present modern building. Turn right into the magnificent **AVENUE RUYSDAEL** which leads to Parc de Monceau through regal wrought-iron gates, the work of Davioud. Before entering the park, you might turn left into rue Murillo, where on a wall at no. 9 you will see some vestiges of the Palais des Tuileries and the Hôtel de Ville, which were rescued when they were set on fire during the *Commune*. By whom and why they were brought to this spot has never been unravelled. One arcade from the Renaissance building of the Hôtel de Ville now stands inside the park.

Parc de Monceau is certainly one of the most beautiful parks of Paris. Unfortunately, considerable parts of it were amputated during the Second Empire. In the 18th century, the area, which extended well into what is now the 17th arrondissement, was basically a hunting-ground and belonged to the Farmer General Grimod de La Reynière, the Lord of Monceau. In 1778 Louis-Philippe d'Orléans, Duc de Chartres and future Philippe Egalité, bought part of the territory and transformed it into a magical park, La Folie de Chartres. A contemporary poet spoke of enchanting grottos, of magical bowers, of the marvel of roses bravely growing among ice (more prosaically, the park had a greenhouse). When the toll walls were built round Paris in 1787, the section that corresponds to today's Boulevard de Courcelles was surrounded by a ditch instead of a wall so as not to obstruct the pleasant pastoral view to the north that pleased the Duke. Similarly, an elegant rotunda was put up instead of an observation post so as not to spoil the environment of the park, with its lakes and islands, vines, water lilies, Greek temples, Chinese pagodas, windmills and fake ruins. Louis-Philippe built himself a sitting-room in the dome of the rotunda, known as the Pavillon Philippe-Egalité, where he would come to enjoy the extensive view.

The Revolution maltreated the park, and it was only at the time of Louis-Philippe that it reverted to its former splendour and became the King's favourite park. With the advent of the Second Empire, however, Paris was handed over to developers and speculators. Over half its area was given over to Pereire who opened up the streets adjoining it; what remained was handed over to Alphand, to lay out an English garden, as elsewhere in Paris. Alphand rescued a considerable number of features from the 18th-century garden, which still ornament the park. The most impressive is a Corinthian colonnade around an oval pool known as the Naumachie. It may have been part of a rotunda that was built by Catherine de Medici, north of the Basilica of Saint-Denis, as a sepulchre for her husband Henri II and for herself.

Exit the park through AVENUE VELASQUEZ, a centre of wealth and splendour in Belle Epoque Paris: the head (*régent*) of the Banque de France, Jean Gouin, lived at no. 4, the owner of the Louvre department store, Monsieur Chauchard, also nicknamed *l'Empereur du blanc* (household linen), at no. 5 and the Milanese financier, Cernuschi, at no. 7. The latter two were great art collectors, which redounded to France's benefit: Chauchard bequeathed 200 paintings to the Louvre, including Millet's famous *Angélus*, while Cernuschi bequeathed to the City of Paris his collection of Far Eastern art. His *hôtel* on Avenue Velasquez was turned into a gem of a museum in 1895 – **Musée Cernuschi** – to house this fabulous collection and many acquisitions that have been added since.

Re-enter the park and leave it through AVENUE VAN DYCK, which leads to Avenue Hoche. Turn round once more for a final look at the magnificent gates, an exquisite sight, particularly in spring, when the trees are in full bloom. Turn right into RUE DU FAUBOURG SAINT-HONORÉ, and walk past the concert hall of **Salle Pleyel**, where the Orchestre de Paris is based, in a home unworthy of a major European capital. Turn right into rue de la Néva and right again into RUE PIERRE-LE-GRAND where a stunning, unexpected sight will meet your eyes: ahead (on rue Daru) is the Russian cathedral **Saint Alexander Nevsky**, with its golden domes glittering, hopefully, on your visit, against a cloudless, blue sky. It was built by Strohm and designed by Keuzmine, members of the St. Petersburg Fine Arts Academy (1859–1861) to replace a small chapel that could no longer accommodate the growing Russian colony at the time of Napoleon III. It was here that Picasso celebrated his first wedding ceremony in 1921, when he was married by Orthodox rites to Olga Khoklova, a member of Diaghilev's *Ballets Russes*. The fact that she was the daughter of an officer in the Czar's army heightened her prestige in the eyes of the Spanish painter. The Russian restaurant opposite the cathedral used to host such people as Stravinsky, Diaghilev and Nabokov.

Retrace your steps, turn left into Boulevard de Courcelles and proceed to PLACE DES TERNES, one of the colourful spots of Paris thanks to its brilliant flower market. If you can, wind up with an excellent meal – alas! not inexpensive – on the terrace of the Brasserie Lorraine overlooking this riot of colours. Their sea-food is real treat.

THE 9TH ARRONDISSEMENT

ANY first-time visitor to the City of Light is bound to land, sooner or later, in the 9th arrondissement, whether to collect mail at the American Express or cash a cheque at one of the neighbourhood's banks, whether to go on a shopping spree at the Galeries Lafayette or the Printemps department store – 'the most Parisian of stores' according to their advertising slogan – before winding up at the Café de la Paix, the meeting point of the international tourist population.

Paradoxically, he will soon discover that apart from errands and shopping there is little for him to do in this practical and business-like area, which he has probably believed to be the centre of tourism of the French capital. He may even have some vague notion of the *beau monde* filing up and down its broad arteries and wonder where it has vanished.

Standing in the middle of this busy neighbourhood, the ostentatious Opera House, le Palais Garnier, is the sole conspicuous remnant of a glamorous past. For here was situated the mythical 'Gay Paris' of '365 Sundays', featuring scintillating, feathered nudes at the Folies-Bergère, and later, the sculpted honey-brown, feline body of 'the Black Pearl', Josephine Baker; Zizi Jeanmaire and her gorgeous legs at Le Casino de Paris; earlier, Paganini and his stunning premiere at the old Opera House on rue Le Peletier, before it was replaced by Charles Garnier's new 'Palace' in the second half of the 19th century, the last word in elegance, the pride of the triumphant bourgeoisie.

Above all, the Grands Boulevards streaming with top-hatted gentlemen in morning coats and slender, tight-corseted ladies – but only the western section of the Boulevards, according to Balzac: 'The heart of Paris today beats between rue de la Chaussée-d'Antin and rue du Faubourg Montmartre.' Indeed, for 60 years the Grands Boulevards were the fashionable promenade of the *beau-monde*, as Monet's and Pissarro's paintings testify, a record length of time for a fickle city and its insatiable society, constantly migrating to new places of pleasure.

It was Louis XIV who first laid out the Grands Boulevards on the southern edge of the arrondissement, then the northern border of Paris. Fortified by his victories over the European nations that had joined forces against him, he replaced the rampart his father had built as a northern defence with an elegant, tree-lined promenade, known at the time as Cours Nouveaux (*cours* meaning 'avenue', 'walk'), so as to distinguish it from the older promenade, Cours-la-Reine, which his grandmother, Marie de Medici, had opened along the Seine (now in the 8th arr.). Soon they would be known as Boulevards, from an old German word '*bulwark*', meaning the top surface of a rampart or the artery that replaces a rampart – which testifies to the military origin of their layout. Little by little magnificent *hôtels particuliers* were sprinkled along their southern side, surrounded by enchanting gardens and enjoying a pastoral view over the hill of Montmartre and its graceful abbey to the north, all of which remained unchanged until the death of Louis XIV in 1715.

The latter part of the Sun King's reign had been marked by an oppressive atmosphere at Versailles, punctuated by the King's recurrent bereavements and enhanced by the influence of his last companion, the austere Madame de Maintenon. But when the King died the nobility were free at last to leave Versailles and return to the city. The exodus was led by the Regent himself, who inaugurated in Paris a new era of light-hearted optimism, of happy-go-lucky financial speculation and of lavish, carefree playfulness and extravagance – in which Louis XV was to join blithely.

Some, however, did not wish to return to the congested neighbourhood of the Louvre, where they had lived before Louis XIV transferred the court to Versailles, and were drawn to the healthier, airy parts north of the Boulevards, much to the satisfaction of bankers, real-estate developers and the best architects of the time – Ledoux, Brogniart, Aubert – who spent the next 100 years slicing up the neighbourhood to accommodate them and the ever-growing number of Parisians who had accumulated fortunes with the rise of capitalism and followed in their footsteps. Significantly, the last mistress of Louis XV, the notorious du Barry, of doubtful birth and easy virtue, had also commissioned the famous Ledoux to build her a mansion here, on rue Laffitte, with a garden extending all the way from rue de Provence to Boulevard des Italiens, but her project was thwarted by the death of the King. Meanwhile, the archeological findings at Pompeii had put classical art on the map and the aesthetic canons of Ancient Greece became the rage among the above-mentioned set. Architects such as Ledoux built them neo-classical mansions, to satisfy their tastes, but the gardens that surrounded them were designed à l'anglaise, according to the vogue of the time.

The new neighbourhood became known as la Chaussée d'Antin after its initial promoter, le Duc d'Antin who, in the early 18th century, had built himself a palatial mansion on rue Louis-le-Grand (now in the 2nd arr.). This hôtel, considered among the most magnificent in Paris, was reached through the present corner of Boulevard des Capucines and rue Louis-le-Grand by way of a causeway (chaussée) that the Duke had built at his own expense. The land around was covered with marshes, which the Order of the Mathurins had transformed into kitchen gardens, as other orders had done elsewhere in Paris. In the 1770s, the Mathurins decided to sell or lease this land to raise funds for the restoration of the Hôtel de Cluny in the 5th arrondissement – thus making their land available for the development of the new quarter.

Several of the streets in the 9th arrondissement bear the names of the enterprising financiers who promoted its development – rue Laffite, rue Le Peletier, rue Taitbout, rue Caumartin, among others. Some of these people settled in the neighbourhood themselves, such as the banker Laffitte, who ended up ruined, and the developer Laborde (commemorated in the neighbouring 8th arrondissement, near Gare Saint-Lazare), who helped to finance the American War of Independence. Others set up their kept actresses or dancers in houses in this area, notably the Maréchal de Soubise who installed the dancer Guimard in a luxurious palace known as the Hôtel Guimard, at no. 9 rue de la Chaussée-d'Antin. It was built by Ledoux and decorated by Fragonard and the young David. Baron von Grimm, a prominent member of society, described the house thus: 'Whilst the costs were borne by Love, Voluptuous Delight drew the plans, and never in Greece did this divinity own a temple more worthy of her worship.' Whereas opinions varied concerning the occupant of the palace (some praised her for her talent, others had no kind word for her, such as the celebrated singer and interpreter of Rameau and Gluck, Sophie

Arnould, who compared her to a little silkworm) nobody disparaged the *hôtel*. It even contained a 500-seat theatre where the best artists of the Comédie-Française, Comédie-Italienne and the Opera performed! Three times a week Mlle Guimard lavished magnificent dinners on carefully selected guests – once on honourable gentlemen of society, once on illustrious artists and writers, and once on female members of the *demi-monde* who took part here in veritable orgies. The financial ruin of the Rohan family and of the Maréchal de Soubise inevitably dragged his protégée down, and by the time she died on 4 May 1816, at the age of 73, pleasure-seeking Paris had totally forgotten her.

After the fall of the *Ancien Régime*, many of the old landed nobility scorned this neighbourhood of new money and retreated into their shell on the beautiful yet obsolete Faubourg Saint-Germain; but others, among them many *émigrés* now back in France, wished to participate in the fun and settled in the exquisite new quarter. Faithful to their roots, however, they would attend commemorative events such as the 'Foreigners' balls (i.e. balls organised for the *émigrés*) and the 'Victims' balls (i.e. balls organised for the direct relatives of victims of the guillotine, who would turn up with red silk threads tied round their bare necks as a gruesome reminder). About 300 of these staunch royalists joined the *Club de Clichy* on rue de Clichy and were known as *Clichois* or *Clichiens*. After an abortive coup on 4 September 1797 a number of them were deported to French Guiana. *Les Incroyables* and *les Merveilleuses* also had their heyday during this period of the *Directoire*; they too had royalist inclinations, but they were no more than pretentious, trendy youths, notorious for their affected speech (particularly the dropping of their 'r's) and for the eccentric dress (the men wore pseudo rags, the women layers of translucid skirts and huge hats), and presented no political threat.

However, this new neighbourhood had more to it than frivolous affectation and vulgar money-bags; the old nobility of Faubourg Saint-Germain obstinately overlooked the fact that cultured members of society had also moved here. One such was the widowed Madame d'Epinay of no. 5 rue de la Chaussée-d'Antin, the one-time patroness of J. J. Rousseau and the benefactress of Mozart in 1788. Madame d'Epinay was living at the time with Mozart's benefactor, Baron von Grimm, and Mozart visited them here together with his mother Anna. After their visit Anna Mozart wrote to her husband about the transformation of the neighbourhood: 'Here in Paris there are a lot of changes since the last time [1766]; the town has grown a lot and expanded in an indescribable way. La Chaussée d'Antin, where Mr Grimm lives, is a totally new quarter with numerous, broad, beautiful streets. Of course, I have not seen many of them yet, but I have a new map of the town, quite different from the old one we had.' We also know from Mozart's letter to his father that on the occasion of that visit Madame d'Epinay offered his mother a beautiful fan, while on their previous visit to Paris in 1766 she had given her a red taffeta dress as a present. After the death of Anna Mozart on 3 July that same year, the couple welcomed Mozart to their home on the Chaussée d'Antin, where he lived in 'a pretty, little room with a very pleasant view'. However, Grimm soon lost interest in Mozart, who was no longer a child prodigy, nor a social animal – in September Mozart left Paris with nothing but ill feeling for its inhabitants and for its superficial musical scene, never to return.

No. 7 next door had been the home of the famous banker Necker, whose wife presided over gatherings which included Buffon, Saint-Lambert, Grimm and others, and who was also the mother of the equally illustrious Madame de Staël, the romantic writer whose childhood home this was. By the time Napoleon had established the *Directoire*, another famous banker was living here, Jules Recamier, whose wife's receptions were as lavish as the premises and a match for her own renowned beauty. The most distinguished members of society gathered here in those years before the First Empire.

Not surprisingly, as soon as Napoleon had established his Empire, many members of the new Napoleonic nobility joined them, notably Hortense de Beauharnais, Queen of Holland, Napoleon's sister-in-law and later to be Napoleon III's mother. She and her husband, Louis Bonaparte, settled on the site of the present no. 17 rue Laffitte and it was there that Napoleon's nephew was born in 1808. However, doubts about the paternity of Napoleon III had been voiced by Napoleon's maternal uncle, Cardinal Fesch, at one time the Archbishop of Lyons, who said, 'When it comes to determining the fathers of her children, Queen

Hortense gets muddled up in her calculations.' Cardinal Fesch chose to settle at no. 68 rue de la Chaussée-d'Antin, much to the disapproval of the Emperor who pointed out curtly that 'La Chaussée d'Antin was not an appropriate neighbourhood for a cardinal'. The Cardinal replied in a letter dated 14 August 1807, that by residing there he wished to 'rekindle by good example the sacred fire of Religion and to disseminate our spiritual support to a neighbourhood almost totally deprived of any'.

The conservative segment of the old, defeated nobility found its spiritual support in its natural environment of the Faubourg Saint-Germain. Vexed at having been ousted from the course of history, the old nobility turned its back on the area where history was being made without it and where France was being catapulted into the Modern Age. Banks and insurance companies, with such reassuring names as 'La Paternelle' or 'La Protectrice', were soon part of the landscape, reflecting the promise of the early days of capitalism. Fashion houses followed in their wake, catering for those towards whom capitalism had been kind. At first these were only small clothing, fabric and mercery shops; later came the grand, enticing department stores, that lured the customer into prodigious spending and ushered in the consumer age. Les Galeries Lafayette and Au Printemps are relics of that age; there were others that have disappeared. Once equipped with the right finery, the upper set swarmed into the cafés and theatres of the arrondissement, both as actors and spectators of the lavish entertainment.

It was in this area too that the press enjoyed a spectacular boom owing to the progress of printing and to the new freedom of expression made possible by the 1848 Revolution. Most of the newspapers set themselves up in the eastern section of the 2nd arrondissement, where cheap labour was available, but some chose the 9th, notably Le Figaro, a literary weekly at the time, which could boast the names of such superb writers as Balzac, Zola, Gérard de Nerval and Théophile Gautier as contributors. Le Petit Journal, La Presse and Le Temps – precursor of the world-famous Le Monde – were all located here, as was Henri Rochefort's ferociously satirical La Lanterne, so called because 'a street lantern can be used for hanging a villain', an echo of the famous song of the Revolution, rendered to posterity by Edith Piaf:

O ça ira, ça ira, ça ira,
Les aristocrates à la lanterne,
O ça ira, ça ira, ça ira,
Les aristocrates on les pendra.

To the lamppost, to the lamppost,
The aristocrats to the lamppost,
To the lamppost, to the lamppost,
The aristocrats will be hanged.

With so much prosperity around, the art market too was bound to flourish, and it did. Dozens of art galleries opened on rue Laffitte and thereabouts, and were still active on the eve of World War I, notably the galleries owned by the famous Bernheim dealers, Georges at no. 9 and Junior (*Jeune*) at no. 8, who promoted Renoir, and whose descendants are still among the renowned art-dealers in Paris. Above all, Durand-Ruel at no. 16 (whose shop had another entrance on rue Le Peletier), the staunch benefactor and undeviating promoter of the Impressionists. 'Without him we wouldn't have survived,' said Renoir, referring literally to their physical survival. Indeed, Paul Durand-Ruel even arranged advance payment for all his protégés. When he decided to organise an exhibition for the 'young school', this is how *Le Figaro* reviewed his initiative: 'The rue Le Peletier is having its troubles. After the fire at the Opera, a new disaster has befallen the quarter. An exhibition of what is said to be painting has just opened at Durand-Ruel's. The innocent pedestrian, attracted by the flags outside, goes in for a look. But what a cruel spectacle meets his frightened eyes! Five or six lunatics – one of them a woman – make up a group of poor wretches who have succumbed to the madness of ambition and dared to put on an exhibition of their work.' The woman in question was Berthe Morisot, referred to as a 'hussy' by one honourable visitor to the exhibition at Salle Drouot, although the reviewer in *Le Figaro* tempered his criticism of her by saying that 'she manages to convey a certain amount of feminine grace in spite of her outbursts of delirium.' New York gave Durand-Ruel quite a different reception when he repeated his venture there in 1886. Unlike the stuffy, conservative French, the American public were receptive to novelty, to the extent that the fortunes of the Impressionist painters changed from then on. If so many of their great paintings now hang in Washington rather than at the Musée d'Orsay, who is to blame?

While not belittling all due respect for Durand-Ruel's sincere love of art, one must say that he was also a sharp businessman. At a time when speculation was the driving force behind expanding capitalism, he had his share of responsibility in turning the picture trade into yet another stock market, in which a dealer, having the monopoly over the works of a given artist, could control supply and demand. Renoir was well aware of this unfortunate trend: 'It's not a picture you hang up on the wall these days, but an investment. Why not frame some Suez Canal shares?' Also on rue Laffitte, first at no. 39, then at no. 41 and finally at no. 6, was the shop of the equally foresighted Vollard, who wrote the well-known biography of Renoir, *Renoir: An Intimate Record*, but is better known today through his portraits by Renoir and Cézanne. In the unlikely premises of the cellar under his shop on rue Laffitte, where he also lived, Vollard stored precious, rare editions, fine furniture and the works of Cézanne which, in his view, 'have not been equalled since the end of Romanesque art.'

With so many galleries proliferating in the 9th arrondissement and so much available cash, it was only too natural for the new auction house, l'Hôtel Drouot, to open in the 9th. At a time when art was becoming a commercial venture, its opening in 1860 at no. 9 rue Drouot, was welcomed by everyone and was soon honoured with a visit by Napoleon III, who came here in person on 8 March and purchased two terracotta pieces for the sum of 12,600 francs.

The community of artists and writers, too, chose to take up residence in the new centre of gravity of the city – a source not only of inspiration, but also of their bread and butter. Two new adjoining quarters, climbing uphill towards Montmartre, sprang up in the early 1820s. La Nouvelle Athènes (1822), bounded by rue Blanche, rue Saint-Lazare and rue de la Rochefoucauld, was named not only in deference to the enlightened centre of ancient Europe, since Ancient Greek culture was all the rage at the time, but also to honour the modern Greeks who had just shaken off the shackles of bondage heroically and gained their independence from the Turks. Saint-Georges (1824), situated to its east and extending roughly from Place Saint-Georges to the church of Notre-Dame-de-Lorette, also absorbed the surplus population of the saturated Faubourg Poissonnière to the east, then an elegant quarter. While such celebrated architects as Lelong, Visconti and Constantin were commissioned to build for the new inhabitants of La Nouvelle Athènes elegant dwellings in neo-classical or Renaissance style, Saint-Georges also had a certain elegant charm, even though it lacked architectural cohesion because of the intervention of several different developers. Alexandre Dumas Père delighted in the new quarter which, he said, 'seems to have been built by a magic wand... It seemed that all of a sudden the sketches of Jean Goujon, Raphaël and Palladio were dug up and opened once more.'

The artist community appreciated the blend of elegance and rusticity of this new neighbourhood, which lay at the gateway to Montmartre, halfway between the prosperous Chaussée d'Antin at their feet and the village of Montmartre on top of the hill. The atmosphere on its southern, sunny slope offered one a foretaste of rural Montmartre and exerted a magnetic power over these new-comers. Here they found a quiet, provincial lifestyle, which they shared with friendly shopkeepers and humble tradesmen, away from the commotion of the Grands Boulevards, yet not too far away... One by one they climbed the slope, Talma, the greatest and most adulated actor of the time being among the first. George Sand, Chopin, Berlioz, Delacroix and Victor Hugo followed later, and, later still, Auguste Renoir. The 9th arrondissement was to become France's laboratory of creativity, the birthplace of new movements and schools and the nursery of future great men. Thus the Lycée Condorcet on rue du Havre, at the time the lycée of the *haute bourgeoisie* par excellence, produced an impressive list of alumni: the Goncourt brothers, the photographer Nadar, the physicist Ampère, the symbolist poets Verlaine and Mallarmé and Marcel Proust. In 1876 the philosopher Bergson walked off with all the awards for science, Latin and poetry. His French teacher thought it sheer madness on his part to persevere with his philosophy! Mallarmé taught English here later and was officially assessed as follows: 'Makes no effort to improve his English, I even doubt that he knows French.' The Baron Haussmann, Léon Blum and three presidents of the Third Republic came out of its ranks too.

If the academic education was dispensed by respectable

professeurs at Lycée Condorcet, creative, experimental schooling was gained through exchanging thoughts and theories (and even crossing swords) with others in one of the arrondissement's cafés, a Parisian tradition that began with the opening of its first café in 1684, the famous Procope (in the 6th arr.), and never failed until after World War II. Each coterie would have its own haunt according to its inclinations, convictions and friendships.

Thus Toulouse-Lautrec, Forain, Willette, Renoir, Maupassant and Zola would gather at La Nouvelle Athènes (not to be confused with the neighbourhood) at no. 9 Place Pigalle. By World War I the place had been entirely refurbished and the pimps and tarts of Pigalle had replaced Manet and his Impressionist friends, of whose presence not a trace was left. It is now quite impossible to raise ghosts from that past and imagine the enthusiastic, bearded youths – Renoir, Van Gogh, Pissarro, Gauguin – engaged in conversation on the premises of what has long been a strip-tease joint, where the sickly, worn out bodies on display are so unlike the healthy, velvety, radiant flesh painted by Renoir. Le Divan Le Peletier, at 3 rue Le Peletier, was another of their haunts, 'a nasty, little, stupid place', according to the Goncourt brothers. From the same source we know of the preposterous verbal jousts between the *réalistes* painters and the *pompiers*. Courbet (a *réaliste*) would always hold forth vehemently, but on one occasion the painter Couture stood up to him and climbed on to a table in order to confront his opponent from a loftier vantage-point. To which Courbet responded by doing the same. Eventually the police were called in to prevent a more violent turn of events.

In 1859 the stately Courbet migrated to the Brasserie at no. 9 rue des Martyrs, followed by Baudelaire, Vallès etc. La Brasserie was the haunt of bohemia and its most honoured regular was Henri Murger, author of *Tableaux de la Vie de Bohème* (better known as the opera *La Bohème*), who sat enthroned at its central table. Alphonse Daudet would make the journey on foot, all the way from his home on the Left Bank, to be part of the excitement, which would commence at around 11 pm. By that time every 'great' man would be seated at his regular table, surrounded by his clique, amid much hubbub and mugs of beer, and partly obscured by the smoke of pipes, an atmosphere described by Alphonse Daudet in *Trente ans de Paris* as follows:

Voici la table des penseurs: ils ne disent rien, ceux-la; ils n'écrivent pas, ils pensent. . . Plus loin des vareuses, des bérets, des cris d'animaux, des charges, des calembours: ce sont des artistes, des sculpteurs, des peintres.

Here is the table of thinkers: these ones, they say nothing, they write nothing, they just think. . . Further on are smocks, berets, animal noises, caricatures, punsters: those are artists, sculptors, painters.

Whilst nothing much constructive emerged from the nights spent at the Brasserie, the literary gatherings at the restaurant Trapp, at no. 109 rue Saint-Lazare, on the other hand, promoted the Naturalist school, which Flaubert, Zola, the Goncourt brothers, Maupassant, Huysmans and others founded officially on its premises on 16 April 1877.

But the main gathering-places of people from all walks of life were the cafés and restaurants of the Grands Boulevards, the backbone of 19th-century Paris, into which converged the world of finance, politics, art and entertainment. They were mostly located on the northern side of the Boulevard, in what is now the 9th arrondissement, so that their terraces would catch the sun. Here business transactions were carried out, political intrigues were schemed, fashions were created and gossip and rumours circulated, providing food for newspapermen. Here too artists and writers got their inspiration. The literary set liked to gather at the celebrated Café Riche, at no. 16 Boulevard des Italiens, and at the Café de Paris, at no. 24 – one of the most fashionable establishments in the first half of the century and Balzac's favourite, which is certainly a recommendation! Zola, Flaubert, Cézanne and their friends were also regulars at Le Café des Grands Hommes, where artists short of cash would pay with a painting, a tradition later perpetuated in Montparnasse. The café was situated on the corner of Boulevard Poissonnière and rue du Faubourg Montmartre, where affluent Paris petered out.

The Grands Boulevards were the meeting point of Tout-Paris (*All*-Paris) – which meant in fact a minute number of privileged few – who, according to Alphonse Daudet, frequented this '*infinitely small* section of Paris between the Gymnase and the Opera,

Notre-Dame-de-Lorette and the Bourse and imagined they were alone in the world. Brokers, actors, journalists; not to mention the bustling busy legions of good *boulevardiers* who do nothing.' All this upper set had migrated from Palais-Royal, the previous centre of pleasure-seeking Paris, where gambling and prostitution had reigned supreme before the puritanical Louis-Philippe shut most of it down.

During the Belle Epoque, from 1871 to the eve of World War I, carefree Parisians congregated on the Grands Boulevards to see and to be seen. The most elegant Parisians displayed the latest fashions at Tortoni, famous for its sorbets, or rubbed shoulders with the great Dukes of Holy Russia, the Prince of Wales and other celebrities, at the plush Maison Dorée, so called because of its glittering, gilded decoration. Gambetta, the man of the people and deputy of the working-class 20th arrondissement, also frequented this dazzling establishment, as did Eugène Labiche, author of 175 vaudeville plays. He and Georges Feydeau raised the genre to a hilarious work of art, very much in keeping with the current tastes of the spoilt middle class. Unaware of the impending cataclysm that would soon engulf Europe, they would flock to the Théâtres de Boulevards to watch the eternal triangle of husband, wife and lover, or vice versa, perpetually engaged in a silly game of hide-and-seek. Boum Boum the clown would entertain them in his famous Cirque Médrano, while others would skate to the sound of a 45-strong orchestra at the fashionable Pôle Nord ice-rink.

Then, on 28 December 1895, in the midst of this whirlpool of festivities, Auguste and Louis Lumière held the first public cinematographic show which was to revolutionise the world of entertainment in the following century. It was held at the Salon Indien in the basement of the very chic Grand Café, at 14 Boulevard des Capucines. When the show was over, the incredulous spectators went to look for the actors behind the screen! The following year the great pioneer, illusionist and magician Georges Meliès showed his own first unforgettable films at the Théâtre Robert Houdin.

More than any other place, it was Charles Garnier's new Opera House that was to embody this Paris of 'perpetual celebrations'. Here, on the grand staircase, in the spacious lounges and foyers, deliberately larger than the plush tiered auditorium itself, the new rich vied with each other in displaying their finery and their glittering jewels.

World War I took Gay Paris by surprise and marked the beginning of the decline of the area. By 1950 Yves Montand was singing about lower-class Parisians coming to the Boulevards with their families on a Sunday afternoon. Three decades later, Charles Garnier's Opera House, the major Second Empire edifice in Paris and today's only testimony of the glamorous past of the 9th arrondissement, was shamefully deemed too 'bourgeois' by a socialist government, indifferent to its historical and cultural associations the world over. A new 'democratic' Opera House was built on the historic Place de la Bastille which cost 25 billion francs (as against the 12 billion originally budgeted for). Although Garnier's Opera has not been shut down, and is now devoted to ballet performances, it has lost its aura and is bound in time to become an empty shell. One journalist has suggested, not entirely tongue in cheek, that, in this age of commercial profit and consumer greed, the best thing would be to raze it to the ground, thus making room for a direct throughway to the Galeries Lafayette!

WHERE TO WALK

THE GRANDS BOULEVARDS AND THEREABOUTS

A walk through today's commercial Grands Boulevards is of no use to those seeking to recapture their elegant past which, except for a few features here and there, largely came to an end with the cataclysm of World War I.

Set out from the western edge of the **BOULEVARD DES CAPUCINES**. The **Olympia music-hall** at no. 28 has managed to survive against all odds. It started when the enterprising manager of the Moulin-Rouge, Joseph Oller, installed a switchback railway he had brought over from Blackpool, which became one of the many 'latest crazes' of thrill-hungry, novelty-seeking Belle Epoque

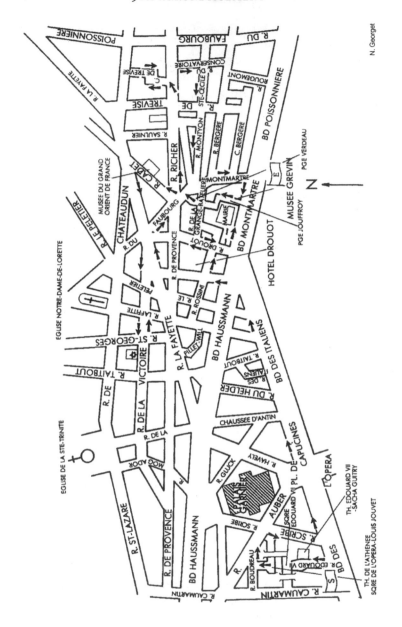

N. Georget

Paris. However, the police ruled that the wooden switchback was a fire hazard and ordered it to be pulled down. Oller, undaunted, opened the Olympia instead on 12 April 1893. In keeping with the prevailing Anglomania, Oller used the term 'music hall' rather than 'café-concert', for the first time in France, and thus became known as '*Le père du Music Hall*'. Oller himself could not speak a word of English, but he had flair, and kept turning to London for new ideas and inspiration.

The Olympia flourished until the late 1920s but had to close down eventually, being unable to compete with the up-and-coming movie industry. On 31 May 1929 its plush red curtain rose for the last variety show, after which it was converted into a picture house. In 1952, however, it was bought by the enthusiastic Bruno Coquatrix and turned back into a music hall, and a most prestigious one indeed!

For the next 20 years it was the Mecca of France's singers and of *la chanson française*. Bruno Coquatrix had the knack of discovering potential talent and in 1953 was the first to set Gilbert Bécaud, '*Monsieur 100,000 volts*', on the road to stardom. All the great names of France were to follow suit – Ch? :s Trenet, Mouloudji, Juliette Gréco, Charles Aznavour, Yves Montand, Jacques Brel. Georges Brassens, on the other hand, deserted it for the humble Bobino on the Left Bank (in the 14th arr.). Some Parisians still recall Edith Piaf's last performances here in 1962 – her tiny figure in a plain black dress, her extraordinarily expressive hands and her heart-rending voice. Others may recall the Beatles' performance in 1964, which created quite a sensation. It was at the Olympia that the great jazz violinist Stéphane Grappelli chose to celebrate his 80th birthday in 1988 and that the Rolling Stones made a historical come back in 1995.

Continue along the Boulevard and turn left into rue Edouard VII. You will come to **Square Edouard VII** with Landowski's statue of the British King and the Théâtre Edouard VII-Sacha Guitry on your right. A little further on is the **Square de l'Opéra-Louis Jouvet** and its theatre, l'Athénée, on the left. This elegant small enclave honours two of the most prominent men of the theatre of the first half of the century and the francophile King of England. The square is best appreciated by night, when the street-lamps create a romantic atmosphere and call to mind the splendour of the neighbourhood a century ago.

Turn right into rue Boudreau and right again into RUE AUBER. On your left is the old Opera House, le Palais Garnier, which can be visited. Like its 20th-century counterpart at La Bastille, it was built for prestige at least as much as for art's sake. In both cases the world was to be dazzled by the greatest, the most beautiful, the most technically advanced etc. opera house in the world, the quality of the performances themselves not necessarily being top priority. While the Bastille Opera had to be ready at all costs for Bastille Day 1989, Garnier's monument was meant to coincide with that of 1867 – the year of the Universal Exposition – but, owing to shortage of funds and bureaucratic sluggishness, only its façade could be unveiled to the public. In both cases a contest was organised by the authorities, and both were won by young unknown architects – the 35-year-old Charles Garnier and the 42-year-old Canadian Carl Ott. The incredible length of time taken to complete both structures and their stupendous costs, which many regarded with a critical eye, are also comparable. But France has always been obsessed by the wish to embody her superlative grandeur in monuments. Opera houses must have been among her favourites it would seem: since Louis XIV set up his first opera house in 1669, 13 other houses have been erected in the French capital!

The Empress Eugénie was bewildered by the neo-baroque style of the new edifice and said so bluntly to Charles Garnier, 'C'est ni du grec, ni du Louis XIV, pas même du Louis XVI.' ('This is neither Greek nor Louis XIV, nor even Louis XVI'). Although somewhat ruffled, the architect retained enough presence of mind to reply, 'Ces styles là ont fait leur temps. C'est du style Napoléon III, Madame!' ('Those styles have had their day. This is in the style of Napoleon III, Madam!').

The painter Renoir was also scandalised by what he called 'that lump of an overbaked brioche', and regretted that Big Bertha had missed it! But some people are rather fond of it and feel that as this is the main example of the magnificence of the Second Empire (although it was inaugurated after its fall), for better or for worse, it should not be lightly dismissed. As you walk up its grand staircase or wander through its splendid foyer, you can picture the

Le Palais Garnier

scintillating Parisian society parading here in their finery, notably on the opening night, 5 January 1875, which was attended by the President of the Republic, the King of Spain, and the Lord Mayor of London in his ceremonial attire, escorted by his sheriffs, sword-bearers and halberdiers. (Charles Garnier was also present but was made to pay for his seat).

The foyer was indeed the centre of gravity of the Palais Garnier, rather than the auditorium with its 2,156 seats. This was where the main spectacle was, where wealth and social status were flaunted and where the real sense of the occasion could be felt and enjoyed. This was exactly what Charles Garnier had intended when he designed the house and he was honest enough to admit it openly.

The tiered, horseshoe-shaped auditorium is beautifully proportioned and enhanced in 1964 by Chagall's splendid ceiling paintings representing nine famous operas and ballets. From its centre hangs the 7-ton crystal chandelier that has made history.

On 20 May 1896, during a performance of *Faust*, it broke loose, crashed through level 5, where no one was sitting, and landed on seats 11 and 13 on level 4, killing one woman and injuring many. This terrible accident caught Gaston Leroux's imagination and triggered off his famous work *Le Phantôme de l'Opéra*. In his distorted – but much more thrilling – version, the sinister phantom penetrates the director's office and forewarns of the imminent catastrophe. The chandelier is shaken loose by the vibrations of the singer's voice and crushes not one woman but several members of the audience.

Even more famous than Leroux's novel was Laemmle's silent movie version of the work with Lon Chaney in the title role. As shipping an entire cast across the Atlantic was a more expensive option, a replica of Garnier's auditorium and its chandelier, as well as the grand staircase where the dazzling masked balls took place, was built instead at the Universal's studio no. 28 in Hollywood. The setting was later used for other movies, notably Hitchcock's *Torn Curtain* and George Roy Hill's *The Sting*. After several versions and remakes of Leroux's legend, Lloyd Weber turned *The Phantom of the Opera* into a box-office success as a musical and has thus contributed to rescuing Charles Garnier's threatened Palace from oblivion. What most people do not know is that the mysterious maze of dark corridors and underground galleries that make up so much of Leroux's backdrop do in fact exist, hidden from the public eye. And the lake that was to play a part in the plot was no fantasy either. A substantial body of water was here when Charles Garnier was planning his edifice and had to be dried up. On the roof of the Palais Garnier there are beehives, yielding honey, apparently, in substantial quantities.

The Palais Garnier should be seen at night in all its splendour, from the Avenue de l'Opéra. It was opened by Haussmann as a stately link between the Opera House and the Palais des Tuileries, the Emperor's residence. The edifice and the avenue were so impressive themselves, that Haussmann deemed it superfluous to plant trees along the avenue, as he did elsewhere.

Turn right into **RUE SCRIBE**, which commemorates the librettist of Fromental Halévy's *La Juive*. The streets surrounding the Opera were named after people who contributed to its productions in the 19th century. On the corner of rue Scribe and no. 14 Boulevard des Capucines, the well-known Scribe Hotel stands on the site of the **Grand Café**. On 28 December 1895 the first public showing of a movie was organised by the Lumière brothers in the Salon Indien, in the basement of the café. Only 33 spectators attended this 20-minute show of ten films (each lasting roughly two minutes) one of which was *La sortie des usines Lumière*, their first film. The spectators were thrilled but the newspaper reporters did not bother to turn up and the event was not even mentioned in the press! Only one far-sighted journalist wrote in *La Poste*:

> *Lorsque tous pourront photographier les êtres qui leur sont chers, non plus dans leur forme immobile mais dans leur mouvement, dans leur action, dans leurs gestes familiers, avec la parole au bout des lèvres, la mort cessera d'être absolue.*

> When all are able to photograph their dear ones, no longer in their immobile shape, but in motion, in action, in their everyday gestures, with words on the tips of their tongues, death will cease to be absolute.

The tickets went for 1 franc each. Three weeks later the takings had soared from 33 francs to 2,000!

Across rue Scribe, the aptly named **Grand-Hôtel** (first known as Grand-Hôtel de la Paix) was also built for the 1867 Exposition, but in this case, met its deadline. It occupied the entire next block of the Boulevard des Capucines, as far as the Place de l'Opéra, and was the most luxurious hotel in Paris, boasting a dumbfounding profusion of styles and features. The archetypal **Café de la Paix** on the corner of Boulevard des Capucines and Place de l'Opéra was decorated by Charles Garnier and was leased out by the hotel. This was the showcase of the Opera, where opera-goers congregated on the performance night, a centre for both the *beau monde* and for musicians and literati – Oscar Wilde, Sacha Guitry, André Gide, Paul Valéry, among others – and Caruso is said to have left his cartoons on the table-cloths. Today this is a meeting-place of the tourist population, inevitably on errands in this shopping area, close to the Galeries Lafayette and the Printemps, the two major department stores in Paris.

At no. 8 **BOULEVARD DES CAPUCINES**, beyond the Place de l'Opéra, was the home of Jacques Offenbach from 1876 to 1880, where he composed the *Tales of Hoffmann*. He died here in 1880, four months before the premiere. At no. 2 is the **Paramount** cinema, which has replaced the old Théâtre de Vaudeville, one of the most famous theatres in 19th-century Paris. It was here that in March 1845 Charles S. Stratton, a native of Connecticut, better known as General Tom Thumb, started his meteoric rise to fame. The 25-inch-tall boy, still only 7 years old, had already been presented to Queen Victoria and was now to meet Louis-Philippe and his court. Théophile Gautier was disgusted by this freak, but Paris adulated the little person who paraded through the streets in a tiny coach befitting his size. Tom Thumb came back to Paris in 1864 with his midget wife and midget daughter. They stayed at the Hôtel du Louvre opposite the Palais-Royal, where he gave a lavish reception. He died in 1883 when only 45, having by then grown to a height of 40 inches.

The Théâtre de Vaudeville occupied the site of a palatial dwelling built by Ledoux in neo-Grecian style for the Prince of Montmorency, one of the loveliest houses in the Chaussée d'Antin. But all is not lost: the wooden panelling of its oval drawing-room has been preserved, albeit in Boston, Massachusetts, and the pavilion of the bejewelled Hôtel Hanover across the Boulevard, of which the façade of Hôtel de Montmorency and its rotunda were a replica, can still be seen in Parc de Sceaux, south of Paris (by the RER train, line B). Originally the home of the Duc d'Antin, the Hôtel Hanover was largely altered by its later proprietor, the Maréchal Duc de Richelieu, one of the most brilliant of Frenchmen, notorious for his prodigal lifestyle and womanising. Not content with the Regent's daughter, her sister and her cousin, the Duke proceeded to carry off three of the Regent's mistresses, after which the Regent decided to remove him from Paris and appointed him Ambassador to Vienna.

His agitated love life – he boasted of having slept with every female in Place Royale (now Place des Vosges) in the Marais, and married for the last time at age 84 – did not seem to wear him out, for he also managed to outlive most of his contemporaries, dying only at 92. This is the more remarkable for the fact that he was born two months prematurely and kept ensconced in cottonwool in a box for three months. Having defeated the city of Hanover, he used the ransom to build this mansion, hence its name. By 1937 there was no room for exquisite 18th-century *hôtels* in the area. Its gracious lifestyle had gone and avid developers were seeking new profits. The mansion was razed to the ground, but the *pavillon* was preserved and reconstructed, stone by stone, in the beautiful setting of Parc de Sceaux.

Continue into **BOULEVARD DES ITALIENS**, named after the illustrious Théâtre des Italiens (in the 2nd arr.), where the Italian troupe performed. Today this is the Opéra-Comique, also known as Salle Favart. after one of its co-founders in the 18th century. During the Restoration the Boulevard was named Boulevard de Gand, to commemorate the Belgian town of Ghent where Louis XVIII, then Comte de Provence, had gone into exile, and its fashionable *Boulevardiers* were known as *Gandins*. Right through the 19th century this was the Grand Boulevard *par excellence*, the backbone of Paris. Between 1833 and 1836 the exclusive Jockey Club occupied no. 34. It had started as a society for the promotion of horse-racing in France but soon became, like its English counter-parts, a select club for titled members and for the privileged who knew how to gravitate around them, about 200 in all. Lord Seymour was their first president.

At no. 28 stood the Théâtre des Nouveautés until 1911, when the opening of rue des Italiens entailed its demolition. This was where Georges Feydeau, the master of vaudeville, triumphed. It might seem odd that someone nourished on literature with a capital 'L' (his father's best friend was Flaubert and he was surrounded in his early years by such writers as Vigny, Baudelaire and Alphonse Daudet) should turn to what many intellectuals consider a minor genre, the vaudeville.

As a matter of fact it was not as minor as may seem and expres-sed deep concern for the stupidity of the new age which would inevitably lead to disaster. Thus Feydeau's characters, engaged in love triangles by way of mechanical ballets, were the grotesque representatives of the new middle classes, gesticulating puppets leaping on to the stage through banging doors and popping out of cupboards like frantic Jack-in-the-boxes, the creations of a pessimistic author, the pathetic products of an unfortunate age, among whom he included himself.

For Feydeau, no less than any of his privileged contemporaries, thoroughly enjoyed the dissolute and eccentric pleasures of Belle Epoque Paris – dining, womanising, collecting works of art (among them dozens of Impressionist paintings at a time when they were still derided) and twice ruining himself in the process. At the last stage of this not atypical journey, he contracted syphilis, not atypically either.

At no. 24, on the corner of rue Taitbout, stood Le Café de Paris, 'The Temple of elegance, where those who were admitted were awarded the diploma of Parisians and Boulevardiers.' Among them were Balzac, Musset, Théophile Gautier and Alexandre Dumas, who often dined here on a veal casserole. Some considered it the best establishment in Europe, although the flight of steps leading up to the dining hall was not quite so famous as that of its next door neighbour, Tortoni, at no. 22, where wonderful sorbets were sold, the 'Berthillon' of those days. At lunchtime its steps were crammed with 'barbarians' (stockbrokers), while the contemptuous dandies came in through the back door. Musset describes how one jostled one's way into the establishment at night, after the show, in order to savour an ice-cream before retiring. On an average summer's night, 1,000 ice-creams were consumed at Tortoni's.

The fabulously wealthy Lord Hertford lived in the *hôtel* next door, on the corner of rue Laffitte. He also owned the exquisite Château de Bagatelle (in the 16th arr.). However, he was never seen on the fashionable Boulevard; unlike his half-brother, the socialite Lord Seymour, he led the life of a recluse, never even bothering to draw open the curtains, and was wholly dedicated to collecting art works. These he bequeathed to his illegitimate son, Sir Richard Wallace (the philanthropist who offered Paris the charming Wallace fountains), and together with the latter's collection they now largely make up the magnificent Wallace Collection in London.

The entire block, now invaded by the BNP (Banque Nationale de Paris, which was privatised in 1993 but has retained its acronym), was lined with the most elegant cafés at the time, where the pleasures afforded the palate were enhanced by the delights that met the eye, among them the beautiful attire of the customers. Café Hardy at no. 20 and Café Riche at no. 16 were particularly renowned during the first half of the century and the saying went, '*Il faut être bien riche pour manger chez Hardi et être bien hardi pour manger chez Riche*' ('One must be quite rich to eat at Hardy and one must be quite daring to eat at Riche'). Café Riche declined during the Second Empire and was referred to then as 'an economical English café to which you invite an acquaintance you are not very keen on...' However, during the Belle Epoque it became the stronghold of the cream of the literati, who appreciated its *haute cuisine*. Café Hardy was pulled down in 1839 and replaced by the most spectacular establishment in the capital, appropriately named La Maison Dorée. The place was a favourite with the royalty of Europe, among them, naturally, the Prince of Wales, later to become Edward VII. Its present owner, the BNP, has preserved its architecture and style, but its one-time gilded balconies no longer glitter. When the café closed down, in the early years of the Third Republic, followed by Tortoni in 1894, the Goncourt brothers saw in this a sign of the 'passing away of the Boulevard des Italiens.'

Turn left into rue Chauchat at the intersection of Boulevards des Italiens, Haussmann and Montmartre, then right into RUE ROSSINI. We shall now enter the arrondissement proper and will be able to grasp its particular atmosphere, where pockets of nostalgia alternate with present vitality, but where concrete has rarely ousted stone.

On your left is the new building (1980) of the auction house, the **Hôtel Drouot**, the main entrance of which is at no. 9 rue Drouot. The Paris auction house, the oldest in the world, was founded by Napoleon when, in the wake of the French Revolution, countless precious possessions were placed on the market. Well before his time, in 1552, Henri II had instituted the first offices of *maîtres-priseurs-vendeurs*, effectively the first professional auctioneers. In 1801 Napoleon appointed 80 auctioneers to his newly created ministerial office, binding the auctioneer on oath to work on a commission basis only (to the exclusion of any profit-making). Few could afford to purchase the office and it was customary for the profession to be handed down from father to son. With the advent of the prosperous Second Empire there was need for a new auction house, which, needless to say, had to be established in what had become the centre of finance and art. Conveniently a mansion that had lodged the distinguished guests of the First Empire was available. It was entirely overhauled and by 1859 was ready to open to the public. Napoleon III went there in person on 8 March 1860. Responding to the decline in prestige of the 9th arrondissement, in 1988 Drouot opened a new outlet at the celebrated Théâtre des Champs-Elysées, on the most glamorous artery in the affluent 8th arrondissement, the Avenue Montaigne. Will that help the house to keep abreast with the high-flying Christie's and Sotheby's, which have unquestionably gained worldwide supremacy? With the opening of the borders and stiff competition from elsewhere within the European Community, many professionals are pressing for reform, for, extraordinary as it may seem to an outsider, Napoleon's rulings largely hold to this day.

If you visit the auction house of Drouot (now known as Drouot-Richelieu to distinguish it from Drouot-Montaigne), you may be disappointed by the shabby aspect of the place. On the morning of an auction the goods are on display and you may be lucky enough to stumble upon a beautiful or interesting exhibition. The auctions themselves take place in the afternoons and are feverish affairs orchestrated by the three-person team of auctioneer-crier-expert and punctuated by the auctioneer's hammer. If you have never been to an auction before, you may feel like an intruder at a ritual reserved for the initiated. You are likely to be right – the majority of the attendants are professional or enlightened amateurs. Do not worry about scratching your nose, but beware of such pitfalls as *style Louis XV*, which does not mean *Epoque Louis XV*! Every Friday *La Gazette de l'Hôtel Drouot* publishes a list of forthcoming auctions and the results of the recent ones. Catalogues are also available.

Among the more sensational sales that took place at Drouot was the occasion in 1878 when the hat Napoleon wore during his Russian campaign went for the modest sum of 175 francs. On 8 May 1951 the furniture from the plushest of the Parisian brothels, le Chabanais, was dispersed here, after the establishment had closed down. In 1991 the famous green velvet couch, with its three bolster pillows, on which Lacan's patients used to lie during their five-minute analysis sessions, was sold here, along with a matching chair, Lacan's desk, headrests used by his patients and books.

As you leave the Hôtel Drouot, you will see several antique, stamp and coin shops which seem like a pleasant extension of Drouot into the street. At no. 6 rue Drouot is the attractive 18th-century Hôtel d'Augny, now the Mairie of the 9th arrondissement. This peaceful retreat, at the back of an elegant, paved courtyard, once belonged to Alexandre Aguado, a prosperous Portuguese Jew who owned le Château-Margaux, the most renowned vineyards of Bordeaux, and who later became banker of Ferdinand VII of Spain. A great lover of the opera, he took Rossini under his patronage. After the downfall of Robespierre this *hôtel* was reputed for its elegant '*bals de victimes*', held by surviving relatives of the Revolution's victims.

Turn left into BOULEVARD MONTMARTRE. At no. 10/12 the Passage Jouffroy, is yet another antiquated arcade built in the 19th century, and full of charm. Browsing through its curiosity shops and their displays of masks, marionettes, old books, old cameras and other curios, makes one feel nostalgic for a past long gone. On your right is the wax museum, another survivor from those days, of which some more later. Passage Verdeau beyond Passage Jouffroy (across rue de la Grange-Batelière) exudes the same nostalgic charm in the same antiquated setting.

As you come out of Passage Verdeau, turn left into rue du Faubourg Montmartre and right into RUE CADET, a bustling pedestrian precinct lined with colourful food shops and stalls, light years away from the old arcades. At no. 16 the Freemasons's temple, le Temple du Grand Orient de France, also houses a museum, where you can see mementos of such prominent members of the brotherhood as the Marquis de Lafayette; Jules Ferry, who had fought for free education for all during the Second Empire, a goal he achieved during the Third Republic; Bartholdi, the sculptor of the Statue of Liberty; and the celebrated anarchists Proudhon and Bakounine. You will also see the armchair of Louis-Philippe d'Orléans, Duc de Chartres, and grandfather of the future King Louis-Philippe, who was also Grand Master of the brotherhood. He was the cousin Louis XVI derided as 'shopkeeper', although he was landlord of both the Palais-Royal and the Parc de Monceau and a richer man than His Majesty. Having adhered to the egalitarian ideal of the Revolution, he became known as Philippe Egalité, which did not ultimately help save his head.

Turn left into rue La Fayette, cross rue du Faubourg Montmartre and continue into RUE DE LA VICTOIRE, where the largest synagogue in Paris stands at no. 44. In the latter part of the 18th century a magnificent mansion stood here, the work of Brogniart, commissioned by the Prince de Soubise for the dancer Drevieux. A garden of arbours, bowers and grottos embellished this architectural gem, although the Prince had lavished even larger sums on Mlle Guimard, as mentioned above. Mlle Drevieux hardly led a monogamous life either – the Duc de Richelieu, the Prince de Conti, the Prince de Condé and the Comte d'Artois (later Charles X), were all her lovers. In 1802 the mansion was occupied by Hortense de Beauharnais and her husband Louis Bonaparte.

In the 1860s, when the only existing Ashkenazi synagogue on rue Notre-Dame-de-Nazareth (in the 3rd arr.) could no longer contain the growing influx of Jews, largely from Alsace (from 2,600 Jews living in Paris under Napoleon to 8,000 in 1840, by 1853 their number had increased to 20,000), the *hôtel* was bought by the Jewish community, torn down and replaced by the present synagogue. The Count Moïse de Camondo, the Rothschilds, the cabinet minister Adolphe Crémieux and others of the great and good attended its inauguration ceremony on 9 September 1874. Although France had been the first country in Europe to emancipate the Jews, in the wake of the Revolution, and many Jews had reached the summit of society, the Empress Eugénie vetoed the initial proposal to place the main entrance of the synagogue on rue de Châteaudun, deeming it inappropriate for a Jewish temple to stand so conspicuously between the churches of La Sainte-Trinité and Notre-Dame-de-Lorette. Nevertheless, on 22 March 1876 the most eminent figures were present at the wedding of Albert de Rothschild and his cousin, Bettina. Emile Zola, also present, commented on the event: 'While watching Paris, filled with wonder and respect, crowding into this synagogue, I thought of the hatred to which the Jews had been subjected during the Middle Ages. . . But time has marched forward, civilisation and justice have gained ground.' Some 20 years later Zola was to revise his opinion, when he wrote his famous *J'accuse* in defence of Alfred Dreyfus. The article, which covered the front page of *l'Aurore* on 13 January 1898, resulted in himself being accused and found guilty of libel. He appealed and the conviction was quashed by the Cour de Cassation on 2 April. A retrial was ordered on 18 July but Zola did not wait to hear the verdict and instead fled to England.

Retrace your steps and turn right into rue du Faubourg Montmartre. A La Mère de Famille at no. 35 is a shop that has been standing since the 19th century and has kept its original setting. Turn left into **RUE RICHER**, the backbone of this other Jewish quarter of Paris which began to develop in the 19th century, with the first mass arrival of European Jews. Today this colourful street has a Mediterranean flavour and is lined with food stores and restaurants typical of North Africa and the Middle East. The Art Déco edifice of the **Folies-Bergère** stands incongruously in this enclave, at no. 32.

The name Folies-Bergère was simply borrowed from the neighbouring rue Bergère. Originally there was a suggestion to name it after the rue Trévise, also near by, but the Duc de Trévise nearly had a heart failure when he heard of the plan to associate his name with such an establishment! Oddly enough, this former house of voluptuous pleasures – '*le seul endroit à Paris qui pue délicieusement le maquillage des tendresses payées et les abois des corruptions qui se lassent*' ('the only place in Paris that stinks so exquisitely of the make-up of bought intimacy and of the despair of weary corruption'), as Huysmans wrote in *Croquis Parisiens* – was previously the property of a venerable religious institution, les Quinze-Vingts! The story goes that in the 16th century a humble dwelling stood on the site, surrounded by fields and washed by the river of la Grange-Batelière. The monk who lived in that house is said to have bequeathed it to the Quinze-Vingts to atone for his penchant for wine.

Be that as it may, when the Folies-Bergère opened in 1858 next to a bedding shop, Les Colonnes d'Hercule, also known as Le Sommier Elastique (the Springy Mattress), it was such a fiasco that it was nicknamed Le Café des Sommiers Elastiques. It was only after the famous *promenoir* (gallery), described by Maupassant in *Bel*

Ami, as well as the bar, rendered immortal by Manet, were added that the Folies-Bergère began to flourish. There was also a magnificent hall with lush vegetation and fountains, creating the voluptuous atmosphere of an Arabian night. However, when in the late 1880s its manager had the extravagant idea of turning the establishment into a concert hall – Le Concert de Paris – it nearly went bankrupt! Not even the patronage of some of the greatest musicians of the day – Gounod, Massenet, Saint-Saëns and Delibes – could save it. Gay Paris was after other kinds of pleasure, and when beautifully-shaped, slender dancers, preferably English, were brought in to replace the dull, lacklustre musicians, and were stripped in spectacular reviews, the public swarmed back and acclaimed them enthusiastically.

In 1907, the famous troupe of English mimes, the Fred Karno Company, came to perform here. Among them was an 18-year-old totally unknown actor by the name of Charlie Chaplin. Two years later, in September 1909, another young beginner made his debut on this stage – Maurice Chevalier then 21 years old. The critic of *Le Figaro* had no kind words for the youth, wondering where such a beanpole came from and why he had been let loose on the stage of the foremost music hall of the capital. Notwithstanding, Maurice Chevalier continued his ascension. In 1911 he was joined by Minstinguett who was engaged to lead the reviews. Her partnership with Chevalier, both on and off stage, lasted for many years.

After the Great War the Folies-Bergère was taken over by Derval, who ran it for nearly 50 years. Derval had it renovated in its present Art Deco style and turned it into an establishment of worldwide renown. Perhaps his most sensational number was *La Perle Noire* starring Josephine Baker, in 1926. Derval had discovered her the year before in the celebrated *Revue Nègre* at the Théâtre des Champs-Elysées and he went into raptures over this magnificent girl who 'would set the stage ablaze.'

He hired her on the spot and she became the highlight of his show. A huge ball, covered with flowers, would descend from the dome of the theatre and land among the musicians. The ball would then open up, revealing the stunning 'Black Pearl' standing on a mirror, almost nude, moving sinuously on the mirror before the ball would close up and carry her off again up to the domed ceiling. The audience was ecstatic. In 1949 Josephine Baker returned to the

Folies-Bergère from New york for a farewell performance. Among other 'greats' who performed here were Fernandel in the 1930s and Charles Trenet in 1944.

Continue along rue Richer and turn left at the **Cité de Trévise**, a peaceful nook enhanced by the trickling water of its fountain. This is a good example of the elegant compounds built in the neighbourhood of Saint-Georges in the first half of the 19th century, which attracted artists and writers. An advertisement for the Cité Trévise in the newspaper *l'Illustration*, dating from 1844, referred to these 'elegant retreats which, whilst ensuring the calm necessary for work, do not remove the scholar from the bustling centre where his interests lie' (the centre being the Grands Boulevards).

Continue along rue Richer and turn right into rue du Conservatoire, named after the National Music Conservatory, which was located here until 1913, when it moved to rue de Madrid in the 8th arrondissement. Its director at the time was Gabriel Fauré. Turn right into rue Sainte-Cécile and rue de Montyon beyond it, then left into **RUE DU FAUBOURG MONTMARTRE**. At no. 7 is the restaurant **Chartier**, which is well worth going into for the experience. For this huge, noisy canteen (1,500 customers a day!) provides a very rare example of genuine Belle Epoque Paris, with absolutely no kitschy extras, and food on the cheap side, though not quite so cheap as in those early days when one paid 60 centimes in advance, for which one would get meat for 20 centimes, vegetables for 10, followed by cheese, dessert and bread for 10 centimes each. Wine was optional, although not included in that price. The atmosphere is still great here, just as it was when the actor Fernandel came to dine here and the Blue Guide to Paris already mentioned Chartier in its 1863 edition.

Turn right into **BOULEVARD MONTMARTRE** and step into **Musée Grévin** at no. 10. The world's first wax museum was opened in 1760 in Berne by the Swiss Jean Christophe Curtis. The Prince de Conti invited him to Paris to start a similar museum. He taught the trade to his niece Marie Gresholtz, who helped him to create his wax figures. During the French Revolution she made a fortune moulding death masks of the guillotined victims. In 1800 she married François Tussaud and soon after opened another wax museum in London, which secured her world renown as the celebrated Madame Tussaud. Although the Musée Grévin is much smaller than its London counterpart (1,100 as against 3,700 square metres), it has a plush, Belle Epoque setting decorated with the works of such artists as Bourdelle and Chéret.

The museum was founded in 1882 by the cartoonist and painter Alfred Grévin, and was the brainchild of Régis Gabriel Thomas, who also helped him to finance and run the Eiffel Tower. Its present owner, his grandson, had the happy idea of founding the Belle Epoque annexe at Les Halles. He claims to have read 8,000 pages of data on that era in order to get everything just right. The main museum on Boulevard Montmartre exhibits models of a mishmash of political leaders, the mediocre side by side with the great, sports champions with film stars and so on. There is an interesting section with major scenes from the French Revolution, and children will love the show at the splendid Théâtre Grévin (where chamber music is also played at times) and the exotic Palais des Mirages.

HEADING NORTH
TOWARDS MONTMARTRE

The next walk will take us further north, to the attractive neighbourhood of La Nouvelle Athènes and Saint-Georges, built in the early 1820s to accommodate the growing numbers of newcomers, mainly from the south of the city, but also from the east, where the elegant Faubourg Poissonnière had become saturated. The area became the stronghold of the Romantic artists who were drawn to its blend of country life and elegance, a tradition maintained by succeeding generations throughout the century. There are so many exquisite nooks hidden here, as well as lovely homes of prominent figures of the time, that the itinerary set out here is, unfortunately, bound to leave some out. Do not hesitate to wander off and peep beyond heavy doors whenever they yield to your efforts (this is more likely to happen on weekdays when some of the digicodes are not used).

Starting at the church of La Sainte-Trinité and heading north

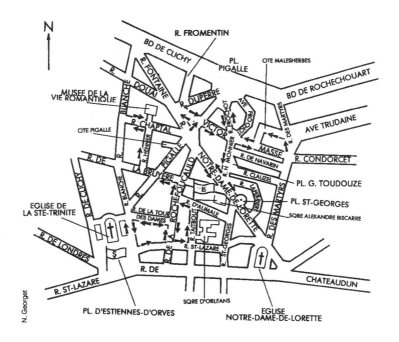

N. Georget

towards Montmartre is the more exciting way of following the itinerary; those who may find this tiring, however, can start at the top and work their way downhill.

The church of **La Sainte-Trinité** on **PLACE D'ESTIENNE D' ORVES** was built between 1863 and 1867 by the architect Ballu, to provide the growing population with an adequate place of worship. It stands conspicuously on a slope, and its eclectic style, so typical of the Second Empire, displeased many. One clergyman wondered whether he was in a lounge, a concert hall or a Parliament! However, the church prides itself on having had Olivier Messiaen as its organist for 40 years. At the foot of the church lie pleasant gardens but surrounded nowadays by heavy, polluting traffic.

Before the Revolution, a huge public-house, the notorious Porcherons, which could seat 600, was located at no. 1 Place d'Estienne d'Orves. The common herd came here to drink cheap wine, but the place was also frequented by some ladies of quality, who liked, from time to time, to mix with the riff-raff and enjoy the company of a rough brute rather than that of an effete gentleman. In 1830 the plot against the Bourbon Monarchy was hatched on these

93

premises. When Louis-Philippe ascended the throne, he closed down all the cafés in the area in order to avert the same fate.

Turn into RUE SAINT-LAZARE. If you are interested in the past, you may first wander off into RUE BLANCHE, where many prominent people once lived. At no. 15 is Le Théâtre de Paris, once Le Théâtre Nouveau, which the famous actress Réjane owned from 1909 to 1918 under the name of Théâtre Réjane. Also on rue Blanche, at no. 21, is the Ecole Nationale d'Art Dramatique. At no. 25 the German Evangelical church has stained-glass windows representing the town of Worms and the castle of Wartburg, where Luther found shelter after his excommunication. At no. 28 rue Blanche is the fire station, which has a vineyard on the premises – six vines in all, nurtured by the fire brigade since 1904! The firemen produce an average of 30 bottles of wine a year. On the second Friday of October the picking of the grapes is celebrated with great pomp. The names on the bottles may sound promising – le Pinot Noir and Chasselas – but the wine itself is almost undrinkable, although the labels are highly sought after by collectors.

Little is left in rue Saint-Lazare to remind you of its past elegance, which was enhanced by lovely public gardens, le Jardin Ruggieri, on the site of the present no. 16/18. In 1783 a pantomime theatre was set up in the gardens where the heroic battle and death of Marlborough were enacted. The burlesque song Malbrough s'en va-t-en guerre, a great hit at the time, was sung as part of the show and it is still part of the standard repertoire of French children under the age of five. At no. 58 stands the house of the painter Paul de la Roche (creator of Les enfants d'Edouard and l'Assassinat du Duc de Guise), built in a refined Italian style, which was much in vogue at the time. A peaceful, countrified drive leads to the back of four houses, occupied by four of the greatest celebrities of the time – the actresses Mlles Mars and Duchesnois on the right, the actor Talma on the left and the court painter of the First Empire, Horace Vernet, in front. This charming, narrow entrance, which they shared, was normally used for coaches but was occasionally invaded by troops of infantry and cavalry, accompanied by drums and horses, all hired to pose for Horace Vernet, who was working on one of his overblown battle scenes designed to glorify the Emperor.

Turn left into rue de La Rochefoucauld, and left again into RUE DE LA TOUR DES DAMES, the elegant hub of La Nouvelle Athènes during its heyday – to judge by its celebrated tenants, if nothing else. The corner house at no. 1 was occupied by the much admired actress, Mlle Mars, who commissioned the sculptor Visconti to add adornments to it. Mlle Mars moved out of this mansion in 1827, after all her gorgeous jewellery had been stolen by her chambermaid's lover. Her jewels were stolen again in 1838, this time by a stranger, who had penetrated the premises by hanging on to the underside of a visitor's carriage. During a costume ball given by Alexandre Dumas at 40 rue Saint-Lazare, a masked person approached Mlle Mars and slipped all the stolen booty into her hand – but the mystery of the robbery was never unravelled. Today the house belongs to a private insurance company, who may permit you to glance into the superbly decorated entrance hall. Mlle Mars had begun her career at the age of 14. At 60 she was still applauded enthusiastically when playing Marivaux's young *ingénues!*

Mlle Duchesnois lived at no. 3. The famous tragedienne started out as a maidservant in the northern town of Valenciennes. In 1802, when only 22, she made her debut in the role of Phèdre at the Théâtre Français. Horace Vernet lived at no. 5/7 and the great Talma spent the last few years of his life at no. 9, where he died in 1826. He was the son of a coachman and his first job was extracting teeth, but he went on to become the greatest actor of his time and was praised beyond the borders of France. A staunch supporter of the Revolution, he provoked a split between Royalists and Republicans at the Comédie Française, in the wake of which, Talma and his followers left the Odéon theatre by the Luxembourg gardens and migrated to Victor Louis's newly-built theatre at Palais-Royal, then known as Théâtre Philippe-Egalité. Talma was also a fervent supporter of Napoleon, in whom he saw the lawful heir of the Revolution. Napoleon rewarded him for his loyalty with the *Légion d'Honneur* and also assembled a prestigious audience, which included several crowned heads, for one of his performances. Talma's revolutionary ideas did not stop at politics; he also shook up theatrical traditions by insisting on archeological accuracy and introducing period costumes, stripping, for example, his Roman or Grecian hero of the powdery white wig he had worn hitherto.

The people of Paris thronged into the streets to pay him a last homage in 1826, all the way from here to the cemetery of Père Lachaise. Today the house is referred to simply as Hôtel Talma and is shamefully allowed to fall into decay.

Not so the two gorgeous houses, on the other side of the street as you retrace your steps. The property of private banking and insurance companies, they remain as evidence of the past glamour of the neighbourhood. The one at no. 4 stands on the site of the old windmill of the Abbey of Montmartre, l'Abbaye des Dames de Montmartre. By the time the street was given its present name, the mill had lost its sails and looked more like a tower. It was first mentioned in 1316 and was demolished only in 1822. Bottles of wine from the reign of Henri IV are said to have been found here. At no. 2 you can see an exquisite example of Palladian architecture, perhaps the best of its kind in Paris.

Back on RUE DE LA ROCHEFOUCAULD, at no. 14, is the **Musée Gustave Moreau** where the symbolist painter had lived. André Breton, who later went on to found the surrealist movement, liked to come here from his neighbouring home on rue Fontaine and the place had a determining impact on his art. The prolific Gustave Moreau left 14,000 works, including some 1,200 paintings and an even larger number of drawings, fewer than half of which are on display for lack of space. Moreau's obsession with the *femme fatale* is a subject of interest in itself, but the house is also a museum piece in its own right and contains an admirable, spiral wooden staircase, typical of the period. Also on display are the painter's couch, table and easel.

Retrace your steps down rue de La Rochefoucauld and turn left into rue Saint-Lazare, left again into rue Taitbout and right into the charming **Square d'Orléans**, at no. 80 rue Taitbout. Built in 1840 on a plot, which Mlle Mars had sold at 100% profit, the Scottish architect, Mr Cresy, tried to emulate the squares of London, and the Regency architecture around Regent's Park, hence the colonnades on the façades of Square d'Orléans. The result was ravishing, though quite remote from anything British – if anything, the graceful fountain in its centre is italianate – and duly attracted some of the most prominent writers and artists, including Alexandre Dumas Père, Chopin and George Sand.

George Sand had been looking for appropriate accommodation for quite some time. A letter written by Chopin on her behalf in 1839 shows that she was so particular in her demands concerning the price, the size, the layout of the different rooms, the exposure and the tranquil environment that she was in danger of sending poor Chopin on a wild goose chase, but apparently the newly built Square d'Orléans satisfied her demands and in 1841 she moved to no. 9. Chopin moved in to no. 5. The garden of the apartment she occupied can be seen behind the fence at no. 82 rue Taitbout.

Turn left into RUE D'AUMALE. At no. 18/22 you will see a beautiful period staircase and an extraordinary period lift, no longer in use but impressive enough to have been preserved. Turn right into rue de La Rochefoucauld, left into rue de la Bruyère – where Jean Cocteau spent his childhood at no. 45 – and right again into rue Henner as far as RUE CHAPTAL. At no. 16 rue Chaptal is the exquisite **Musée Renan-Scheffer**, also known as the **Musée de la Vie Romantique**. This was the house where the painter Ary Scheffer settled with his family after arriving from Holland in 1830.

The Italianate ochre-coloured house, in a style much cherished during the Restoration, has been restored in its original simplicity and good taste, with its charming paved courtyard and an alley lined with trees on either side. Artists and writers used to gather here on Friday nights, among them Ingres, Delacroix, Liszt, Chopin, George Sand, Turgenev and Lamartine. Charles Dickens came here three times a week for two months in 1856 to sit for his portrait by Ary Scheffer. Dickens liked the portrait although he did not find it a very good likeness of himself and wondered what his friends in London would say when they saw it in the National Gallery, for which it was destined. Ernest Renan, who had written *inter alia* a major work on the origins of Christianity, married Ary Scheffer's niece (hence the name of the museum), whose granddaughter bequeathed the house to the City of Paris in 1956. In 1972 it was converted into a museum and great care was taken to recreate faithfully the setting and atmosphere of those days: each piece of furniture, each braid and tassel, each piece of upholstery, each wall hanging was chosen with an eye to authenticity.

Of all the glorious participants of those 'Friday nights' it is George Sand who is commemorated here permanently. This came about through a happy combination of circumstances. It so happened that George Sand's granddaughter had bequeathed the writer's memorabilia to the Musée Carnavalet, and the City of Paris, owner of both museums, took the judicious step of transferring it to this more suitable environment, so much like her successive homes on the neighbouring rue Pigalle and at Square D'Orléans. You will appreciate the collection which blends naturally into the charmingly outdated rooms, and the exquisite silence, broken only by the song of birds and the trickling water of a fountain. If it were not for the bright blue uniforms of the municipal attendants, you would mistake the place for the private home of a friend in some sleepy provincial town and almost expect George Sand, Liszt, Delacroix, Turgenev and the others to walk in, accompanied by the langorous sound of a piano.

Between 1896 and 1962, the celebrated Grand-Guignol theatre was situated at no. 20, offering a mixture of morbid humour and horror. The public wallowed in it. The audience might gasp and clutch each other for comfort and occasionally a female spectator would swoon – but they always came back for more. Some writers and playwrights too enjoyed the experience of having their baser emotions pandered to: Maupassant, Guitry and Courteline are known to have frequented the establishment. When the real horrors of life reared their heads in two ghastly world wars, it took more than *Grand Guignol* to move the new generations. The management, adjusting with customary Parisian ingenuity to new trends, replaced horror with sex and the theatre was converted into a strip-tease cabaret, which eventually closed down in 1962: this kind of business does better on the more garish boulevards that border the arrondissement to the north than in the discreet side streets. The accessories of the original theatre – pistols, whips and other instruments of torture, as well as a coffin and a guillotine – were sold at auction.

Walk back along rue Chaptal up to RUE PIGALLE, named after the 18th-century sculptor who lived at no. 1 until 1785, then at no. 12 rue de La Rochefoucauld, where he died the same year, aged 71. Pigalle was a sincerely pious person, who devoted much of his artistic talent to religious themes. He would probably have been vexed to see his name associated all over the world with the most lewd area in Paris. George Sand and Chopin lived together at no. 16 before moving into two separate houses at Square d'Orléans. George Sand entertained the Romantic circle and Chopin gave piano lessons. The painters Pierre Bonnard and Emile Vuillard shared a studio on the 6th floor of no. 28, Victor Hugo lived for a time at no. 55 and Baudelaire lived at no. 60. As you walk up rue Pigalle to your left, you will come to **RUE DE DOUAI** on your left and **RUE VICTOR MASSÉ** on your right. At no. 50 rue de Douai stood the *hôtel* of the opera singer Pauline Viardot, sister of the celebrated Malibran. It was here, during his visit to Paris in 1856, that Charles Dickens was introduced to George Sand, who was a regular visitor to the house. Another member of that artistic circle, Turgenev, actually occupied an apartment on the third floor of the *hôtel*. The painter Degas lived for 30 years on the third and fourth floors of the house that stood at no. 37 rue Victor Massé. From here he would climb up the Butte Montmartre to visit Suzanne Valadon on rue Cortot, watching the postures and gestures of the laundresses on the way, who did not appreciate this at all: 'Dirty old man!' they would cry out. 'It's disgraceful at your age!'

However, the most famous address on rue Victor Massé was the rowdy cabaret Le Chat Noir, at no. 12, where the wit and spirit of the Montmartre *chansonniers* were born. The cabaret moved to this respectable street in 1885 from the Boulevard de Rochechouart further north (in the 18th arr.), where it had first opened, partly because it lacked space, but mainly to escape the seedy environment of the previous premises and the riff-raff that lurked around. The decor of the cabaret was eclectic, with medieval artefacts alternating with biting cartoons. Leading artists performed here, the best remembered being Aristide Bruant, whom Toulouse-Lautrec immortalised in his wide-brimmed black hat, red scarf and black boots. Claude Debussy would sometimes lead the singing. All segments of established society – the bourgeois, the capitalists, the clergy and, of course, the Jews – were targeted by the sharp, satirical tongues of this stronghold of bohemia!

Today rue Victor Massé, and its continuation, rue de Douai, boast a multitude of music shops, a hangover from the time when Place Pigalle was an art and music market of sorts, where painters would come to look for models and conductors for musicians. Now the younger generation come here for music scores, electric guitars and other instruments for playing the kind of music that is popular today. For classical music they have to travel further west, to the neighbourhood of Europe and rue de Rome in the 8th arrondissement.

Turn left into RUE DES MARTYRS, the old, steep road that led to the Abbey of Montmartre and which is named after the martyrdom of Saint Denis and his two companions, Eleuthère and Rustique, all three beheaded in Montmartre. Today rue des Martyrs is a bustling street, lined with colourful, enticing food shops, and its shopkeepers are as friendly and smiling as those of the days of Renoir. At no. 9, at the bottom of the street, was the famous Brasserie, the nightly haunt of bohemia, described in detail by Alphonse Daudet in *Trente Ans à Paris*. Turn left into the Cité Malesherbes, worth strolling along for the sake of its elegant 19th-century architecture. Continue along rue Victor Massé. On your right is the **Avenue Frochot**, a gem of a countrified alley which has survived unexpectedly, just around the corner from the seedy dives of Pigalle.

This explains why it is, unfortunately, kept locked to outsiders, even during the day. It was built in 1827 and commemorates the Prefect of the Seine who in 1805 gave the houses of Paris their street numbers. The alley developed without any preconceived plan, which accounts for the charmingly eclectic architecture of its houses. Hence the cottage lodge of the concierge on the right which has little in common with the fabulous Art Deco glass panels on the left, a vestige of the Round Theatre which was built here in 1929 and was the first of its kind in France. The experiment, however, lasted only 13 years because the landlord, hoping to make a profit through real-estate transactions, refused to renew the troupe's lease. From the outset the Avenue Frochot attracted, understandably, writers, artists and musicians. Victor Hugo, Alexandre Dumas, the musician Charles Lamoureux, the painter Alfred Stevens and, especially, Toulouse-Lautrec, once lived here. So did film director Jean Renoir, just before World War II when he went into exile in the United States, and today this is the home of the opera singer, Régine Crespin. It was also appreciated by François Truffaut who came here to shoot one of the scenes of *Les 400 coups*.

Rue Frochot, west of Avenue Frochot, leads to PLACE PIGALLE. It looked quite different around 1870, when the Impressionist painters and their writer friends used to gather at the Nouvelle Athènes café at no. 9. Here they would engage in animated conversations with Emile Zola, Maupassant and others. Jean Renoir, the painter's son, however, recorded that the intellectual atmosphere of the café did not last for long. By the time he himself visited the place with Cézanne's son, even before the Great War, the pimps and tarts of Place Pigalle had replaced the artists and 'complete decadence had set in, an irremediable downfall.' Running due south in the axis of Avenue Frochot is RUE HENRI-MONNIER, the subject of beautiful illustrations by Gavarni. At no. 13*bis* is another little jewel, a charming, provincial house, standing behind a paved courtyard cloaked in green plants. The street leads to the picturesque PLACE GUSTAVE TOUDOUZE, a charming spot with its typical Fontaine Wallace trickling with water, an ideal stopping-place for a snack.

RUE NOTRE-DAME-DE-LORETTE meets rue Henri-Monnier a little further south, and will take you to the charming PLACE SAINT-GEORGES which gave its name to the entire neighbourhood when it was built in 1825–6. The elegant fountain in its centre honours the 19th-century cartoonist Gavarni who lived on rue Saint-Georges and devoted many of his drawings to the neighbourhood's girls of easy virtue, the *Lorettes* – so called after the church of Notre-Dame-de-Lorette down the road – and who owed their existence to Gavarni, according to Charles Baudelaire.

The Hôtel Thiers at no. 27 stands on the site of Thiers's original mansion which was razed to the ground during the civil war of the *Commune*. Adolphe Thiers moved here when he married the daughter of Monsieur Dosne, the chairman of the company which financed this new development. The people of Paris, the *Communards* or *Fédérés*, had particular grudges against Thiers who, they believed, had become a turncoat, betrayed their cause and compromised with the Prussian enemy (there were persistent rumours of wheeling and dealing behind closed doors). Acting out of caution, Thiers had transferred his government to Versailles, from where he launched his attack on Paris. The desperate *Communards* retaliated by setting fire to as many symbolic landmarks

Place Saint-Georges

as they could during the 'bloody week', which began on 24 May 1871 – the Tuileries, the Hôtel de Ville among others, and, understandably, the home of their most treacherous enemy. His art collection and library, however, escaped their wrath, thanks to the persuasiveness of their friend and supporter, the painter Courbet. The *Commune* was defeated and Thiers's *hôtel* was reconstructed within a few years. The library, specialising in 19th-century Paris, is open to the public and the premises, like many of the city's monuments, can be rented for functions or meetings. When Thiers died in Saint-Germain-en-Laye his body was brought back to the newly-built mansion and his funeral was celebrated at the church of Notre-Dame-de-Lorette down the road.

Like the church of La Sainte-Trinité, on the western edge of the new neighbourhood, the church of **Notre-Dame-de-Lorette** was to provide the growing population with a place of worship on its eastern edge. However, religious fervour was not a dominant feature in these parts and the term '*Lorette*', ironically, was to be invested with connotations other than spiritual. The old social order had collapsed and upward mobility became possible. Women of easy virtue thus stood a good chance of bettering themselves, if they knew how to go about it. Those aspiring ladies – embodied by Zola in the character of Nana – longed to meet a prince or a minister who would lavish jewellery and gifts on them and set them up in a glittering mansion, even though he might ruin himself and his family in the process. Every afternoon they would walk down the hill to the Boulevards in search of the man who would propel them into the *Grand Monde*. They must have been appetising, if we are to believe Delacroix, who wrote to George Sand how struck he was by 'a magnificent *lorette* of the tall sort, all clad in black satin and velvet, who, when alighting from her cabriolet, with the nonchalance of a goddess, let me see her leg up to her belly.' However, few *lorettes* attained the social summits they craved. Some ended in squalid hovels, others left for the New World. Some were locked up in the ghastly mental home of La Salpêtrière and there were also cases of suicide. How could it have been otherwise in a century of economic and social upheavals, filled, inevitably, with tantalising decoys, false hopes and promises betrayed? This was especially true of the 9th arrondissement, where the century had struck its roots, and which extended uphill above the Boulevards, that irresistible riband of bewitching glitter.

No. 28 Place Saint-Georges has an extraordinary façade in *troubadour* style, that is, a blend of neo-Gothic and neo-Renaissance, richly sculpted with allegorical figures and graceful motifs in the Ancient Greek style that was once so popular. Despite the stupendous expenses incurred, this was a purpose-built house and at one time Paul Gauguin lived here. In the middle of the 19th century the ground-floor flat to the right was occupied by the notorious courtesan, La Païva – one of the few aspiring women of her generation who did not stumble – while awaiting the completion of her mansion on the Champs-Elysées. Her adventurous life was sketched in the previous chapter.

If you take RUE NOTRE-DAME-DE-LORETTE uphill, you will come to a grotty building at no. 58, Delacroix's studio and home between 1845 and 1857. If the entrance door yields, you will be appalled to find the hall inside, with its stucco sculpted decorations, in a similar state of neglect. The place does little honour to the painter who, on moving from here to Place de Fürstemberg on the Left Bank said: 'I cannot leave this humble place, these rooms, where for so many years I have been alternately melancholy and happy, without feeling deeply moved.' The charming **Square Alexandre Biscarre**, across the street as you retrace your steps downhill, is more refreshing – a treat in early spring, when clusters of cheerful daffodils herald the new season.

THE 10TH ARRONDISSEMENT

LA GARE DU NORD, the terminus of all trains from the North, was the Englishman's gateway to Paris during the reign of the railway. Located in one of the dismal arrondissements of the French capital, the enthusiastic newcomer, full of happy anticipation, was dumbfounded: 'Where are the Boulevards? where are the Champs-Elysées?' was George Moore's *cri de coeur* upon his arrival early one morning in 1873. A 'tall, haggard city' met him instead: 'Pale, sloppy, yellow houses; an oppressive absence of colour; a peculiar bleakness in the streets. . .' and 'miserable carriages'. Three years later Emile Zola gave the following description of the area and its inhabitants in *L'Assomoir*: '. . . *et les poitrines se creusaient, rien qu'à respirer cet air, où les moucherons eux-mêmes n'auraient pas pu vivre, faute de nourriture.*' ('. . . and the chests were hollow merely from inhaling this air, where even gnats could not live, for lack of food').

Although Zola was referring to the even more destitute population outside the city's toll walls (now the 18th arr.), there was not much difference between the two and during the day their routes often converged, as the latter came into Paris in search of livelihood, 'the throngs of workers, surging into Paris by way of the gaping street of Faubourg Poissonnière.' They also shared the Lariboisière hospital, just north west of the Gare du Nord, the limbo of the wretched.

On the southern edge of the arrondissement, at the bottom of rue du Faubourg Saint-Denis, which runs along the eastern flank of the Gare du Nord, stands the stately Porte Saint-Denis in the middle of a heavily congested crossroads, an incongruous feature in this unsavoury neighbourhood. Those who are well versed in Parisian history will remember that rue Saint-Denis, beyond the gate, was the royal and sacred way of the capital and the Porte Saint-Denis its royal gateway, even as recently as the 19th century. Queen Victoria, 'head of the Empire on which the sun never set' passed under this triumphal arch only two decades before her fellow countryman and subject, George Moore, wrote the lines above. This was in 1855, on the occasion of her visit to the Universal Exposition. However, because of the turbulent turn of events in France during the 19th century, culminating in the definitive death of the Monarchy, Queen Victoria also happend to be the last sovereign to have completed this ritual that dated back nearly a thousand years.

The arch itself, like the Porte Saint-Martin to its east, was erected only at the time of Louis XIV. Having crushed his foes and feeling secure in his newly acquired military superiority, Louis XIV proceeded to demolish the old city walls and replace them with the fashionable, shady Grands Boulevards described earlier, and also took the opportunity to commemorate his victories with these two monuments. The Porte Saint-Denis, built by Blondel, commemorates the capture of Maastricht and the crossing of the Rhine: two allegories, designed by Girardon, represent Holland, distressed, sitting on a dying lion, and the Rhine astounded. No effort was spared to glorify and flatter the Sun King, and Blondel planned the monument in every detail. A broken sword was placed in one of the lion's paws, a sheaf of arrows in the other, and more arrows scattered around. A Latin inscription listed all the spectacular conquests of the great King, achieved in a record time of 60 days, an edifying example for that other megalomaniac who ordered the restoration of the gate in 1807. However, fearing competition, even from a predecessor long deceased, Napoleon had the words *Ludovico Magno* covered with bronze so as to dim their glitter. He need not have gone to the trouble – no one ever stops in front of the monument to read the inscription. Besides, few people in France today know Latin. The rebels who fought at the foot of the monument in July 1830 and February 1848 did not give it much thought either, being much too preoccupied with fierce street fighting in the cause of liberty.

It was not so much the two arches as the newly laid out Grands Boulevards that were to affect the development of the arrondissement, as they did that of the neighbouring 9th. These pleasant, shady promenades were a great draw to Parisians and were lined with places of entertainment and pleasure, most of them ephemeral. Of course this section of the Boulevards, which lay east of rue du Faubourg Montmartre – the social divide, beyond all doubt, according to Balzac and Alfred de Musset – was not in the same league as the stylish Boulevard des Italiens. Nevertheless, Alphonse Daudet, in the second half of the 19th century, placed the edge of the territory of Tout-Paris as far east as the Gymnase, the very popular theatre at no. 38 Boulevard de Bonne Nouvelle. This prestigious theatre, which opened in 1824, enjoyed the patronage of the Duchesse de Berry and regularly staged works of the playwright Scribe. The theatre had an impressive list of comedians, notably the renowned actresses Déjazet and Rachel, who both made their debuts there.

At about this time, too, when the *beau-monde* of western Paris occasionally ventured east to the irresistible Boulevard du Temple, the permanent funfair and theatreland of lower-class Paris, their route led them unavoidably through the stretch of Boulevards that bordered the 10th arrondissement. The Boulevard du Temple, meanwhile, had spilt west into the 10th, and the theatres of the Boulevard Saint-Martin were much the same as those of the Boulevard du Temple.

As a matter of fact, the entertainment on the Boulevard du Temple had actually originated in the 10th arrondissement, having roots in the Foire Saint-Laurent which was held every summer, in theory from 25 August (day of Saint-Laurent), for a variable duration – initially eight days but eventually up to three months – under the shade of chestnut trees. Acrobats and mimes, puppet shows, exhibitions of deformed creatures, street entertainers of all sorts delighted the crowds thronging among stalls which displayed cooking utensils, crockery, toys, gingerbread, jars of jam and a thousand other things.

Those street performers were good! In fact, they were so good that the *Comédiens français* and the *Comédiens italiens* who enjoyed a monopoly of the profession kept a jealous eye on them and clutched at every opportunity to thwart their activities. The entertainers astutely devised tricks to circumvent the restrictions that were placed on their means of expression: No dialogues on stage? In that case the repartee would be spoken off-stage, while the next actor took his place on the stage! The effect was unexpected and hilarious. The spectators were delighted.

Not so the official royal troupe, La Comedie-Française: when, during the Regency, the entertainers (with the renowned couple

Favart in their lead) started scattering verses among the lines of prose, and singing them to pleasing melodies, thus giving birth to a new genre – *l'opéra-comique* – their success was such that the alarmed Comédie-Française used all its lobbying power to silence them once and for all. From then on entertainers were banned from the streets altogether, except for dancers and acrobats. The Comédie-Italienne tried to muscle in on the fair, but the public did not care for them. The demise of the theatre at the fair, competition from two more recent fairs on the present Place de la Concorde (in the 8th arr.) and Jussieu (in the 5th arr.) and the development of entertainment on the Boulevards all combined to bring about the decline of the fair and its final closure during the Revolution.

The Foire Saint-Laurent had never been a match for the elegant Foire Saint-Germain (now in the 6th arr.), which was held in winter and was attended even by the Kings of France. On the whole it catered to a more modest collection of country people, artisans and shopkeepers, as the following verse indicates:

> *Ne croirais-tu pas comme moy*
> *Que cette femme avec son lustre*
> *Fust épouse de quelque Illustre?*
> *C'est la femme d'un Paticier,*
> *Cette autre l'est d'un Epicier. . .*

> Would you not believe, as I do,
> That this woman with her lustre
> Was the wife of some man of mark?
> She is the wife of a pastrycook
> This other of a grocer. . .

In due course, as the neighbourhood became more prosperous, thanks to the opening of the tree-lined promenade, which attracted Parisians and therefore trade, knick-knacks and trinkets, even luxury items made their appearance on the stalls too.

The new promenade was counterbalanced, however, by the open sewer – *le Grand-Egout*. It ran from the Temple area, where it had originally been fed by the waters of Belleville and the Pré-Saint-Gervais, east of Paris and was now a putrid, evil-smelling mire and a source of epidemics. Its southern branch ran along the site of the present rue Notre-Dame-de-Nazareth (now the 3rd arr.), the northern branch along the present rue du Château-d'Eau and rue des Petites-Ecuries in the 10th arrondissement. Only a century later, when the sewage system had eventually been covered over, did wealthy people settle here in any great numbers. Their splendid mansions were built by such talented and respected architects as Ledoux, who moved into the area himself. If you use your imagination as you walk around rue du Faubourg Poissonnière and the parallel rue d'Hauteville, you may be able to picture what some of today's shabby houses and courtyards looked like before the Industrial Age.

When the area began to open up to urban development, negotiations took place between the various religious orders that owned the land and developers out to make profits. The order of Saint-Lazare had no reason to complain about the deals it struck, but the naïve nuns of Les Filles-Dieu fell prey to a certain cunning Monsieur Goupy. When they finally woke up to his trickery, they took legal action against him but this seems not to have affected him, for he went on with his shady but profitable real-estate operations in the neighbourhood up until the Revolution.

Before the opening of the Grands Boulevards, the sparsely populated country that lay beyond the city walls was still a damp area, even though hundreds of years had passed since the community of Saint-Laurent had drained its marshes, the residue of the prehistoric Seine. As elsewhere in the Paris area, the land was used as vegetable gardens (*marais*), tended by local people and religious orders. No doubt the annual fair gave the area an economic boost, particularly to the Order of Saint-Lazare, having obtained the concession for the fair from Louis VI in the early 12th century – hence its early name, Saint-Ladre, a version of Lazarus.

The Order had been founded to treat the leprous, and a leper house was built for that purpose on its prosperous grounds, which extended west of rue du Faubourg Saint-Denis. The house is first mentioned in historical records in 1122. Before leaving for the Second Crusade in 1146, Louis VII stopped at Saint-Lazare on his way to the Basilica of Saint-Denis to collect the banner, proof of the link between the royal house and the Order. Soon their premises became one of the four official stations of royal processions into the city and of royal funeral processions to the Basilica of Saint-Denis. Before the Revolution a square tower stood there, surmounted by a cross and decorated with *fleurs-de-lys* and the statues of Saint Louis and his two sons, Philippe III le Hardi, Comte de Nevers, and the Comte de Clermont. Philippe III actually stopped here with the coffin of his father, which he carried barefooted on his shoulder, all the way from Notre Dame to Saint-Denis. The last remains to have been brought here were those of Louis XV in 1774, by which time the royal household had lost its lustre. The funeral of Louis XV was a lonely affair, attended by a single member of the nobility, Charles de Rohan, and accompanied by the jeers of the hostile public. In the Middle Ages, however, the prestige of both the king and the station were such that a special building was erected to accommodate His Majesty, le Logis du Roi, where he received the oath of obedience from the various orders. All this, obviously, contributed to reinforcing the ties between the royal authorities and the Order of Saint-Lazare and accounts for the granting of the preferential rights of the fair to the Order. The fair turned out to be a lucrative business indeed, which the Kings were quick to catch on to. By the time of the business-minded Philippe Auguste the profits were running so high, that he decided to take possession of it and transferred it to the site of what would soon become the central market of Les Halles.

It was not until the 17th century that the Order was again permitted to hold its annual summer fair. By then leprosy had been conquered and the leper-house had closed. The newly established Mission of Saint-Lazare, which was founded in its stead, went to great expense to erect permanent pavilions, just south of the present Gare de l'Est, along pleasant alleys shaded by chestnut trees. However, the fair was now known as Foire Saint-Laurent, after the original community that back in the 6th century had settled here, drained the marshes and developed the area, and were indeed the founding fathers of the 10th arrondissement. The Norsemen had wiped out this flourishing community and burnt down its church in 886, after which the Order was almost forgotten. However, despite the age-old omnipresence of Saint-Lazare in these parts, it never totally disappeared.

Since the leper-house was now vacant, it was turned into a prison whose inmates were sent here with a sealed letter from the King (the notorious *lettre de cachet*), often at the instigation of the prisoner's own family. Many a prodigal son and adulterous husband were locked up in this relatively comfortable prison for a term of a few months, although this was by no means a rest cure either – upon their arrival they were given a sound lashing by a servant of the Order. An old etching depicts the writer Beaumarchais undergoing this treatment: he is seen with his breeches down, being lashed energetically on his generous posterior by a member of the Order, under the chagrined eye of the Comtesse Almaviva. The playwright was detained at Saint-Lazare for a few days in 1785 over the issue of his audacious play *Le Mariage de Figaro*. Questioning the basis of ruling-class privilege, the play presented a threat to the existing social order – which, indeed, toppled over four years hence.

Even when the premises were used as a prison during the Revolution, they were under a fairly lenient regime. One of the inmates wrote in a letter, 'The advantageous situation of Saint-Lazare, as for its spaciousness, its fresh air, and the view it offers, cannot be compared to that of an obscure, narrow prison, deprived of fresh air and surrounded all round by high walls. . . My room, situated on the third floor, looks out through a very large window, onto the middle of a very beautiful inner courtyard, beyond which stretches an immense park that blends into the panorama of the faubourgs and the countryside, ending at Mont Valérien on the horizon.' By the early 20th century all this had changed. Saint-Lazare had become a women's prison, described by Léon Daudet as 'one of the most pathetic sites in Paris' and 'the limbo of the female city dweller'.

The siting of the leper-house in the Middle Ages, was based on the common-sense notion that the victims of this dreadful contagious disease should be removed from the centre of the city. The same consideration led Henri IV to choose this remote area for the new hospital he built in 1606–7 for victims of the raging plague epidemics. L'Hôtel-Dieu, hitherto the only hospital in Paris, was centrally placed on the Ile de la Cité, obviously not a location where victims could be effectively quarantined. Besides, its overcrowded premises had become inadequate to service growing needs, especially at times of epidemic – not that the new hospital solved the problem of space, for even there every bed was shared by five patients! The hospital was named Saint-Louis after the pious Louis

IX, who had himself died of the plague. Today this is the oldest surviving institution in the 10th arrondissement and one of the most beautiful architectural examples dating from the reign of Henri IV.

For reasons of geography, too, the main gallows of the city that came under royal jurisdiction was set up in this area. It was all right to chop up or quarter people in the centre of Paris, but you could not leave dangling bodies to rot there. A plot of land was therefore sought in an uninhabited spot, remote enough from the city but also of sufficient height so as to be seen by everyone, inspire terror far and wide and serve as a warning to would-be wrongdoers. The word *gibet* (gallows or gibbet) is believed by many historians to derive from the Arabic *djebel* (mountain).

A site answering the requirements was found along the road to Germany, on the present rue de la Grange-aux-Belles, north of the Hôpital Saint-Louis. This was confirmed in 1954, during the construction of a garage at no. 53, when the bases of two stone pillars and some human bones were discovered. It was not a very high mound – though high enough for Henri IV to erect his battery there in 1590 for his siege of Paris – but it stood out well among the fields. (This was open countryside, of course, the hospital having been built only four centuries later.) The site was bought from the Comte Fulco, the lord of vast expanses in these parts, including those he had sold to the Order of Saint-Lazare – hence the distorted name Montfaucon.

Of course, many wretched victims were hanged for no crime of their own. One such was the noted Pierre de la Brosse, chamberlain by appointment of Saint Louis, and also physician and Minister of Finance. He was the favourite of Philippe III le Hardi, the son of Saint Louis, which naturally aroused the jealousy of rivals, who succeeded in bringing him to trial on the false allegation that he had poisoned the heir to the throne. He was executed in 1276. Other prominent figures were to meet the same fate as a result of personal rivalries: Enguerrand de Marigny (in 1315), who had rebuilt the Royal Palace on the Ile de la Cité for Philippe le Bel, Pierre Rémy (in 1328), who had himself supervised the construction of the new, permanent, stone gallows three years earlier, Jean de Montagu (in 1409) who had repaired them; and the 72-year-old Semblançay (in 1527), the financial superintendent of François I,

whose execution was immortalised in the satirical lines of the poet
Clément Marot:

Lorsque Maillart, juge d'Enfer, menait
A Montfaucon Samblançay l'âme rendre,
A votre avis, lequel des deux tenait
Meilleur maintien? Pour le vous faire entendre,
Maillart semblait homme que mort va prendre,
Et Samblançay fut si ferme vieillard,
Que l'on cuidait, pour vrai, qu'il menât pendre
A Montfaucon, le lieutenant Maillart.

When Maillart, judge of Hell*,
To Montfaucon led Samblançay to give up his soul,
Which of the two, in your mind,
Had the better demeanour? To enlighten you,
Maillart seemed the man whom death would take
And so sturdy an old man was Samblançay,
That one truly believed that it was he who led
Lieutenant Maillart to be hanged at Montfaucon.

The victim, however, could take comfort from the fact that, if a
miscarriage of justice was discovered to have occurred, he would
be released from the noose – *dépendu* – and receive honourable
burial in the parish churchyard, which vouchsafed his rehabilita-
tion. This did not restore him to life, but that was spiritually of
little consequence.

The size of the gallows in the kingdom depended on the rank of
the authorities they came under – two pillars for a lord, four for
a baron, 16 for a king, and therefore for Montfaucon. It could
accommodate as many as 64 bodies at a time and was often used to
full capacity. The sight of dozens of bodies dangling against the
north-eastern horizon was thus an integral part of the landscape in
medieval Paris. The bodies were left to rot in the open and were
taken down only when there was need to make room for others.
They would then be thrown into a mass grave at the foot of the
gallows, where they joined the mutilated remains of the wretched
victims of public executions. Since the hanging of women was considered indecent, condemned women were instead buried there
alive, a custom that persisted until the end of the 15th century. The

*The prison of Châtelet

113

grave was guarded by archers against mobs of witches who coveted the hearts of the victims for the preparation of philtres. In keeping with the a highly hierarchical nature of this society, the gallows were divided into an upper and a lower section and the condemned were hanged in a higher or lower position according to their social rank. However, a condemned man could be pardoned if a woman of the Order of the Filles-Dieu agreed to marry him or if the rope broke during the hanging.

The famous medieval poet François Villon was one of the fortunate few whose neck was spared, though, in his case, not by the capricious intervention of Fate, but by the Parliament of Paris, which in 1463 cancelled his death sentence, after which he vanished and was heard of no more. Nevertheless, he left for posterity one of the masterpieces of French poetry, *La Ballade des Pendus*, which he wrote while awaiting his hanging, immortalising the chilling gallows of Montfaucon:

> *Frères humains qui après nous vivez,*
> *N'ayez les cuers contre nous endurciz,*
> *Car, se pitié de nous pouvres avez,*
> *Dieu en aura plus tost de vous merciz.*
> *Vous nous voyez cy attachez cinq, six:*
> *Quant de la chair, que trop avons nourrie,*
> *Elle est pieça devorée et pourrie,*
> *Et nous, les os, devenons cendre et pouldre.*

> Brother men who after us shall live,
> Let not your hearts against us hardened be,
> For if you take pity on our poor souls,
> God will return his mercy upon yours.
> You see us here hanging, five or six,
> Our flesh, once too well nourished,
> now rots, torn by beaks, devoured,
> And we, the bones, dissolve to dust and ashes.

The gallows of Montfaucon fell into disuse only in the early 17th century, when the hospital of Saint-Louis was built next to it. A new gallows was built further out, in what is now the 19th arrondissement, but it was much smaller and not quite as horrendously forbidding.

The Industrial Revolution brought about rapid change in what was to become the 10th arrondissement, which was accelerated by the building of the Canal Saint-Martin, followed later by the two railway stations, Gare du Nord and Gare de l'Est. Already in the 16th century there had been a project to dig a canal to bring the water of the river Ourcq into Paris, and thereby increase the city's water supply and provide it with an additional waterway. In 1520 François I had voiced the idea of a canal but the first concrete proposal was put forward by Henri IV, as part of the monumental Place de France (discussed in the chapter on the 3rd arr.).

His assassination in 1610 nipped the scheme in the bud. Louis XIV also showed an interest in the idea of a canal but his ministers Colbert and Riquet (the latter had built the Canal du Midi) died before the scheme could be carried out, and it was Napoleon who eventually did. Indignant at the sorry state of the dried-up fountains of Paris – no match for those of Rome – the Emperor resolved to give his capital flamboyant fountains that would equal or surpass them. So eager was the Emperor to astonish the world, however, that the work was carried out with too much haste. On 2 December 1808, during the inauguration ceremony of the Canal de l'Ourcq (in the 19th arr.) and in the midst of enthusiastic applause, the canal wall burst and its waters gushed into the Bassin de la Villette (also in the 19th arr.).

It did not remain there for long, as its surface was permeable, and by March all the water had gone. It took another three years before the first fountain was supplied by the river Ourcq. This was the Fontaine du Château-d'Eau, which stood in the middle of what was then Place du Château-d'Eau, now Place de la République. It was inaugurated amid great pomp on 15 August 1811, to coincide with Saint Napoleon's Day, previously known as the Roman Catholic holiday of the Assumption. The fountain has since been moved to La Villette in the 19th arrondissement, on the eastern edge of the city. Napoleon was never to see the Canal Saint-Martin, however: it was built in 1822, a year after his death and six years after he had lost the throne.

The opening of the canal triggered off the massive industrialisation of the 10th arrondissement. A few industries were already scattered here and there in the 18th century, notably les Petites et Grandes Ecuries, in charge of the royal horses, harnesses, saddles and coaches, and the porcelain workshops of the Comte d'Artois and of the Duc d'Angoulême. There was a silk workshop and next to it a marble stonemason's works. Other industries followed suit in the 19th century, among them the famous gold- and silver-smith Charles Christofle, whose business developed into a famous crystal glassworks, purveyors of the court. Many examples of their work can be seen in the showrooms and museum in rue de Paradis. The internationally renowned shoe manufacturer Pinet also started his trade here in the 19th century, while the famous equestrian statue of Henri IV, which stands on the Pont-Neuf, was cast in one of the arrondissement's foundries.

Manufactured goods entered Paris by way of the canal, bringing both prosperity and misery. While luxury shops opened on the Grands Boulevards, gloomy warehouses loomed out of the fog along the new waterway. These in their turn attracted the new railway and determined the choice of location for the future Gare du Nord (1846) and Gare de l'Est (1850). Though promising prosperity to some (and also, in the case of the Gare de l'Est, of paramount strategic importance against the Prussian enemy), the railway ushered in the inevitable social downfall of the 10th and the defacing of its environment. Poverty-stricken people moved in to supply the necessary hands for its growing industries. After the defeat of France by Prussia in 1870, waves of refugees from Alsace-Lorraine arrived at the Gare de l'Est and settled in the 10th arrondissement. The many well-established *brasseries* (originally brewery) in the arrondissement, specialising in Alsacian *choucroute* (sauerkraut) washed down with beer, were first introduced into the capital by these refugees. Much less welcome were the Jews who alighted at the Gare de l'Est, first from Alsace like their Gentile predecessors, then, at the beginning of the 20th century, from Eastern Europe, and in the 1930s from Germany and Austria. In 1933 the writer Paul Morand complained in *Le Temps* about the 'really Biblical vicinity' of the Gare de l'Est.

In more recent years the Gare de l'Est has been used by many illegal immigrants, who have helped to swell the ranks of the multiracial population of the 10th, among whom is a large proportion of Africans, Turks and of Tamils, who have created an enclave for themselves, off the Faubourg Saint-Denis. Thus the 10th arrondissement, though it can boast little opulence, can certainly pride itself on human diversity. And although it may have few monuments, its canal is unique. The gaudy neon lights around the junction of the Boulevards de Strasbourg and Saint-Denis, are a sham glitter that may appeal only to the uprooted, lonely hearts, but the 10th also houses one of the prestigious jazz clubs in Paris, the New Morning, as well as one of its most exciting theatres, Les Bouffes du Nord, where Peter Brook staged such world-renowned productions as *Carmen* and the *Mahabharata*. Along with the plush decoration of the Théatre de la Porte Saint-Martin and the Théâtre de la Renaissance on the Boulevard Saint-Martin, they are vestiges of a tradition of entertainment which began way back at the Foire Saint-Laurent and reached its climax during the days of perpetual partying that was the Belle Epoque.

On 14 November 1994, at 12.23 pm, the first passenger Eurostar train to connect London and Paris by way of the Channel Tunnel pulled in at the Gare du Nord. A medley of UK nationals poured out of the train, euphoric for having made the historic journey, delighted with the free champagne they had been served on board. All the media were present to scrutinise those extraordinary first-timers, who, similarly to their ancestors of nearly two centuries ago, *les Anglais* (read *all* the inhabitants of the British Isles), aroused much curiosity among the native French, especially the incongruous Bobby, the red-headed kilted bagpiper and some exotic eccentrics. With Waterloo station only three hours' away, the 10th arrondissement has become London's next-door neighbour and, once more, the Englishman's gateway to Paris.

FROM THE GARE DU NORD
TO THE PORTE SAINT-DENIS

Pour moi, le dixième, et que de fois ne l'ai-je pas dit,
est un quartier
de poètes et des locomotives . . . étayé par deux gares.

For me, the 10th, and how many times have I said so,
is a neighbourhood
of poets and locomotives . . . propped up by two railway stations.

Léon-Paul Fargues, *Le piéton de Paris*

One of the two stations, **la Gare du Nord**, was the gateway to Paris
for all British visitors in the days before aviation (as it has become
once more for those using the Eurotunnel train). Coming to Paris
for the first time, they would certainly be aware of the locomotives
but had no inkling of the poets. The City of Light would come as a
culture shock and they might, with reason, feel baffled and let
down. You will begin this walk by following in their footsteps and
perhaps you will understand their first disappointment, except
that you will have been forewarned. The station is easily accessible
by the RER (take the rue du Faubourg Saint-Denis/rue Dunkerque
exit), although it is not advisable to linger here. Try to come on
Saturday afternoon so as to include the Hôtel de Bourienne in your
visit (open 2–4 pm) – the jewel in the crown – and also enjoy the
bustle of Faubourg Saint-Denis.

The railway being the driving force of the economic and social
revolution of the 19th century, the Gare du Nord (as well as the
Gare de l'Est) largely determined the growth of the 10th arrondissement and the shape it has taken. The first station, built in 1846,
soon proved inadequate and had to be replaced by a larger one.
However, It was not completed until 1865, and a special line was
therefore laid to the Gare de l'Est in 1855 to enable Queen Victoria
to disembark when she came to visit the World Fair. The station is
attributed to the gifted Hittorff, but how much of it was actually
his work has not been ascertained. Unkindly treated by the environment, the station's façade nonetheless deserves your attention

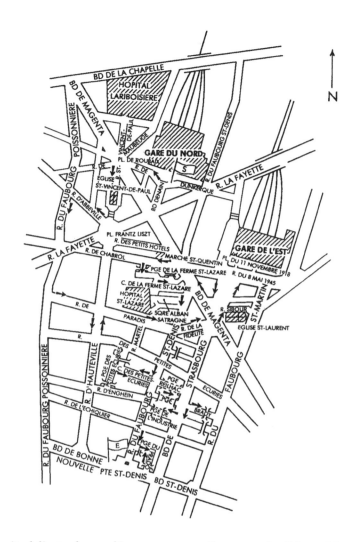

BD DE LA CHAPELLE
HOPITAL LARIBOISIERE
BD DE MAGENTA
POISSONNIERE
R. VINCENT-DE-PAUL
R. DE MAUBEUGE
R. DU FAUBOURG ST-DENIS
GARE DU NORD
PL. DE ROUBAIX
R. DE
S
R. DU FAUBOURG
R. D'ABBEVILLE
EGLISE ST-VINCENT-DE-PAUL
R. ST.
BD DENAIN
DUNKERQUE
R. LA FAYETTE
PL. FRANTZ LISZT
R. DES PETITS HOTELS
R. LA FAYETTE
R. DE CHABROL
MARCHE ST-QUENTIN
GARE DE L'EST
PL. DU 11 NOVEMBRE 1918
PGE DE LA FERME ST-LAZARE
R. DU 8 MAI 1945
C. DE LA FERME ST-LAZARE
HOPITAL ST-LAZARE
R. DE
PARADIS
SQRE ALBAN SATRAGNE
R. DE LA FIDELITE
BD DE MAGENTA
R. SIBOUR
ST-MARTIN
EGLISE ST-LAURENT
R.
R. D'HAUTEVILLE
DES
R. MARTEL
ST-DENIS
PETITES
STRASBOURG
R. DU FAUBOURG
PGE DES PETITES ECURIES
R. DES PETITES ECURIES
PGE REILHAC
PGE
ECURIES
R. D'ENGHIEN
PGE DE L'INDUSTRIE
BRADY
POISSONNIERE
R. DU FAUBOURG
R. DE L'ECHIQUIER
PGE DU
BD DE
BD DE BONNE NOUVELLE
E
PTE ST-DENIS
BD ST-DENIS

N

C. Carrier

for its delicate glass and iron structure, a fine example of the architecture of the time. Twenty-two monumental statues represent a
wide spectrum of cities of the north, including London, Brussels,
Berlin, Vienna, St. Petersburg – but also such close neighbours as
Compiègne, all of which are connected by rail to the Gare du Nord.
Arising above them, at the top of the pointed roof of the station, is
Paris, twice their size, overpowering them all, a proud eagle by her
side. Likewise, a number of the neighbourhood's streets are named
after cities and towns in Northern France, such as rue de Dunkerque just in front of the station, well-known for its Belle Epoque

brasserie, Le Terminus Nord, at no. 23. The restaurant is well worth a meal in a genuine setting and atmosphere. Head west along rue de Dunkerque and turn left at Place de Roubaix into rue Saint-Vincent-de-Paul.

You will reach the back of the impressive **church of Saint-Vincent-de-Paul**, which you will skirt clockwise along pleasant, drowsy streets to reach its front, overlooking PLACE FRANZ-LISZT. Like the neighbourhoods of Saint-Georges and La Nouvelle Athènes further west in the 9th, it was built in the early 1820s. The architecture is of the same dignified simplicity, and the same serene atmosphere prevails here as there, a suitable setting for Liszt and his friends. The church of Saint-Vincent-de-Paul enjoyed the collaboration of Hittorff. Baron James de Rothschild, chairman of the Compagnie des Chemins de Fer du Nord, had been so impressed by Hittorff's work here that he commissioned him to help with the Gare du Nord. The church stands on an elevated site with a sweeping panoramic view. The steep steps that lead up to it add a picturesque touch to the site, and the charming garden rolling down the slope provides this busy section of the city with a happy touch of greenery. Inside the church, the colourful frieze in the nave was painted between the years 1848 and 1853 by Hippolyte Flandrin. The church commemorates the charitable Saint Vincent – '*le grand saint du grand siècle*' – who, in the early 17th century, a time of both appalling poverty and religious fervour, dedicated his life to the poor.

Born in 1581 to a peasant family in the Landes (south-western France), the energetic Vincent had already become chaplain to Marguerite de Valois by 1610. Before this, he had been abducted and sold to an alchemist in Tunis, where he lived for three years before managing to escape back to France. Soon after, he was put in charge of the education of the children of the great Prince de Gondi, but it was the poor and the foundlings that he wanted to educate, and it was the pain of the wretched that he wanted to relieve. After serving as chaplain to convicts condemned to the galleys, Vincent was appointed head of the Visitation Order and of the Collège des Bons-Enfants, which was situated in the quarter of Saint-Victor (now Jussieu, in the 5th arr.). In 1625, with the financial help of Madame de Gondi, he founded a mission to educate the peasantry and train for the priesthood those peasants of the Gondi estates who were deemed suitable. So successful was he that the premises he was using soon proved inadequate. The Order of Saint-Lazare, on the other hand, had ample space now that its leper house had become obsolete. The Order had already allotted some space to the canons of Saint-Victor a century earlier, where they had set up a house of correction, later to become the prison of Saint-Lazare. The current prior of Saint-Lazare, desperate to find a use for the remainder of his premises, was happy to hand them over to Vincent for such a noble cause and Saint-Lazare became the seat of the Mission of Saint-Vincent-de-Paul and the residence of their prior. Thus, the priests of the Mission came to be known as *Lazaristes*, although there was no link between the two. Vincent went on to found another institution, Les Filles de la Charité, on the site of the present nos 94–114 rue du Faubourg Saint-Denis, whose inmates devoted all their energy to the economic and social welfare of the area. He also opened a hospital on the site, Saint-Nom-de-Jésus (now Fernand Widal), at no. 200 rue du Faubourg Saint-Denis, where beggars were offered shelter whilst being nursed by the neighbouring Filles de la Charité and given spiritual assistance by members of the Mission across the street.

So great was the aura of Monsieur Vincent, as he was affectionately called, that King Louis XIII died in his arms. When the holy man died in his turn in 1660, at the age of 84, he was buried in a silver reliquary in the choir of the original 13th-century church of the Order of Saint-Lazare. Eleven paintings depicting his life were added to the church after his beatification. The members of the Mission and the other occupants of the place were expelled during the Revolution but were allowed to keep the remains of Saint Vincent, except for the precious silver reliquary, which was confiscated and sent to the Mint. For over a century thereafter, the Saint's remains were lugged around Paris and even across the border as far as Belgium and London. Only after the Great War were they brought back to France, enclosed in a new reliquary that had been made for them during the Restoration and deposited over the high altar of the Lazarist convent, now established on rue de Sèvres (in the 6th arr.). The Mission's church survived the Revolution, but in a sorry state, and in 1823 was demolished. Although the paintings were dispersed, they were largely preserved. Some can still be seen in Paris, notably in the Lazarist church of rue de Sèvres and in the church of Sainte-Marguerite (in the 11th arr.).

Continue west of the church along RUE FÉNELON. An impressive 1900 façade at no. 9, decorated with ceramics, celebrates the different civilisations that contributed to this craft. Turn left into RUE D'ABBEVILLE. Lovers of Art Nouveau will delight in the profusion of sculptures at nos 14 and 16, though they may feel uneasy about the eerie presence of an owl and a bat above the spectacular plant-like motifs at no. 14; the voluptuous figures that decorate no. 16 by way of caryatids are more inviting.

Turn left into RUE DU FAUBOURG POISSONNIÈRE, previously known as le Chemin de la Marée, both of which names refer to the fish from the North Sea that were carted through it to rue Montorgueil, where the fish section of the central market of Les Halles was located. Only the eastern side of the street belongs to the 10th. The real-estate development of the area goes back to 1644 when the stretch of land lying west of Faubourg Poissonnière, in what is now the 9th, was sold off by its owner to be parcelled up. The humble houses that were built on the site came to be known as La Nouvelle France, possibly after a local tavern. When the land of Saint-Lazare, in what is now the 10th arrondissement, became available for development in its turn, the new neighbourhood was misnamed La Nouvelle France.

Like the parallel rue d'Hauteville, rue du Faubourg Poissonnière is studded with late 18th-century *hôtels*, reminiscent of a time when the upper crust was only too happy to settle in these airy parts, blessedly remote from the crowded hub of the city. The enlightened Baron Philippe Frédéric de Dietrich, a renowned member of the Académie des Sciences, who was also a writer and a musician, lived at no. 106. During the Revolution he was appointed first constitutional Mayor of Strasbourg and it was in his Strasbourg home that his guest, Rouget de l'Isle, first sang a composition of his own – the patriotic *Marseillaise*. None of this helped the Mayor to save his neck and in 1793, aged 45, he climbed the steps of the guillotine.

The barracks of the Garde Républicaine at no. 82 replace the late 18th-century barracks, which had been built by the unscrupulous developer Goupy, who, as was mentioned above, had little compunction about doing the Filles-Dieu out of their property. Before 1770, only the Musketeers were allocated barracks in the capital, while other soldiers had to lodge with private families scattered all over town, often making a nuisance of themselves when rolling in drunk. The Maréchal Biron, the head of the army, took the initiative of building barracks for the different companies and this was one of the five erected at the time. Goupy let the premises to the State, drawing a substantial profit, but they remained in the hands of his family until 1827, which then sold them to another private person. They were purchased by the State only in 1830. By 1926 they were deemed too dilapidated to warrant repair and were replaced by the present building. Some of the old sculptures have been preserved, nonetheless, and can be seen on the present façade. Today the barracks is still known as La Nouvelle France, after the name attached to the neighbourhood and which may refer to the young ruffians, who in the 17th century were abducted in the area's taverns and deported to Canada, then known as La Nouvelle France. The above mentioned tavern, La Nouvelle France, stood across the street.

Behind the building at no. 60 is tucked away a late 18th-century *hôtel*. Its garden can be perceived from rue de Paradis. It contains a stone lionesses which may have been brought over from the Tuileries. The house at no. 58 was also built by Goupy on the land he had appropriated from the Filles-Dieu. The owner of this formerly magnificent *hôtel*, the councillor J. B. Titon, was guillotined in 1793, after which his widow had to let out the mansion and eventually it lost its glamour. Some remnants of its faded glory can still be detected on the ochre-coloured façades overlooking the inner courtyard and in the elegant wrought-iron staircase on the right, but the garden with its little neo-classical temple, fountain and grotto are all gone. In the 19th century Alexandre-Charles Sauvageot lived next door, at no. 56, where he amassed an impressive collection of Renaissance art, which he later bequeathed to the Louvre. Sauvageot was also an excellent violinist who, after having been awarded first prize at the Conservatoire, became the leader of the Opera orchestra, an activity he later exchanged for a post in the customs administration – there is no accounting for tastes! The painter Corot also resided in this house and died here in 1875 at the age of 79. He had a studio on the neighbouring rue de Paradis. The mansion at no. 52, a lovely example of Louis XVI architecture, was also built by Goupy, for the painter Deleuze. The Parnasse poet Sully Prudhomme, first recipient of the Nobel Prize for Literature in 1901, was born in 1839 at no. 34.

The one time palatial *hôtel* at no. 30 is now being converted into a block of 57 flats. Among its owners in pre-Revolutionary days was a wealthy tax collector, François Nicolas Lenormand, whose main claim to fame was to have been married to Marie Louise O'Murphy, to whom he may have owed this profitable post. After being the mistress of Louis XV, by whom she had a daughter, she married a gentleman, became a widow, then married Lenormand. Meanwhile, she bestowed her charms upon the Contrôleur Général des Finances to Louis XV, l'abbé Terray, who may have created her husband's office especially to please her, and who may also have, rather than her husband, fathered her second daughter. Widowed again, she married the last Foreign Minister of the Monarchy. Mlle O'Murphy, as she was commonly called, was also Boucher's model and as such can be seen in the guise of Boucher's *Odalisque Blonde* now hanging in Munich's Neue Pinakothek.

Retrace your steps and turn right into **RUE DE PARADIS**. This unlikely neighbourhood has been Paris's showcase of porcelain and crystal since the Restoration, when the Comte d'Artois, later to become Charles X, and his son, the Duc d'Angoulême and last Dauphin of France, were the first to set up porcelain workshops here, soon to be followed by others.

Before browsing along the street, turn right into **RUE D' HAUTEVILLE**, also once lined with palatial homes such as the little mansion tucked away in the courtyard of no. 54 and, especially, the **Hôtel de Bourienne** at no. 58, hidden behind a commonplace building: just ring the doorbell and you will be let in.

Begun by Madame de Dompierre in 1787, in 1790 the *hôtel* was bought by a wealthy sugar manufacturer from the West Indies, whose daughter, the Creole Fortunée, inherited the house in 1792. She was the beautiful, sparkling and intriguing Madame Hamelin, the friend of Napoleon and Josephine, who during Napoleon's reign set the tone in Parisian society. Fortunée had the place redecorated in the style of the *Directoire*, but by 1801, ridden with debts, she had to sell the house. The buyer was Antoine Fauvelet de Bourienne, one of those figures who managed to wade their way through the political upheavals of French history: after a close friendship with Napoleon, during which time Josephine became the godmother to one of his daughters, he was disgraced, but managed to resurface during the Restoration and to return to France with Louis XVIII and the other *emigrés* of Ghent (*Gand*, in French), the *Gandins*. Louis XVIII appointed him head of police and from 1815 to 1824 his *salon* was one of the most brilliant gathering places in the city, thanks to the sparkling wit of his wife, which largely compensated for her unfortunate looks. The *hôtel* was redecorated at the time of Bourienne and this is the way it has been left since.

In 1886 the house became the property of Charles Tuleu, a prosperous printer who had worked with Monsieur de Berny, Balzac's partner in 1828. Balzac had opened a printing-house a year earlier on rue Visconti (in the 6th arr.) but was unsuccessful and handed it over to the son of his much older friend and mentor, Madame de Berny, who turned it into a prosperous venture. A portrait of Balzac and another portrait of Madame de Berny can be seen in the study. Photos of present-day members of the family also decorate the house, reminding the visitor that the Hôtel de Bourienne is still lived in. Its present owners are the great nephews of Monsieur Tuleu and the printing-house he built at the back of the garden still stands, now converted into an outpatients' clinic. The winter garden with its marble floor, the dining-room with its magnificent painted wooden panelling in the style of Wedgewood china, the exquisite drawing-room with its Carrara marble fireplace, the tender blue ceiling of the boudoir with its exotic birds and delicate Cupid and Psyche in its centre, above all, the bathroom with the infinite reflection of its mirrors, combine to make an exceptional example of *Empire* and *Restauration* styles. Do not omit to take your time and enjoy the lovely gardens, so unexpectedly serene in this busy part of present-day Paris.

Retrace your steps and continue along RUE DE PARADIS. No. 18 first housed the retail outlet of the Choisy-le-Roy pottery, where gorgeous ceramics were on sale. In more recent times the Musée de l'Affiche et de la Publicité occupied this marvellous setting.

However, in 1991, unable to raise the funds to renew its lease, the museum had to leave the 10th arrondissement, where it had been much cherished, and move to the premises of the Musée d'Arts Décoratifs on rue de Rivoli (in the 1st arr.), thus depriving the 10th arrondissement of its fabulous collection of 50,000 bills and posters from all over the world. The premises are now used as an art gallery, **le Monde de l'Art**, and you can still admire the stunning 1900 ceramics in the entrance hall, the main hall and the staircase. The floor is still covered with the original tiles of the Choisy-le-Roy pottery. In 1831 the prestigious Saint-Louis and Baccarat crystal manufacturers, suppliers to Kings, Princes and Presidents, opened a showroom and distribution centre at nos 30 and 30bis. Today the **Musée des Cristalleries de Baccarat** can be visited at no. 30bis and items can be viewed and bought at the enormous showroom, which covers an area of 4,000 square metres.

Cross rue du Faubourg Saint-Denis and walk into rue de la Fidélité. You will reach the junction of the Boulevards de Magenta and Strasbourg. Across the Boulevard Strasbourg is the **church of Saint-Laurent** with its little square. An early basilica, first mentioned in 558 by the great historian and Bishop of Tours, Grégoire de Tours, stood approximately where the present church is, namely along the old Roman cardo (now Faubourg Saint-Martin). Around it lived a sparse, rural population, on the marshland that the religious community helped them to drain. Coffins from the Merovingian era (481–639), were found here around 1680.

After the devastation wrought by the Norsemen in the 9th century and the destruction of the shrine, it took another three centuries before a new basilica was erected in its place, to be replaced in the following century by a parish church. The latter in its turn was replaced in the 15th century, except for the original tower. In the course of its long history the church was inevitably tampered with, enlarged and renovated several times, and different periods and styles have left their mark on the building – hence the outside frieze at the back of the church dates from the Renaissance, while the portal is 17th century. The flamboyant neo-Gothic style that dominates it overall bears the mark of the 19th century, as does the spire. Having been used as various 'temples' during the Revolution, the church escaped demolition and its presbytery was

even converted into the first Mairie of the newly created arrondissement (then the 5th).

The famous Foire Saint-Laurent, described above, extended
north of the church into what is now the courtyard of the Gare de
l'Est and was held here from 1633 until the Revolution.

The **Gare de l'Est** was even more important strategically than
economically, for this was the departure point for the eastern
front, scene of periodic confrontations with the then eternal
enemy – Prussia, then Germany. Later, it was also from here that
French youths left for Germany on an indefinite mission of Oblig-
atory Work, as part of the humiliating sanctions inflicted by the
forces of Occupation during World War II. More tragically, many
of France's deportees left from the Gare de l'Est on their journey
East, never to return. Some commemorative plaques can be seen
inside the station, though few passengers ever bother to read them
or give a thought to those dark days.

The Fair of Saint-Laurent declined towards the end of the 18th
century and was closed down altogether during the Revolution. A
covered market replaced it in 1836 but it too was closed in 1852 to
make room for the Boulevard de Strasbourg. The **Marché Saint-
Quentin**, at 81/85*bis* Boulevard de Magenta is one of the two
markets that replaced it (the other being the Marché Saint-Martin,
discussed below). Its typical 19th-century iron structure and its
local colour warrant a detour, even though it is only a poor man'
version of the glorious fair. It is closed between 1 and 3.30 pm on
weekdays, on Sunday afternoons and all day Monday.

Walk into **RUE CHABROL** which runs south of the Marché
Saint-Quentin. It is named after the Prefect of the Seine in 1899. At
the time when France was enflamed over the Dreyfus Case, Jules
Guérin, the founder of Le Grand Occident de France, a notoriously
anti-Semitic and anti-Freemason movement, resisted a 37-day
siege on the roof of the one-storeyed house at no. 51, nicknamed
'*Fort Chabrol*'. Forty supporters joined him on the roof on 13
August 1899. In order to reinforce the siege and secure Guérin's
surrender, the water was cut off and buses were diverted from the
street to prevent his many supporters from throwing provisions
to the rebels from the upper deck. However, he and his friends

managed to resist until 20 September, when they finally exhausted their food and wine supply. On 4 January 1900 Jules Guérin was condemned to 10-years' imprisonment.

Retrace your steps and turn right and left into the **Passage** and **Cour de la Ferme-Saint-Lazare**, reminders of the medieval institution of Saint-Lazare, the life and soul of the neighbourhood, then wholly dedicated to work for lepers. Saint-Vincent's Mission, which replaced it in the 17th century but kept the same name, was the first religious institution to have suffered from the impetuous fury of the Revolution. The *Patriotes* ransacked the building, believing they would find corn (which they did) and weapons (which they did not), meanwhile stripping the place of whatever they could lay hands on. The members of the Order were chased away and the forces of the Revolution established a prison here. Among its political detainees was the greatest poet of the time, André Chénier, who began as an enthusiastic supporter of the Revolutionary ideal but was repelled by the nasty turn it took in 1793, and notably by the execution of the King. He also sided with Charlotte Corday after her murder of Marat – an unwise step for which he was first sent to the prison of Saint-Lazare and then transferred to the Conciergerie for his trial and death sentence as 'enemy of the people'. On 25 July 1794 he was led to the guillotine on the present Place de la Nation, only two days before Robespierre's own downfall. It was during those few tragic months of seclusion at Saint-Lazare that he wrote one of his best-known poems, *La Jeune Captive*, a homage to another prisoner, Mlle Aimée de Coigny, who, unlike Chénier, survived the Revolution, along with the Comte de Montrond. The two had even managed to become lovers within the prison walls and were later married. Saint-Lazare became a women's prison after the Revolution and remained so until 1935, when it was razed to the ground. In 1963 the Square Alban Satragne was laid out on part of its grounds. Only the courtyard and the chapel, built by Victor Baltard's father, have been preserved.

If you like multiracial, colourful street scenes, walk down RUE DU FAUBOURG SAINT-DENIS to the bottom of the street as far as the triumphal arch built by Blondel to commemorate the ultimate victory of the Sun King over his European enemies. A proliferation of narrow side-alleys on either side of rue du Faubourg-Saint-Denis creates an atmosphere of an Oriental bazaar, miles away from Paris. Turn left into the **Passage Reilhac** at no. 54 and have a look at its graceful fountains and succession of tiny courtyards, home to children from all parts of the world who play together in perfect harmony. On the other side of rue du Faubourg Saint-Denis, at no. 63, is the picturesque **Cour des Petites-Ecuries** where the King's coaches and harnesses were made and repaired in the second half of the 18th century. The workshops were naturally on the ground floor, while the craftsmen – coachbuilders, gilders, varnishers, saddlers, etc. – lived upstairs. The most prominent craftsman, Monsieur Aubert, lived in the house that stands on the north-west corner, at no. 63. Today this is the famous Belle Epoque **Brasserie Flo**, attracting hearty eaters from all over Paris into this out-of-the-way nook. Unfortunately, the establishment is now no longer unique and other celebrated establishments such as La Coupole at Montparnasse (in the 14th arr.), Le Boeuf sur le Toît, on rue du Colisée off the Champs-Elysées (in the 8th arr.), Terminus Nord and Julien (both in the 10th arr.), have been bought out and are part of the prosperous Flo chain, which hires 800 employees and caters daily for 5,000 visitors. There is also a Brasserie Flo under the cupola of Au Printemps department store, not to mention two in Barcelona, and another in Tokyo! Thank God, the premises of this early Brasserie Flo have remained intact.

Brasserie Flo

Retrace your steps and continue walking down rue du Faubourg Saint-Denis. Turn left at no. 46 into the **Passage Brady**, a tiny, ramshackle enclave of Tamils from the Indian subcontinent, who have taken up residence in this charming 19th-century arcade and filled it with the smell of spices and incense of the East. You will notice the profusion of Indian restaurants and grocery shops, but also barber shops, swarming with customers on Saturday afternoons. A profusion of video tapes provides the community with a major cultural link with its roots. Indians are voracious film-goers and it is India, not the USA, that has the biggest film industry in the world.

Beyond the Boulevard Strasbourg, the Passage Brady becomes an open air alley, and specialises in the rental of fancy costumes for both adults and children. Retrace your steps to the Boulevard Strasbourg. The **Passage de l'Industrie**, running parallel to the Passage Brady, will take you back to rue du Faubourg Saint-Denis. Here you will find a profuse display of hair rollers, and hairdressing accessories, alongside wigs in all colours of the rainbow.

Two greengrocers, on either corner of rue de l'Echiquier and rue de Metz, burst with the cries of vendors and overflow with enticing, bright-coloured vegetables and fruit – an exciting scene in contemporary Paris, from which native Parisians are strangely absent.

Passage Brady

At no. 16 rue du Faubourg Saint-Denis, further down, is the Brasserie Julien in its Art Nouveau setting. Here again they serve a traditional Alsacian *choucroute* (sauerkraut), preceded by a dish of oysters, as is customary among the French, and washed down with beer or Riesling wine from Alsace – a pleasant way of winding up. As you leave, take a look at the **Passage du Prado**, at no. 12, now home to textile workshops but once the departure point of the stage-coaches for Saint-Denis, a reminder that you have been strolling down the ancient sacred and royal way.

EAST OF RUE DU FAUBOURG SAINT-MARTIN

This walk starts at the **Mairie** of the 10th arrondissement, at 72 RUE DU FAUBOURG SAINT-MARTIN, a massive, ostentatious building inspired by the Hôtel de Ville and which was put up at the beginning of the 20th century. Behind it, at 6 rue Pierre-Bullet, the **Music Conservatory** of the 10th occupies one of the most exquisite buildings of the arrondissement, a rare vestige of its late 18th-century elegance. What you can see is merely the rear pavilion of what used to be the Hôtel de Gouthière, a beautiful building with a lovely garden, which disappeared with the opening of rue Bullet.

Gouthière, a great chiseller and gilder and inventor of matt gilding, created some magnificent works after the designs of Ledoux, Houdon and others. The King's entourage snapped these up and soon he became supplier to the court. Nevertheless, he went on living a hard-working, simple artisan's life, except for one great self-indulgence he allowed himself – owning a gigantic mansion, which he commissioned from the famous Métivier. But Gouthière was unable to pay for his house and ended up ruined, not because of his own extravagance but because he could not recover the debt of 765,000 pounds owed him by Madame du Barry, the notorious and last mistress of Louis XV, who with ruthless nonchalance, simply refused to pay. After the Revolution poor Gouthière tried to retrieve his due and took action against the State, sole holder of du Barry's estate, but in vain: Gouthière lost the case and died in utter destitution in 1813.

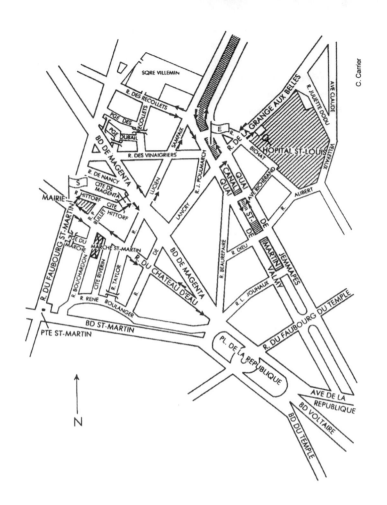

On the corner of rue Bouchardon and rue du Château-d'Eau, which runs south of the Mairie, stands the other indoor market of the arrondissement, **le Marché Saint-Martin**, a modest substitute for the Foire Saint Laurent. Recent reconstruction has made it more functional but has also taken away much of the charm.

Rue du Château-d'Eau leads to **PLACE DE LA RÉPUBLIQUE**, today a polluted, noisy place with little aesthetic appeal, but, unquestionably, a focal spot in the modern history of the capital. First opened by Napoleon, it was then known as Place du Château-d'Eau, after the spectacular Fontaine du Château-d'Eau by Girard that stood at its centre. It was fed by the newly built

Bassin de La Villette and the Canal de l'Ourcq, and with its eight proud, crouching lions, spitting great spouts of water into the air, was intended to put Rome's fountains to shame. It was inaugurated with great pomp by Napoleon on 15 August 1811, a date deliberately chosen to coincide with the newly established holiday of La Saint-Napoléon in lieu of the Catholic Assumption. However, Napoleon was soon ousted and whether Rome was shamed or not we do not know; but the fountain pleased the natives, and the Place du Château-d'Eau, hitherto no more than a vast street junction, became a favourite promenade, a source of inspiration to Daumier and Gavarni, and, from 1836 on, an exquisitely colourful sight on Mondays and Thursdays when a flower market was held here.

This happy state of affairs did not last for long: Haussmann's programme for recreating Paris, which in the 10th arrondissement included the construction of the Boulevard de Magenta, brought about radical change; the place was enlarged to its present dimensions and lost its intimacy and soul. Girard's fountain, once Napoleon's pride, looked insignificant on this vast expanse and was dispatched to La Villette, to decorate the entrance to its cattle market. Davioud was commissioned to erect a more monumental fountain, also decorated with inevitable lions, but it too was exiled elsewhere (to Place Félix Eboué in the 12th arr.) because the newly arisen Third Republic required something more emblematic. Having settled comfortably into their victory, the authorities set about distributing symbols of the new order throughout Paris, and in 1879 the Place du Château-d'Eau was renamed Place de la République. In 1884, on the symbolic date of 14 July, a gigantic allegorical statue representing the Republic took up position in the centre of the square, the meeting point of the 3rd, 10th and 11th arrondissements and scene of many militant, working-class gatherings. Which is why Haussmann had astutely placed the military barracks at no. 12, then known as la Caserne du Prince-Eugène. It replaced Daguerre's Diorama and its adjoining laboratory, where between 1822 and 1835 Daguerre worked on perfecting Niepce's extraordinary invention of the photograph. Next to it stood the celebrated Vauxhall d'Eté, one of the city's centres of pleasure during the Restoration.

Thus came to an end a world of picturesque bustle and local colour, which was, in fact, an extension of the extraordinary Boulevard du Temple (see next chapter). The fun deserted the streets and migrated to new places of pleasure, as ephemeral as their predecessors. Extending along the southern side of rue du Château-d'Eau, all the way to rue de Bondy (today Renée Boulanger), the monumental Grand Café Parisien called itself '*le plus grand café du monde*'! An army of waiters, over 100 strong, was employed to serve a daily clientele of several thousands. In keeping with the contemporary spirit of gigantism and extravagance, the management spared no expense and neglected no opportunity to dazzle and entertain. On rue de Bondy was a monumental gate ornamented with allegorical caryatides that served as reminders that commerce and industry were the source of the opulence of the interior. The café's centrepiece was a fantastic clock which indicated not only seconds, minutes and hours but also months, years and centuries, even the phases of the moon.

In 1881 a Panorama replaced the café, another colossal, ephemeral establishment, of which the ground floor alone – an enchanting winter garden – could seat 5,000 guests. It was named Le Panorama-National in keeping with the patriotic fervour of the day, and on the circular inner wall of its huge rotunda was a mural depicting a heroic episode of the Prussian War, known as *The Defence of Belfort*. In 1892 all this splendour disappeared to make room for the **Bourse du Travail** (trade-union centre), for which there was probably more need in this working-class neighbourhood.

Back on rue du Faubourg Saint-Martin, turn right into rue Hittorff, named after the famous architect who had helped the Baron Haussmann with much of the city's reconstruction and embellishment. Continue along the Cité Hittorff and the Cité de Magenta, then turn right into Boulevard de Magenta and left into rue Lucien Sampaix, past rue des Vinaigriers, where several houses from the 18th century can still be seen.

Turn left again into RUE DES RECOLLETS. The imposing walls of the **Hôpital Villemin**, once the military hospital of Saint-Martin, surround the site of what used to be the Couvent des Recollets, first founded by Henri IV. His wife, Marie de Medici, laid its cornerstone. During the Revolution it suffered the same fate as the other religious institutions and lost, among other things, its prestigious library of over 30,000 volumes, although the 17th-century cloister, staircase and chapel have survived intact. A patch of its grounds has also been rescued and turned into a small garden, le Jardin Villemin – a much appreciated bit of green space in this congested area, complete with a children's playground, all too rare an amenity in these parts.

Retrace your steps on rue des Recollets and continue up to the CANAL SAINT-MARTIN, along quai de Valmy to the right, then cross over the bridge and continue into RUE DE LA GRANGE-AUX-BELLES. The Hôpital Saint-Louis, on your right, was probably designed by Claude de Chastillon and executed by Claude Vellefaux, who also built the magnificent Place des Vosges. Here too the architect chose to alternate red brick and stone (a characteristic feature of the architecture of the time of Henri IV and Louis XIII) and tried to create an attractive environment for its patients and staff. Brick, however, was expensive at the time and surfaces were often just painted to simulate brickwork. When brick went out of fashion by the 18th century, most of it was plastered over. A wall and a moat surrounded the beautiful compound, and soldiers and even watchdogs were posted around it to prevent pestilence-ridden patients, doctors and nurses alike from escaping and spreading disease. On the other hand, nobody considered allocating each patient a separate bed and it was quite customary for four or five patients to share the same one. It was only in the 18th century that the Swiss Guards were granted the privilege of sharing a hospital bed between two.

When the first epidemic broke out at the time of Louis IX, rumours had it that it had been deliberately brought over and spread by the Jews. The saintly King encouraged this theory. A notorious anti-Semite, he had already compelled all the Jews to wear the yellow badge well before the outbreak of the epidemic. The plague was in fact brought over from Damascus to Marseilles aboard a ship carrying damask fabrics. This piece of information was concealed from the public to avoid creating panic, which only helped to spread the epidemic further, since no appropriate measures were taken to avoid it. The King contracted the disease and died of it himself, which is why the hospital was named after him.

As you visit the old premises, you will come to the Pavillon Gabrielle – which, contrary to legend, was not one of Henri IV's love-nests. It has, on the other hand, been used by medical students who have given vent to their pornographic self-expression in the form of wild graffiti on the inside walls of the pavilion. The penchant for pornography, known as *l'esprit carabin*, is traditional amongst medical students, called *les carabins* because they were protected from the angry public by soldiers armed with carbines (guns).

The hospital chapel was built outside the walled compound because it was not used by the patients, who had their own oratories in two of the corner pavilions. Henri IV dedicated the chapel to Saint Louis, hence his statue on the façade. The second statue is of Saint Roch, the patron saint of the victims of the plague. Henri IV, though, was never to attend the first ceremony held here on 14 July 1610, which, ironically, became his own memorial service, two months after his assassination by Ravignac on rue de la Ferronnerie in Les Halles.

The modern hospital has maintained its old calling to a certain extent, since it specialises in skin diseases. It is situated discreetly out of sight from the old hospital, so as to preserve the architectural harmony of the latter, which, some claim, is even more beautiful than Place des Vosges. It is worth a visit for its elegant architecture and serene surroundings, a tribute to the administration's efforts to create a humane environment for the patients.

And now for the CANAL:

Le douzième aussi a ses locomotives, mais il a moins de poètes.

The 12th too has its locomotives, but it has fewer poets.

Léon-Paul Fargues

As a child of the 10th arrondissement, Léon-Paul Fargues can be suspected of bias, but on arriving at the Canal Saint-Martin you may be inclined to agree with him. Considered by some as the highlight of the arrondissement, the Canal warrants an outing in itself and should preferably be seen both by day and by night. The poet in you can walk along its banks and/or discover it by boat, all the way from the Bassin de la Villette to the Musée d'Orsay on the Seine. Bear in mind that the trip is very slow because the boat has to wait at each lock and you will need to allow several hours for this wonderfully old-fashioned and relaxing experience.

You should reach the Canal through rue de la Grange-aux-Belles, once the site of the gallows of Montfaucon, vestiges of which were found in 1954 at no. 53 together with some human bones, as reported earlier. Today an extensive glass roof lets the light pour into the new, airy premises of an artists' centre at no. 37, drawn to the proximity of the Canal. Across the Canal, at no. 102 quai de Jemmapes, stands the picturesque **Hôtel du Nord**, which rises on its other side, immortalised by Arletty in Marcel Carné's movie by the same name. The hotel was earmarked for demolition to make room for a modern block of flats in this more expensive strip of the arrondissement. Besides, it was argued, the building was of no architectural value and Marcel Carné's movie was not at all shot on the site but in one of the studios in Boulogne (west of Paris and also gone by now). Demolitionists further argued that at the end of Eugène Dabit's novel, on which the film was based, the hotel was actually pulled down. Conservationists and sentimental film-lovers countered that the hotel must be preserved, if only out of respect for the author, who was the son of the hotel-keepers and grew up there. Finally a compromise was reached: the old façade has been preserved and renovated, masking a totally new construction, a trick often used in Paris these days, thereby gradually turning the city into a sham. A 250-square-metre gallery devoted to the cinema has opened on the ground floor. One can only hope that the entire corner with its two antiquated cafés, which bear such picturesque names as le Café du Pont Tournant and l'Ancre de la Marine – relics of old working-class Paris – will also be preserved.

In contrast to this exquisite spot the rest of the canal is lined with commonplace blocks of flats, so wrong in this environment. Ignore them and concentrate on the canal itself – a lovely sight with its romantic iron foot-bridges arching over it and reflected in the grey waters – whose placid atmosphere evokes the northern plains of Flanders. The nine locks are a spectacle in themselves:

whenever a trippers' boat or a barge approaches, strollers and cyclists stop and flock to the canal banks or the bridges to watch the lock-keeper opening the gates. Here time has come to a standstill. Adults and children alike watch the level of the water rise or fall for the umpteenth time. Others have their eyes riveted to the rotating turn bridge, always with the same fascination when the bridge finally connects up with the street and the neighbourhood comes back to life and goes on with its business. This is the only place in Paris where motorists are prepared to wait patiently for the manoeuvre to be completed and where serene anglers have not been scared off by the motorcar. The eternal *boules* players add to the prevailing provincial nonchalance. Paris is miles away.

Canal Saint-Martin

THE 11TH ARRONDISSEMENT

W HEN the last decade of the 20th century witnessed the collapse of communism throughout the Soviet empire and her European satellites, proletarian traditions lost their grip on the 11th arrondissement, the vanguard of French class struggle ever since 1789. As protesters march between Place de la Nation, Place de la République and Place de la Bastille – the three cardinal points of working-class militancy – one is struck by the dramatic fall in their ranks. Even the First of May parade no longer galvanises the labouring masses; the red banners are few and far between and its once wholehearted *Internationale* has lost its conviction. As the 20th century draws to a close, many comrades have deserted the ranks to join the celebrations of Le Pen's National Front in front of the statue of Jeanne d'Arc, in the 1st arrondissement.

It was on the southern edge of the arrondissement, in the wretched Faubourg Saint-Antoine, that rumbling discontent was first channelled into working-class consciousness and into organised action against exploitation. When word was spread on 28 April 1789 that Monsieur Réveillon, the painted-paper manufacturer on rue de Montreuil, was planning to reduce his workers' wages, the Faubourg Saint-Antoine rose up in a violent insurrection. Monsieur Réveillon had not anticipated such a reaction, for the lowering of wages he had intended was proportionate to the drop in the price of bread fixed by the authorities to ease social tension. His 400 workers had a different idea of fairness and Réveillon, terrified, ran for his life and sought shelter in the neighbouring Bastille, the ominous fortress looming west of the Faubourg. It took the intervention of the troops and a death toll of 30 to put down the revolt, but any wise ruler should have sensed that further trouble was brewing. . .

King Louis XVI had been hunting on 14 July. Upon his return he noted in his diary:

> *Aujourd'hui, rien'*
>
> Today, nothing'

The account Charles Dickens left of the day is somewhat different:

> A tremendous roar arose from the throat of Saint Antoine, and a forest of naked arms struggled in the air like shrivelled branches of trees in a winter wind: all the fingers convulsively clutching at every weapon or semblance of a weapon that was thrown up from the depths below. . .
>
> *A Tale of Two Cities*

Although the heroic storming of the Bastille boiled down in effect to nothing more than the liberation of the seven prisoners still detained there, as described in the chapter on the 4th arrondissement, the demolition of the formidable fortress was another story.

A wily charlatan called Palloy took charge of this arduous task, awarding himself the title of *démolisseur de la Bastille* for the occasion. Disposing of the stones of the fortress proved even more arduous. Some were used to build the Concorde bridge (see chapter on 8th arr.), but what about the many others? Palloy came up with the idea of chiselling miniature model Bastilles out of them, which he sold as souvenirs, not unlike the little Eiffel Towers we can see today. In January 1790, 93 miniatures were offered as gifts to the newly created *départements* (districts) of France securing for Palloy a substantial profit. Palloy's patriotic activities connected with the Bastille took other forms as well. In June 1790 he oversaw the solemn burial of some old remains found in the prison's cells. The Bastille having proved a disappointment by failing to provide living proof of oppression, the dead of earlier times were pressed into service instead as victims of tyranny, their remains enjoying national recognition. A monument to them was erected, bearing a pompous inscription and also the Latin signature *Petrus Franciscus Palloy, amicus patriae*. When Louis XVI was executed in January 1793, Palloy the Patriot, turned *chef* for the occasion and concocted a dish which he named *tête de cochon farci* and which also allowed him to increase his revenue.

The politically symbolic demolition of the Bastille by the *sans-culottes* was fraught with unanticipated consequences. With the overthrow of both church and monarchy, it was the entire medieval edifice that was being challenged and, first and foremost, its constraint upon freedom, as advocated by the Enlightenment. To working-class Paris this meant, above all, the inalienable right to perpetual revelling, a right so far reserved for their social betters. No longer content with the annual fairs of Saint-Germain and Saint-Laurent conceded by the church, the people of Paris now demanded festivities on a permanent basis and it was on the Boulevard du Temple, the north-western boundary between the 3rd and 11th arrondissements, that these took place – an obvious location since this was the eastern proletarian section of the semi-circular Grands Boulevards, the spacious, tree-lined promenade laid out by Louis XIV between the Madeleine and the Bastille.

As the hitherto squeezed city shook off its girdle and spread to the new boundary (the toll walls completed on the eve of the Revolution), its citizens and those of its former suburbs also broke free and converged on the pleasure-grounds of the Boulevards. Emulating the privileged classes in the western parts, working-class Paris thronged to the Boulevard du Temple where, enjoying a lull between two revolutions, it indulged in an uninterrupted fête for nearly half a century, to which bears witness the following verse:

> *La seul' prom'nade qu'a du prix,*
> *C'est le Boul'vard du Temple à Paris*

> The only promenade worth anything
> is the Boulevard du Temple in Paris.

A strip of the Boulevard du Temple, barely 200 metres long, was turned into a theatreland, where the entertainment was not confined to the playhouses that lined it but spilt out into the Boulevard itself. According to poet Gérard de Nerval, the show outdoors was even more fun than those indoors. The spectator-turned-actor unwittingly provided a wealth of material for Daumier, Gavarni, Grandville and other cartoonists and sometimes took part in real-life dramas as emotional as those enacted on stage.

The mornings, however, were reserved for the natives of the neighbourhood who created a scene of village life – a 'prologue' of sorts – with its inimitable street criers in their colourful garb, selling water and other necessities. By midday they had all vanished, making room for the first rolling of drums and clashes of cymbals announcing the *parade* – that street spectacle involving buffoons and tumblers which preluded the show and was meant to lure the spectators into the playhouses. Borrowed heavily from the Italian farce, the priceless Bobêche, a sly character sporting a red jacket, yellow knickerbockers, blue stockings and an orange tailed-wig with a red riband would outdo his slow-witted, rustic counterpart, Galimafré.

It was knockabout comedy full of oafish puns, saucy innuendoes, mistaken identities and occasional scuffles, which delighted the unsophisticated crowds gathered around the trestles. More popular still were clownish Paillasse (Pagliacci), mischievous Policinelle, dazzling, scheming Arlequin and old Cassandre, in their Gallisised versions, who brought back nostalgic, emotionally charged childhood memories and perpetuated the pre-Revolutionary traditions of the fairs of Saint-Germain and Saint-Laurent, whose jugglers, acrobats, conjurors, animal tamers, monsters and puppeteers moved to the Boulevard du Temple with the new century. Of all the artists on the Boulevard, it was the tightrope-walker who carried on the most essential heritage of the medieval fair: through perfect body control that transcended mere acrobatic skills, he conveyed an imponderable dream-like quality that offered the spectator a magically enchanting experience, as he moved about suspended in mid air.

However, after a time, the rope limited his freedom of expression and his performance became tedious, which is why he eventually turned to mime, an art that gave him fuller scope, a necessity on a fairground where the show must never cease. Although he came down to the ground, he retained all the glamour of the tightrope-walker, and all the mimes hired by the famous Théâtre des Funambules ('tightrope walker', in French) had first to excel on the rope, notably the Bohemian-born Gaspard Deburau, the heart-rending, fragile Pierrot immortalised by Jean-Louis Barrault in *Les Enfants du Paradis.*

'Children of Paradise', as Marcel Carné poetically dubbed the people of the Boulevard du Temple, because they were as guileless as the childlike inhabitants of the Garden of Eden, but also because the only seats they could afford in these twopenny theatres were those in the gods, called *paradis* in French. They would arrive well ahead of time and settle down to eat a pick-nick of chips, sausages and cooked apples bought on the Boulevard, those seated in the first row either using the balustrade as a counter or sitting on it with their feet dangling off the ground. Deliberately or inadvertently, food and greasy paper were dropped on the heads of the better-off spectators below, along with sarcastic comments and insults.

The actors too were treated to either vociferous approval or boos, catcalls and the pelting of cooked apple cores, hence the French expression *recevoir des pommes cuites*. Easily gullible, the audience would get so involved in this world of make-believe that the borderline between reality and fiction became blurred. Like modern pantomime audiences, they would cry out warnings to the hero about to be stabbed by the villain, or to the heroine on the verge of sipping a poisonous drink. In fact they were not far wrong. Five-hour-long melodramas ending in a pool of blood were not confined to the stage, and although the Boulevard du Temple was nicknamed Boulevard du Crime after the fictional thrillers, real crime was not uncommon, as to be expected among such excitable crowds when so much destitution lurked in side alleys. Even Deburau unintentionally fell into that trap when he killed a tramp in self-defence. Although he was acquitted, his sense of guilt never left him and he never again played the part of Pierrot, who stabbed a ragman in order to steal from him a costume with which to seduce the coquettish Colombine. Instead he adopted the lanky, pallid, pathetic stage persona of the eternal victimised pariah.

The enthusiasm and responsiveness of the gullible spectators in the gods were largely guided and channelled by the claque, who, with masterful timing could provoke a roar of applause or a flood of tears to suit the strategy of the theatre director. Even an idolised actor like Frédérick Lemaître could not do without the support of the claque, and, when the latter remained obstinately silent after his performance in *Robert Macaire*, he was not called back to the stage. Frédérick Lemaître knew very well that his employer had used this device to bring him to heel. Once on the stage, however, the actor enjoyed a considerable degree of latitude, inherited from his mischievous ancestors of the fairs. In the endless melodrama *l'Auberge des Ardets*, put on at the Ambigu, Frédérick Lemaître, in the lead, turned the role into a comic one without bothering to consult the authors. Likewise, inspired by one of the neighbourhood's vagabonds, he adopted the costume of a dandy vagabond which became his trademark, somewhat like Charlie Chaplin. Yet, when he took it with him to the rival Folies-Dramatiques to play the lead in *Robert Macaire,* the owner of the Ambigu sued him for stealing his moral property.

During the ambivalent reign of Louis-Philippe, freedom was by no means unlimited: like the tightrope-walker, the population of the Boulevard du Temple had to find out for itself how far it could go. When the celebrated grotesque puppet Guignol took to thrashing Louis-Philippe, the authorities banned the show. The Boulevard rags, sold in great quantities by vociforous hawkers, were the authorities' main target, since they could contain subversive messages. On the other hand, no one troubled with the Mardi Gras carnival, the climax of the year, when social distinctions disappeared behind seemingly innocent disguises, allowing criminal hands to settle private accounts. On Ash Wednesday, a motley stream of humanity surged forth from the toll barriers of Belleville, known as La Courtille because of its open-air taverns(*courtille,* originally a walled-in property), where untaxed wine was served, and hurtled down the slope to the Boulevard du Temple in a maelstrom of frenzied rounds. Thousands of people came from all over Paris to take part in the *descente de la Courtille,* and not only the mob. The mob, however, particularly relished it, hurling flour over their betters who were comfortably seated in their barouches, a custom which has been revived of late by students and which causes a lot of disturbances in public transportation. Alfred de Musset, an eyewitness, may have sensed the ominous nature of this force:

> *Les voitures de masques défilaient pêle-mêle, en se heurtant, en se froissant, entre deux longues haies d'hommes et de femmes hideux, debout sur les trottoirs. Cette muraille de spectateurs sinistres avait, dans ses yeux rouges de vin, une haine de tigre. Sur une lieue de long tout cela grommelait . . . de temps en temps un homme en haillons sortait de la haie, nous vomissait un torrent d'injures au visage puis nous jetait un nuage de farine.*

Carriages of masked passengers paraded pell-mell, bumping, jostling against each other, between two long hedgerows of hideous men and women, standing on the pavements. In this wall of sinister spectators, with eyes bloodshot from wine, could be read the hatred of a tiger. For the length of a league could be heard their muttering

... now and then a man in rags would emerge from the hedge, spit out a shower of abuse then hurl at us a cloud of flour.

La Confession d'un enfant du siècle (1836)

Louis-Philippe did not dare interfere with those festivities but was well aware of the state of mind of the arrondissement. After all, it was the Faubourg Saint-Antoine that had risen up in July 1830 and which, after a three-day insurrection, known as *Les Trois Glorieuses*, brought him to the throne of France in place of the Bourbons. It was political tactics on his part that led him to hold the annual commemoration of that revolt in these plebeian parts, rather than in western Paris. He had chosen the Boulevard du Temple for the itinerary of the royal procession, because it was the promenade of working-class Paris *par excellence* and because it ran conveniently into the symbolic Place de la Bastille, where the actual ceremony of commemoration took place. For symbolic reasons too Place de la Bastille was likewise chosen as the final destination for the remains of the victims of the insurrection.

A plaster and wood model of a monumental elephant stood there at the time, providing shelter to such street urchins as Gavroche in Victor Hugo's *Les Misérables*. Napoleon, yearning to take India from England, liked the emblematic beast and intended to replace it with a bronze model and turn it into a fountain, with water from the new canals of Ourcq and Saint-Martin spurting out of its trunk. The bronze would have been melted down from guns captured from the Spaniards and would have enhanced the empire's glory and the Emperor's ego.

But the Empire had collapsed before the project was carried through and the July Monarchy erected the Column of the Bastille in its stead. This was surmounted by the gilded sculpture of the Génie de la Bastille, which represents Liberty breaking off its shackles and spreading light all around. Funeral vaults were built into the foundations, destined to hold the remains of the 504 identified victims of the insurrection, hitherto buried in the gardens adjoining the Louvre to the east. Next to them lay some mummies brought over from Egypt by Napoleon and transferred here from the damp basement of the Louvre Museum where they had decayed. A pompous ceremony to the sound of Berlioz's *Symphonie funéraire et triomphale*, commissioned for the occasion, accompanied the transfer of the victims' remains to the vaults of the Bastille in 1840. It is believed that they were laid to rest alongside several contemporaries of Ramses II. As for Berlioz, appalled by the quality of the performance, this is what he said:

La musique est toujours ainsi respectée en France, dans les fêtes ou réjouissances publiques, où l'on croit devoir la faire figurer . . . pour l'oeil.

Music is always thus respected in France, in public celebrations and rejoicings, where it is believed one should present it . . . to please the eye.

In March 1848, 196 new victims of the 1848 February Revolution were brought here for burial. On 24 July the triumphant people of Paris paraded the throne of Louis-Philippe through the Boulevards on its way to the Bastille Column where they burnt it down, thus doing away with royalty once and for all.

Louis-Philippe had been taking a gamble when he challenged the crowds of the Boulevard du Temple by appearing before them in person. Although rioting was restricted to the narrower side streets, beyond the reach of the troops, the dense crowds on the Boulevard gave cover for some political agitation there as well. It was on the Boulevard du Temple that Guillard de Kersausie, a leader of an underground organisation, was arrested on 17 April 1834, but it was in the narrow streets around Saint-Merri that riots broke out and were brutally suppressed by the troops.

When one soldier was wounded by a shot said to have been fired from one of the buildings along the Boulevard, the troops stormed the building and massacred all its inhabitants one by one – women, old people, no one was spared. The following day the National Assembly congratulated the troops on their deed!

Ignoring these signals, Louis-Philippe brazenly advanced into the minefield of the Boulevard du Temple on 28 July 1835. At no. 50, a certain Fieschi, having installed his infernal machine of 25 guns tied together like organ tubes, was posted behind a window, waiting for the King to pass at the head of the National Guard. Fieschi had chosen that spot, opposite the opulent Café Turc, assuming, rightly, that the King would slow down to acknowledge its cheering royalist clientele.

Suddenly, his 25 guns, charged with grapeshot, exploded all at once and within seconds 40 people were lying on the ground. Eleven died on the spot, among them the Maréchal Mortier and the Duc de Trévise, but the King escaped with no more than a slight scratch on his forehead. Ignoring the casualties strewn about him, he turned to the Guard and said, 'Gentlemen, let us proceed!' The following day he was seen as usual strolling with his family in the Parc de Saint-Cloud, carrying his umbrella. . . Fieschi, just as self-composed, climbed to the guillotine with his two accomplices on 19 February 1836.

Stability was achieved only after 1850, once Napoleon III grabbed the reins of power. In order to put an end to the political unrest – in the past 25 years the government had been unsettled no fewer than 9 times! – he ordered his Prefect, the Baron Haussmann, to remodel the urban layout of the capital. Medieval Paris, a maze of dark crevices, had provided an ideal territory for urban guerrillas and a nightmare for troops to control. Obviously, Haussmann could not wipe out the entire arrondissement but he could at least carve through it a network of thoroughfares so that troops could move quickly and break down insurgency, often manifested in barricades.

Du Boulevard du Temple à la barrière du Trône, une entaille
. . . des entailles partout, Paris haché à coups de sabre, les veines
ouvertes. . .

From the Boulevard du Temple to the barrier of the Trône, a gash
. . . gashes everywhere, Paris slashed by a sabre, its veins slit. . .

Emile Zola, reported in *La Curée.*

Thus the Boulevard du Prince-Eugène (now Boulevard Voltaire) was carved through the axis of the arrondissement in 1857 to allow for the speedy passage of troops between Place du Château-d'Eau (a simple crossroads at the time, now Place de la République) and Place du Trône (today Place de la Nation). The vast new esplanade that replaced the crossroads and was later renamed Place de la République, to mark the advent of a new regime, encroached on a sizeable chunk of Boulevard du Temple. Broad arteries radiated from it, including what is now Avenue de la République, which facilitated movement into and out of the area.

A final obstacle, the Canal Saint-Martin, was also removed

thanks to Haussmann's ingenious idea of covering it up with yet another artery, the Boulevard de la Reine-Hortense (now Richard-Lenoir), which connected Place de la Bastille and Place de la République. The last insurrection of the 19th century, the 1871 *Commune*, was to prove Napoleon III and his Prefect right, even though it was Thiers, the head of the provisional government of the budding Third Republic, who was the beneficiary of the initiative.

Indeed, the barricades erected by the *Communards* during the *semaine sanglante* ('bloody week') of May 21–28 against the inexorable advance of the *Versaillais* (the government's forces) through Haussmann's broad arteries proved totally inadequate and the week ended with the massacre of 20,000 to 30,000 *Communards*. On 28 May, after eight days of heroic yet hopelessly useless resistance, 1,900 of them were shot dead at the prison of La Roquette, in the 11th arrondissement.

Napoleon III had other considerations as well. Impressed by London while in exile there, he wished to modernise and embellish his own capital and to encourage its development. This necessitated the opening up of means of access to the new railway stations. Work on such a scale would help launch the construction industry and revitalise the economy. It would also provide work for 100,000 people and alleviate discontent. After all, had not Napoleon III designated himself a socialist Emperor? However, he felt no compunction in allowing destitute people to be evicted in the process and be pushed out of the 11th, into insalubrious, derelict quarters on the periphery of Paris – the farther out, the safer for the establishment. The Boulevard du Crime, the magical lifeblood of the arrondissement, had been dismembered and was no more.

Rue de Lappe, with its cheap bars and dance halls, would later become a dingy, ramshackle substitute for the Boulevard du Temple. Frequented by defiant, troublemaking *apaches* in their bell-bottom trousers and shapeless caps, and by their female appendages, the *gigolettes*, this was the sort of place that attracted such people as Henry Miller and was romanticised by the likes of Léon-Paul Fargues. Inhabited by metal-workers in pre-Revolutionary days, it became in the 19th century the headquarters of the Auvergnat colony.

Back in the 18th century these hardy mountain people used to come to Paris by way of the Allier river and the Briare Canal to sell the coal of their native Brassac. Upon arrival they would saw up their barges, sell the wood as well as the coal and return home on foot. It was not long before they settled in Paris permanently, earning a living by salvaging and selling the scrap-iron that came their way around rue de Lappe. When water came to be in demand, they converted to the tough trade of water-carriers. Every morning they could be seen on the Boulevard du Temple in their traditional costume, two buckets of water dangling from a yoke on their shoulders, crying out, '*A l'eau!*' or '*Ao! Ai!*' or '*Oia!*', the first syllable being voiced from the head, the second projected from the chest, so as to be heard on the top floors.

They had come up to Paris to improve their lot, and did so doggedly, step by step. Soon they added coal to water in the winter months, and when modernised Paris had been supplied with water, they substituted wine for water as their stock-in-trade. Before long the one-time hawkers set up shops selling coal and wine, which also served as rudimentary cafés, and the celebrated *bougnat* (from *charbougnat*, originally a collier or coalman) became no less of a Parisian institution than the *bistro*.

Not content with owning practically all the establishments – including cheap hotels – in the area, the resourceful, thrifty (some say parsimonious) Auvergnats now set about conquering the café industry of the entire capital, which is largely in their hands to this very day. Remonecq, Balzac's Auvergnat character in *Le Cousin Pons*, demonstrating the same dogged perseverence, started out selling scrap-iron and ended up a prosperous antique-dealer after a frugal life dedicated to work and piling up his savings.

In the dance halls of rue de Lappe, which were also frequented by members of the strong Italian community, who had arrived here via the nearby Gare de Lyon, they danced their native *bourrée* to the music of their traditional bagpipes known as *musettes*. In 1905 their fellow-countryman Monsieur Bouscatel, the owner of Le Bouscat, joined forces with the Italian accordionist Peguri and invented what would become a world-renowned type of accordion music known as *musette*. It was in Le Bouscat, Monsieur Bouscatel's *bal-musette* on rue de Lappe, that this popular music was performed for the first time. Thus, what came to be taken for a typically Parisian musical lore was in fact the joint invention of two members of the outside communities of the 11th and combined the Italian sense of melody with the Auvergnat sense of rhythm.

A third community was soon to join them. With the decline of the Ottoman Empire, the first Jewish refugees from Turkey, Greece and Bulgaria settled down on rue Sedaine, preparing the ground for their fellow-Jews. The café Le Bosphore became the social meeting-place of this 'Little Turkey'. Having alighted at the Gare de Lyon after a journey from Marseilles, one of the Ottoman Jewish passengers found that there was no-one waiting to meet him. Totally at a loss, he sought the help of a cab-driver, who, on hearing the taveller's country of origin, drove him straight to Le Bosphore, where, sure enough, his cousin was found!

Like all new arrivals then and now, he must have had to settle for one of those dismal hotel rooms, which, like the neighbourhood cafés, were nearly always owned by Auvergnats. Relationship between the two communities was harmonious, all the more so since they were involved in different economic sectors. The Ottoman Jews dealt in clothing, household linen, hosiery, mercery and some oriental rugs. At times these would be seen spread out in a courtyard as had been the custom in the Levant.

These Mediterranean Jews took time out to socialise around a game of cards, the men in the café, the women at home. By contrast, the Eastern European Jews who arrived in the arrondissement a generation later were hard working and turned the clothing trade into an industry. Today this industry has largely been taken over by Jewish immigrants who arrived from North Africa in the 1960s. Exploding with dynamism and ambition, they have spread here from their Sentier stronghold (in the 2nd arr.) and given the neighbourhood a further boost. But the concentration of Jews in the arrondissement was so large even before their arrival, that during World War II one of the major round-ups of the Jews of Paris took place in the Gymnase Japy in the 11th arrondissement. As one survivor put it, out of 30 families living in his building, only two were not rounded up. Some Jews who had kept their Turkish citizenship were more fortunate since, paradoxically, they benefited from the protection of Germany's ally, Turkey.

While their predecessors have bettered themselves by now and moved out, preferably west, today's new arrivals – Africans, Blacks or Arabs – still have to live in derelict hotel rooms in some seedy streets of the arrondissement. Today these are often at the mercy of being evicted and at risk from fires or gas explosions. As communism and trade-unionism have lost their appeal in working-class Paris, fundamentalism is gaining ground among immigrant Moslems. Wearing beards, white abayas and turbans, these members of the French branch of the Al Jama'at al Tabligh movement are to be seen on rue Jean-Pierre Timbaud, at the foot of Belleville, where their shrine, the Mosque of Omar, is located. Significantly, the neighbourhood used to be the stronghold of the Communist Party and, ironically, the mosque stands on the site of the general hospital belonging to the metalworkers' section of the the C.G.T. (la Centrale Générale des Travailleurs), the communist-orientated trade union. No less significantly, one of the movement's leaders is a former Maoist! One last gesture in honour of working-class struggle was nonetheless granted the arrondissement in 1991, when the statue of Léon Blum, the first president of the *Front Populaire*, was erected on Place Léon Blum, opposite the town hall.

In 1976 the painter Dominique Thiolet settled in a new studio at 5 rue de Charonne, ushering in a new era for the 11th arrondissement. The arrival of other artists in the southern section of the arrondissement around the Bastille and the renovation of the area were the first step of an overall process of gentrification of eastern Paris. By 1985 the association Le Génie de la Bastille (called after the golden 'spirit of liberty' which surmounts the Bastille column) boasted 40 participating studios and over 100 artists. A year later Jean-Pierre Lavigne, a major art-dealer on the contemporary Parisian scene, opened his spacious, three-storeyed gallery at 27 rue de Charonne and dazzled the neighbourhood with the first exhibition in Paris of Andy Warhol's silk screens. By now nearly 200 artists and writers have taken up residence in what has become the new trendy area of Paris, among them the Japanese fashion designer Kenzo. Brochures and leaflets speak in highfaluting terms of their spiritual or ideological motives when settling around the 'place' (i.e. Place de la Bastille) 'generating freedom and movement'.

In point of fact, they came here initially because they could not afford to settle in places like Saint-Germain-des-Prés, and, with the building of the new Opera well under way, it was reasonable for them to assume that the neighbourhood would soon become desirable. Furthermore, as old trades – metalworks, spinning mills – were dying out, many workshops became vacant and could be purchased at low prices and converted into 'lofts'. It was in the Bastille area that the frenzied vogue for lofts, emulating Manhattan, began in the 1980s. These were located on the ground floor usually, because that was where the workshops were located, but in Parisian terminology they became 'lofts' nonetheless. Kenzo too followed the trend when he converted the premises of a metal factory into a fabulous Japanese-style residence. Cafés, night clubs and restaurants followed, turning the Bastille into the new 'in' neighbourhood of Paris.

There is no place here now for characters like the 'white gypsy' Jo Privat, the 'King' of the rue de Lappe, also known as 'le Seigneur de la Bastille'. His accordion has long been silent. It was the instrument of the people, and nobody wants the people any more, so Jo Privat has taken to the bottle. . . In 1936 he played for the first time at the celebrated Balajo on rue de Lappe, a classier establishment than the average dance hall, frequented by slender pimps in their gaudy ties and pointed patent shoes. 'Paris has buggered off,' he says today, 'and we have not noticed it.'

rue de Lappe

The residents of the neighbourhood were less willing to throw in the sponge. In May 1992, having gathered 500 signatures, they succeeded in rescuing the 100-year-old grocery, Aux Produits d'Auvergne, at no. 6 rue de Lappe.

WHERE TO WALK

FROM PLACE DE LA BASTILLE
AND BACK AGAIN

During your exploration of the 11th arrondissement, you will not see any spectacular landmarks; instead, you will gain insights into the changing social make-up of Paris, even more so here, perhaps, than anywhere else, as you will be catapulted straight from the birthplace of proletarian Paris and of its ancestors, the *sans-culottes* of Faubourg Saint-Antoine, to the focal point of up-to-date, contemporary Paris. Since rue du Faubourg Saint-Antoine is the cradle of Proleterian Paris, this will be our starting point.

Set out from **PLACE DE LA BASTILLE** and remain on the northern pavement of **RUE DU FAUBOURG SAINT-ANTOINE** (the southern pavement belongs to the 12th arrondissement). The furniture shops that line the street cater mainly to the lower middle classes and no longer produce the works of art that embellished the courts of France and Europe before the Revolution. However, reproductions of items from that golden age are still displayed here in great numbers, often turned out in the back alleys and courtyards of the street, where some French cabinetmakers and carpenters still work alongside their Chinese counterparts. At times you will even be greeted by the wonderful smell of sawdust. More rarely you will come across the odd specialist in metal plating – gold, silver, copper – struggling to perpetuate old traditions. These side alleys are the highlight of this walk, as they have all preserved their original architecture, designed for an industrial society in the making. At present the buildings are being spruced up one by one, especially around the Bastille (but those further out are fast following suit), and as they are metamorphosed into green havens, their hubbub fades into peaceful tranquillity. Local papers periodically reiterate

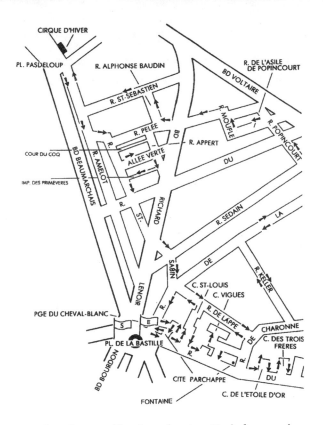

their protests against the gentrification of eastern Paris, bemoaning its lost soul, but there is no putting the clock back and the result has been beneficial to locals and enchanting to the visitor, who can discover new delights at every corner. The wreckage here has been minimal; instead, down-at-heel constructions have merely been improved and renovated, thus enabling some of the hard-working inhabitants of Faubourg Saint-Antoine to retire comfortably after drawing a decent profit from the sale of their property. By the same token, the newcomers, who arrived here predominantly in the 1980s, were able to acquire spacious premises at affordable prices, a privilege reserved to very few in Paris. Furthermore, by converting the shabby workshops into 'lofts', the run-down alleys into patios and vacant corners into picturesque havens, they have contributed to the embellishment of the neighbourhood.

At the gateway to the Faubourg to the left, on the north-eastern edge of Place de la Bastille, lies the first of these back alleys, **le**

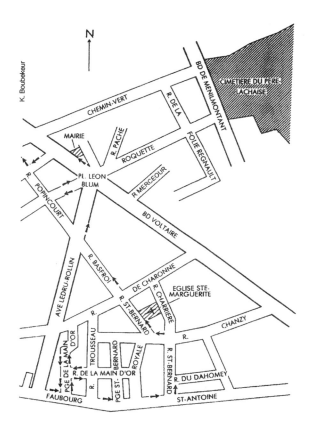

Passage du Cheval Blanc. The name of the alley, like many of the others in the neighbourhood, is reminiscent of an old street sign. The present sign, which reads *Loisir Provence Mediterranée*, is more in keeping with the lifestyle of today. Pink geraniums and lavender waft their fragrance outside the pompous, glittering entrance of Claude Deco, an establishment that has obviously 'made it' and has little in common with the image of Faubourg Saint-Antoine conveyed by Dickens's *A Tale of Two Cities*. Mind you, in those days too, some of the more talented craftsmen prospered and lived in comfort here, and the best even gained the favour of the court.

Next door is the more understated workshop of Monsieur Texier, an artisan who perpetuates the craft of gold and silver plating. His entrance is unfussy but the smell inside is wonderful!

Retrace your steps and walk into **RUE DU FAUBOURG SAINT-ANTOINE**. This was the scene of social unrest from 1789 on and it is not surprising that in 1835 the Corsican Fieschi found in this nest of anti-royalists an accomplice, a certain Pépin, for his attempt on the life of Louis-Philippe. Monsieur Pépin owned a grocery shop at no. 1, at the back of which they hatched their plot, together with a third accomplice. It was to be executed on Boulevard du Temple during the annual royal procession of 28 July, the anniversary date of the three-day Revolution – *Les Trois Glorieuses* – that had brought Louis-Philippe to the throne in 1830 .

The next alley, the **Cité Parchappe**, leads back to the Passage du Cheval Blanc, revealing a different, attractive angle of the typical 19th-century construction with its workshops on either side. At the rear end facing you, a house with a red-tiled roof and green shutters evokes an old French village or a film set for an oldie. On your left as you enter, however, is the **Cour de Février**, where the first signs of gentrification are apparent by way of a studio selling lithographs next to a jeweller's workshop. The adjoining alley, the **Cour de Mars**, is also in the process of converting its workshops into 'lofts'. The house at the back is being renovated and its warm, wooden beams uncovered and polished, which in Paris is always a sign of moving up the scale. The lovely old stones are also brought out to advantage. Even the outside toilets have been spruced up – a vestige of those days, not so long ago, when modern conveniences were unknown. The **Cour d'Avril** is still in its derelict condition, notably its staircase, evidence that this was until recently a slummy neighbourhood. The **Cour de Mai**, on the other hand, is now sleek and whitewashed, equipped with digicode security, Venetian blinds, indoor plants and all the usual paraphernalia. Accordingly, it has been taken over by contemporary activities, such as multimedia and a concessionary for Apple computers. You would be hard put to it to find a traditional workman in his *bleu de travail* (blue overalls), although a messy old cabinetmaker's workshop has fortunately survived at the back.

Do not hesitate to press the button of no. 33 and push open its heavy door: inside is an enchanting genuine, ancient timber house and also a rare 17th-century staircase. On the left is another old house with wrought-iron ornamentation, albeit in a very sorry condition – it is of no consequence when everything is bursting with a riot of greenery. A table and chairs, tucked away in a nook at the back of the courtyard, behind this lush vegetation, surely a pleasant retreat in summer. At no. 45 a 19th-century factory-like building stands intact, with its characteristic sloping roof, red-brick wall and a tall, slender chimney-stack.

The next alley, at no. 47, quaintly called **Nom-de-Jésus**, is charmingly decorated with green creepers. A native old-timer still runs the furniture business opposite, but the premises on the left have been taken over by a Chinese who sells lacquered furniture from his own motherland. Peep also into no. 55, a picturesque sight with its glass roof and profuse vegetation. No. 57 on the main street contains a beauty salon, full of the aquatic paraphernalia meant to create a stress-free, soporific environment for a clientele that is lightyears away from the *tricoteuses* and other such shrews, their revolutionary predecessors of two hundred years ago.

Cour Viguès at no. 59 is another peaceful spot, with cobblestone paving, a couple of trees and rambling ivy.

At no. 61, the early 18th-century elegant fountain, la Fontaine de Trogneux, commemorates a well-known brewer of Saint-Antoine. It has long since dried up but water once used to spurt out of the mouth of the sculpted lion. Three other fountains were erected in the area at the time, for which there was a pressing need in a fast-growing suburb totally devoid of any other source of water.

There is an extraordinary glass canopy at the back of no. 71 but the highlight is no. 75, the astonishing **Cour de l'Etoile d'Or**. You enter a village-like alley, the kind you would expect to see on the rustic hill of Montmartre. A bright pink cottage with bright green shutters is the first thing you see; it has been decorated with an amazing *trompe-l'oeil* of doubtful taste – a kitschy set straight from an operetta – but charming all the same. A pretty 18th-century house stands on the right, then undoubtedly the property of a prosperous craftsman, who embellished it with a frieze of palm leaves. Inside, the bannister of a listed staircase is sculpted with motifs of the four seasons. Two elongated houses stand next to it, contributing to the rustic atmosphere with their pocket-sized front gardens, overgrown with lush vegetation. Ahead is another 18th-century house with an original sun dial and leading to a second courtyard.

In the **Cour des Trois-Frères**, at no. 83, three glass canopies run in succession across the alley, imparting to it character and even a certain elegance.

The further you get from the Bastille, the more the working-class atmosphere prevails, particularly once you reach no. 133, **Le Passage de la Main d'Or**, a notorious slum not so long ago, now inhabited by representatives of Paris's various ethnic groups. On RUE DE LA MAIN D'OR, to your right, stands an old café with the words *Bois Charbon Vin & Liqueurs* still displayed on the shop window, a heart-warming sight, harking back a century to the days when the resourceful Auvergnat colony settled in the 11th arrondissement and diversified their activities by selling wine in addition to coal. Before long they converted all their outlets into cafés and set about conquering the entire café industry of Paris (which is still predominantly in their hands). On the window is also the old-fashioned term *casse-croute* (a 'bite') – today one speaks of *sandwichs*, spelt in French without an 'e' in the plural – as well as *téléphone*, a relic of the time, only 20 or 30 years ago, when the ownership of a telephone line in Paris was not a privilege enjoyed by everyone and could take as many as two years to obtain. Nor has anybody bothered to change the old advertisements that must have been posted on the walls since the 1950s. L'Ami Pierre across the street is yet another genuinely French, old-fashioned café. A furniture-polisher runs an untidy-looking shop and there is even a violinmaker in the street, based in a tiny, run-down shop, so remote from the smart premises of his better-off colleagues around rue de Rome.

Retrace your steps and continue along the Passage de la Main d'Or past the Turkish-Kurd restaurant (a curious combination at this time in history). On your left is a well-known fringe theatre by the same name, popular among intellectuals. It too has to share its pretty, cottagey premises and the inevitable geraniums with a cabinetmaker.

Back on RUE DU FAUBOURG SAINT-ANTOINE, notice the wonderfully messy hardware shop at no. 151. It sells a mishmash of door handles, knobs and other bits and pieces and proudly displays two yellowed photos of the old establishment (which has hardly changed). However, there is no plaque to commemorate the killing of the Republican deputy Baudin on top of the barricade that was erected here on 3 December 1851. Napoleon III had just carried off his coup and Baudin, infuriated, had come over to stir up the Faubourg Saint-Antoine, which was naturally in ferment. Defiantly mounting the barricade he had just helped to erect, he declared that he would show the world how one gets killed for 25 francs a day (to preserve a day's wage), at which very moment he was accidentally hit and killed by a shell.

Turn left into RUE SAINT-BERNARD. At no. 8 an astounding structure of ironwork and glass houses an impressive medley of furniture in an old courtyard. Rue Saint-Bernard is a neighbour-hood street which sells tools, varnish – whatever craftsmen, joiners or carpenters may need. Aware of our fast-changing world, one of the shops has chosen to calls itself Aux Produits d'Antan ('Ye products of yore'). An Algerian *boui-boui* (dingy bistro) rivals it for authenticity, serving inexpensive couscous to an all-male clientele of North Africans. The old Belle-Epoque shop window at the corner of rue du Dahomey has attractive ceramics painted with chinoiserie, rather than the usual motifs of the French countryside.

Ahead is a rural-looking church, with an attractive, slate bell-tower surmounted by a weathercock and pleasantly surrounded by trees. The industrial world, however, intrudes in the form of a couple of tall, slender, black chimney-stacks rising against the sky to its right. This is the **church of Sainte-Marguerite**, tucked away in these side streets, unknown to most Parisians. Yet in the 18th century, and more precisely from 1725 on, it became the centre of attraction of every Parisian, nobles and commoners alike. For on 31 May in that year, during the procession of the Holy Sacrement, Madame Anne Charlier de La Fosse, a cripple for 20 years, was suddenly restored here to health. Consequently, the Archbishop of Paris, Cardinal de Noailles, decreed officially that it was a miracle and ordered a solemn procession to be held to mark it. The impact on Parisians of the recovery of Madame de La Fosse was such that when she died 35 years later a huge crowd attended her funeral. Her remains were laid in the prestigious Jesuit church of Saint-Paul-Saint-Louis in the Marais, of which Sainte-Marguerite was only a suburban branch. The churchwardens of Sainte-Marguerite per-sistently requested that the precious remains be handed over, but to no avail, and their humble little shrine had to content itself with a commemorative plaque.

But fate stepped in 35 years later bringing Sainte-Marguerite some other venerable remains instead, or, at least, so it was believed. On 10 June 1795 at 5 in the afternoon, a mysterious funeral procession, made up of a sergeant and eight soldiers, a few municipal guards, some officials from the Temple, an undertaker and several other men, four of whom carried a coffin, entered the graveyard discreetly from the northern side of rue Saint-Bernard. Having left the Temple, they had followed the route of rue du Temple, rue de Bretagne, rue du Pont-aux-Choux in the 3rd arrondissement, then rue Saint-Sébastien, rue Popincourt, rue Basfroi and rue Saint-Bernard in the 11th. The coffin was laid in the common pit with no preliminaries, no religious ceremony and no flourish. At nightfall the gravedigger exhumed the coffin, extracted the nails to open it and, satisfied that the skull had been sawn off, nailed the lid back on, marked it with a *fleur-de-lis*, then placed it in a lead coffin before moving it to the western church wall, leaving it partly jutting into the graveyard.

Some 50 years later, and again 50 years after that, the remains were exhumed to be authenticated by forensic surgeons, who all stated categorically that the remains belonged to a youth aged 18 or more. They were certainly not those of a 10-year-old and equally certainly not those of the Dauphin, supposedly deceased in the tower of the Temple on 8 June 1795. What if someone else's remains had been substituted for the Dauphin's and for the skull, sawn off at the Temple, a rumour that spread with increasing persistence during the Restoration? After all, in 1794 the child had been thrown into solitary confinement to vegetate in a pitch-dark cell, where nobody could check on his fate. Some believed he eventually died in the cell, which was plausible under such circumstances, but the death would have been kept secret as it deprived Robespierre of a precious hostage. It is surmised that a feeble-minded youth was substituted for him in the cell and that the Dauphin was buried at the foot of the Temple tower, where, in fact, some remains were later found.

Upon their return to France, Louis XVIII and Charles X set out energetically to find the remains of their brother Louis XVI and their sister-in-law, Marie-Antoinette, but they were circumspect enough never to undertake to look for the Dauphin, dead or alive. . . Meanwhile, as many as 43 pretenders claimed the throne of France, but all of them were tripped up by the same question, 'What happened at the Temple on 22 January 1793 at 9 in the morning?' None of them could give the correct answer, that the royal family came to submit to and kneel before their seven-year-old new king. The mystery of the Temple child has never been solved and when a new investigation was undertaken at the church in 1980 no remains were found at all.

In the once-spacious graveyard of Sainte-Marguerite, where the guillotined victims of Place de La Bastille and those of the *Fronde* * were laid side by side with the humble inhabitants of Saint-Antoine, there remains today only one tomb. Surmounted by a little white cross, it bears the inscription: L. . . XVII 1785–1795, a strange but moving memorial to France's last king of the *Ancien Régime.*

The graveyard disappeared and a garden replaced it. Recently a crèche was also opened here, just next to the humble tomb of the 'Temple child', but most parents are unaware of the existence next door of this historic site. At present it can only be reached through a door on the left-hand side of the church. The door is normally kept locked but will readily be opened for the visitor, except during mass. The church too deserves attention, being one of the few old churches of Paris to have survived. Note the pure, architectural lines, the harmony and the antique feel created by the low ceiling of the older nave. There are also some excellent paintings and sculptures, although these are hard to appreciate in the dim light. Among them are paintings relating to the life of Saint Vincent de Paul, which were brought here during the Revolution, after the Mission of Saint-Lazare, which he had founded in the 10th arrondissement, had been closed down. As you walk out of the church, go round to its south-west corner to admire the pretty, slate bell-tower, framed from this angle by a cluster of trees – a lovely picture, especially on a sunny afternoon.

Continue along rue Saint-Bernard. At no. 42 is a stunning courtyard where creepers vie with lavender and geraniums. There is a charming cottage invaded by creepers and a rickety wooden staircase. A terrace decked with bright geraniums and shaded by a parasol adds an ultimate touch of idle bliss.

* The princely revolt against Louis XIV in August 1652.

You will now reach the junction of **rue de Charonne**, a country lane leading to the village of Charonne from the Middle Ages until the early 17th century. RUE BASFROI ahead was one of the strongholds of the Jewish immigrant community in the early decades of the 20th century. Fleeing persecution and poverty in eastern Europe, they brought their traditional clothing trade with them to the 11th arrondissement. Some settled on rue Basfroi, where, a generation earlier, their fellow-Jews from the Ottoman Empire had already established themselves. Here too early signs of gentrification are perceptible, notably at no. 8 which has been pleasantly renovated. The old workshops have been converted into 'lofts', while strings of creepers span the alley overhead and green bushes and fragrant lavender line it on either side. An extraordinary jumble of goods for the film-maker is available for hire at no. 21/23, from old bus-stop signs to Wallace street-fountains, from accordions and trumpets to old prams and walking sticks, anything to help him recreate old times. Even a skeleton is on hire here, for those seeking to create a bone-chilling atmosphere.

Continue on rue Popincourt, turn right into rue de la Roquette and continue to PLACE LÉON BLUM, the hub of the arrondissement. Haussmann's surgery is spectacularly noticeable in the 11th arrondissement, for here, in particular, evil had to be extirpated for obvious political and strategic reasons. A prime example is the Boulevard Voltaire (then Prince-Eugène, after Napoleon III's nephew), which splits the arrondissement lengthwise, running all the way from Place de la République (then Place du Château-d'Eau), where the military barracks was situated, past this newly created roundabout, to the strategic Place de la Nation (then Trône). Prince-Eugène disappeared from both Boulevard and Place with the fall of the Second Empire, to be replaced by Voltaire. In 1957 he in turn was ousted on the latter by Léon Blum, the leader of the *Front Populaire* who became head of state in 1936 and initiated major social reforms, such as the 40-hour working week and annual paid holidays. With its imposing, characteristic **Mairie**, Place Léon Blum is the only spot in the arrondissement that has this solemn, yet somewhat pleasantly provincial aspect. This is one of the earliest Mairies in Paris, built at the time of Haussmann. In May 1871 it was taken over by the *Communards* who retreated to it after they had burnt down the central town hall of Paris, l'Hôtel de Ville. Six hostages, whom Thiers had refused to exchange for the socialist leader Auguste Blanqui, were brought here to be executed on 24 May, among them the Archbishop of Paris. After a week of ruthless and unspeakable brutality on the part of the *Versaillais* (Thiers's government forces), the *Commune* was defeated and the Mairie offered little shelter to the few survivors. The *Versaillais* advanced inexorably eastwards, massacring every *Communard* they could lay hands on.

RUE DE LA ROQUETTE is not of Haussmann's making, but he successfully integrated it into his modern street network, making it run through the present Place Léon Blum, more or less at right angles with Boulevard Voltaire. Back in the 17th century this was a rural road leading to a convent by the same name. Whether the name was derived from a yellow flower called *rochette* that grew on the estate or from the name of a previous landlord, Monsieur Rocquet, is not known for sure. What is known, however, is that the size of the domain was spectacular by today's standards, extending roughly as far as the present rue du Chemin-Vert, rue de la Folie-Regnault, rue Mercoeur and rue Popincourt. The main buildings of the convent were situated around the present rue Pache (second to the left from Place Léon Blum). Its destiny followed the same pattern as many other such domains, beginning as private property, then once in decline being passed on to a religious institution, and later abolished by the French Revolution. In earlier times it was often the reverse, when religious institutions, anxious to increase their revenue, sold their domains into secular hands.

In the 19th century rue de la Roquette became the 'sinister way' taken by the hearse and the funeral processions heading for the new cemetery of Père Lachaise in eastern Paris, jolting uphill towards Boulevard Ménilmontant. In *Paris Vécu* Léon Daudet described it as 'the principal sorrowful way of Paris, the road of funerals'. He was speaking from personal experience, having accompanied the body of his father, Alphonse Daudet, along this route in December 1897, '*à pas lents, (mon) chapeau à la main.*' ('At a slow pace, hat in hand'). The Dreyfus Case had only just begun, which explains why both Emile Zola, later to write the famous article *J'accuse*, in defence of Dreyfus, and Drumont, author of the rabidly anti-Semitic *La France juive*, attended the funeral, each holding one of the cordons of the catafalque; Zola, however, was on the left, Drumont on the right. Léon Daudet espoused Drumont's theories and became one of the founders of *L'Action Française*, the fanatically anti-Semitic movement that led logically to the persecution of the Jews during the last war. For the time being he was absorbed with the death of his father and with the funeral, writing, 'As to the participation and emotion of an immense multitude, no funeral, not even that of Victor Hugo, surpassed the funeral of Alphonse Daudet.' In November 1923 he passed along the same morbid route beside the coffin of his son Philippe, who had been involved with the Anarchists and died in mysterious circumstances.

At that time two ghastly prisons stood on opposite sides of the street, a little further up: the women's prison, La Petite-Roquette, built in 1836 on the site of the present no. 143, and the men's prison, La Grande-Roquette, erected the following year on the site of no. 168. Every now and then the guillotine would make an ephemeral appearance in front of the men's prison – 41 times between 1840 and 1880. Among the victims were also a couple of women from across the street, the last of whom was executed on the snowy dawn of 6 February 1946. Jules Vallès, one of the heroes of the *Commune*, gave a spine-chilling description of the last moments of the prisoner:

> *La grosse porte de la prison roule sur ses gonds. C'est le moment terrible. C'est à ce moment que La Pommeraye qui avait été jusqu'alors impassible, pâlit: l'oeil devint vitreux, les jambes fléchissent. L'échafaud est débout, à vingt pas en avant sur la place.*

> The big door of the prison rolls on its hinges. This is the terrible moment. It is at this moment that La Pommeraye, who up until now has been impassive, turns pale: his eyes are glazed, his legs sag. The scaffold is standing, twenty steps ahead, on the square.

A contemporary who was present at one of those public executions described the vociferous delight of the 'teeming, screaming, drunk, revolting' mob. Unlike Alphonse Daudet, all that the wretched guillotined prisoners received by way of homage was the discreet mention on their death certificates, 'died on rue de la Roquette, no. 168'. The men's prison was torn down in 1900, the women's only in the 1970s. An attractive garden now replaces it, a welcome patch of greenery in a busy neighbourhood, oblivious to the misery of the past.

If you have the energy, you may wish to stroll through rue de la Roquette as far as RUE KELLER which has been strikingly upgraded and is lined with art galleries and an assortment of shops that cater for the 'hip' (*branché*) crowd, selling Spanish tapas, tracts on zen philosophy and desert boots. On rue de la Roquette, just before rue Keller, one can take in some spiritual nourishment at the Théâtre de la Bastille, followed by a meal in one of the restaurants across the street, which are not surprisingly geared to theatre-goers and are decorated with theatre bills. One of them, the Cyrano, honours one of the most prominent characters in French drama who, according to tradition, found final refuge at the Dominican convent at no. 94/8 rue de Charonne, in this arrondissement. Next to the theatre, at no. 84, a new synagogue was opened in 1960 for the ex-Ottoman community, which also serves as a community centre and a place of study. It is named after Isaac Abravanel, the great philosopher and treasurer of Ferdinand, King of Spain; like all his Jewish brethren, he was exiled from his kingdom in 1492.

Retrace your steps to Place Léon Blum and walk into RUE SEDAINE, behind the Mairie to the left. The street has somehow managed to retain a little of the flavour of the early decades of the 20th century, when it was home to the Jews of the Ottoman Empire. Le Bosphore, their 'port of disembarkation' nearly a century ago, is still in existence at no. 74, although who can tell for how much longer? When the Jews arrived here from the Gare de Lyon, they found themselves among easy-going members of their community playing a relaxed game of cards in an atmosphere that was reassuring for these anxious newcomers who realised at once that here they would find support through the first stages of their adjustment to a foreign land.

Some of the shop windows on rue Sedaine and the neighbouring RUE POPINCOURT still display outdated household linen, the main item they traded in lackadaisically when they first arrived, replacing little by little sheet-metalworkers, tinsmiths, blacksmiths and coal merchants of yore. Most of the children of the linen merchants have now gone and a new wave of North African Jews has transformed these two streets into a branch of the Sentier (the rag-trade neighbourhood in the 2nd arr.), overflowing with gaudy junk clothes, teeming with honking delivery vans and brimming overall with vitality. And then, in the midst of all this maelstrom of energy, as you cross the threshold of no. 7 rue Popincourt to your left, you will hardly believe your eyes – for here time has come to a standstill! A one-time **synagogue** of the Ottoman community, which has kept intact both its decorations above the entrance door and its entire interior structure with the traditional women's gallery, has been turned into a gathering-place for the male members of the community who, now, as then, are wholly absorbed in an eternal game of cards under the protection of a reassuring, thick veil of cigarette smoke. Occasionally someone might bring a dog along but the wives are conspicuously absent – they have their own activities. Repeating the same ritual day after day, and totally insulated from the speedy world careering outside, this congenial group leads a satisfied self-contained life, outside both time and space.

Continue along rue Popincourt. The street commemorates a hamlet by this name which lay around the present junction of Boulevard Voltaire and rue de la Folie-Méricourt, originally on the fief of Jean de Popincourt, the President of Parliament in 1403–13. It was officially annexed to Faubourg Saint-Antoine in 1702.

At no. 12 across the street, another picturesque alley pleases the eye with its abundant vegetation and its spacious 'loft' at the back. As you continue along rue Popincourt, step into no. 27 where the owners and workers of a household-linen wholesalers are too busy to notice in the doorway the charming stucco sculptures of chubby cupids and pretty musical instruments. The occupants of no. 41 have gone all out to turn their courtyard into an oasis of delight: it is a ravishing sight with its bright blue chairs, mosaic table and its riot of flowers. Notice also the neighbouring *boulangerie* at no. 45, on the corner of rue du Chemin-Vert, with its listed Belle-Epoque ceramic window and pretty gingham curtains. It sells wonderfully hot croissants and *pains au chocolat* (chocolate croissants) at 4 in the afternoon.

Continue to rue de l'Asile Popincourt and turn left, then on to rue
Moufle as far as the BOULEVARD RICHARD-LENOIR, a dismal neighbourhood from which alcohol provides a rare escape.
Indeed, on your right you will notice a bar-restaurant surmounted
by a huge bottle and bluntly named La Grosse Bouteille, which is
one way of bringing a cheerful note into the area. Boulevard
Richard-Lenoir was built by the Baron Haussmann over the Canal
Saint-Martin, depriving the arrondissement of a lovely water-
course – but the authorities had more urgent priorities in their
struggle against the troublesome working classes. This hitherto
drab avenue, the home of Commissaire Maigret, has lately been
remodelled into a new garden with many more trees and
ornamented with a succession of fountains as part of the
renovation scheme of eastern Paris. The new plantings are meant
to show to advantage the basement windows of this covered
section of the canal, which are particularly impressive when seen
from a boat underneath, as they let the sun rays through.

The annual ham and scrap-iron fair was held on the Boulevard
Richard-Lenoir during Holy Week, until as recently as 1980 when
it was transferred to the Parc Floral in the Bois de Vincennes. The
tradition of the ham fair began in the Middle Ages and, like some
other annual fairs, was then held in front of the Cathedral of
Notre-Dame, the social hub of the medieval city. However, unlike
most fairs, which eventually petered out, it was perpetuated
through the centuries until the Revolution. Only in the 19th
century did it wander around for a while before finally settling on
Boulevard Richard-Lenoir, where a flee market was added to it, to
the pleasure of Parisians who much regretted its departure.
However, the colourful open-air market on the Bastille side of the
boulevard (Thursday and Sunday mornings) is still there, at times
enhanced by jolly buskers.

Cross the Boulevard and continue into rue Pelée, then turn right
into rue Alphonse Baudin. At the corner of RUE SAINT-SÉBAS-
TIEN, the Bar de la Gaieté belies its name, being the kind of place
where one drowns one's daily sorrows in alcohol. This was already
a cheap drinking establishment in the 18th century. On the eve of
the Revolution Paris had 7,000 such establishments – five times the
number of bakeries! – and Parisians absorbed a yearly average of

200 pints each. Under such circumstances the savage brutality of the mob during those chaotic days is not surprising . . . and it is needless to dwell on the quality of the wine they had to make do with. However, the wine sold in this place must have been worse than most, for even its down-and-out customers accused it angrily of selling them beetroot juice!

Rue Saint-Sébastien commemorates the King's company of bowmen, whose patron saint was the martyr Sébastien. The bowmen used to train around Place de la Bastille, but their gathering-place was on the corner of rue Saint-Sébastien and the present Boulevard Beaumarchais. Set up originally to protect the King, they gradually became the protectors of civilians and thus fore-runners of the *gendarmerie* ('men of arms').

Turn left on rue Saint-Sébastien and continue to rue Amelot, which runs along the moat of the city walls built by Louis XIII. Our itinerary will continue to the left, but if you wish to see the only remaining vestige of the old world of entertainment, turn right and continue to the pretty PLACE PASDELOUP and its festive **Cirque d'Hiver.**

Built by Hittorff for his Emperor in 1852 as a winter counter-part to the Cirque de l'Impératrice on the Champs-Elysées, it was named Le Cirque Napoléon III. On 11 December 1852, barely a year after his coup, and seeking more legitimacy for his rule, the new Emperor came over in person for the inauguration, hoping to rally over the people of eastern Paris to his support by means of *panem et circenses.* In a bid to gain popularity by turning Paris into a beautiful pleasure-ground, he hired the most talented artists to embellish even the most underprivileged parts of the city. Hittorff put great efforts into turning this round pavilion into a gem comparable with those on the Champs-Elysées, and invited such venerated sculptors as Pradier and Bosio to decorate it. Every Sunday afternoon the composer Etienne Pasdeloup con-ducted the orchestra he had founded to offer classical music to the general public at reasonable prices, a tradition that has been maintained to this day (albeit on other premises). Elitist music-lovers may turn up their noses at the quality of the orchestra but it has undoubtedly given generations of Parisians a lot of pleasure. With the fall of the Second Empire this winter circus was renamed prosaically Le Cirque d'Hiver, while its counterpart on the Champs-Elysées was renamed Le Cirque d'Eté. The famous Bouglione family took it over in 1934, enchanting 1,600 spectators at each performance. But the circus culture declined (circuses are now altogether banned from urban centres, for obvious reasons of hygiene and congestion) and in the early 1980s the Bougliones let out the magical premises to Kenzo and Gaultier for their fashion shows and to television companies. The premises are also periodically used for musicals and children's shows. On these occasions the audience can appreciate their splendid Second Empire decorations, to which impressive murals were added in the 1920s representing such circus heroes as Auguste Auriol, Charlie Chaplin and the Fratellinis. Outside, only the Bar du Cirque and the Bar du Clown, on either side of the pavilion, recall the golden age of the circus. As for the Boulevard du Temple beyond, not a trace is left of its thrilling past, not even a commemorative plaque.

Retrace your steps and continue along RUE AMELOT. At no. 74 you will see another attractive example of the recent transformation of the neighbourhood: a former factory is now a pretty hotel, with a patio, conservatory and spacious premises for functions and seminars, appropriately located within a few minutes' walk from the up-market Bastille area. No. 70 next door is what remains of an 18th-century factory, with the clock at the back of the courtyard that punctuated the workmen's days and the bell on the street side that announced meal breaks. With the advent of the machine in the 19th century, working hours were stretched beyond reason, while the lunch break shrank to half an hour. One must hope that the new owners will preserve these relics in deference to their toiling predecessors.

Turn left into RUE SAINT-SABIN. A pleasing alley at no. 60, on your left, now bursts with flowers. It also bears the picturesque name of La Cour du Coq, a reminder of a long gone rural past. Walk into the next alley on your left, the Allée Verte. At the end of the alley, on your left, stands a whitewashed building with bright green shutters, ablaze with geraniums, a veranda lush with honeysuckle and a conservatory with thickly growing palms and laurels.

A romantic lamppost adds a final enchanting touch to this oasis, dubbed in all simplicity l'Espace Vert.

Retrace your steps and turn left into **rue Nicolas Appert**, another former workmen's compound. On a mural at no. 5 Victor Hugo can be seen rubbing shoulders with Sophocles, Shakespeare, Molière and Marivaux, and with later playwrights – J. P. Sartre and Samuel Beckett. Philippe Rebuffet, who painted it in 1985, is seen on the right, adding a last touch of paint to the theatre curtain.

Turn right into the **Impasse des Primevères** (primroses), reminiscent yet again of long gone pastoral days in a working-class neighbourhood. Back on rue Saint-Sabin, you will reach Boulevard Richard-Lenoir once more and enjoy its successful renovation. A charming footbridge has been added to it, to mark the boundary between the market section and the recreational gardens. It serves no utilitarian purpose but creates the illusion of crossing a waterway, which is precisely what the landscape gardeners had in mind, who wished to bring up to the surface the presence of the underground canal.

As you continue along rue Saint-Sabin, notice the alley at no. 16, overhung with a bower of wistaria and other creepers – unquestionably one of the most ravishing nooks in the neighbourhood. If you pause at the corner Café de l'Industrie beyond, you will get a view of its lavish vegetation through the window.

Back at the BASTILLE area and on RUE DE LA ROQUETTE, you have reached the south-western patch of the 11th arrondissement which in the 1980s cast off its proletarian past to become the latest 'in' place in Paris. Paradoxically, it was in the shade of the new people's opera – the institution that was to bring enlightenment at affordable prices to the *peuple* on its own native territory – that the up-and-coming chose to settle. Paradoxically too, it is this neighbourhood, so essentially of Parisian stock and so much part and parcel of the history of Paris, that is fast losing its Parisian identity, swapping it for a cosmopolitan one with a strong North American flavour and Latin American overtones.

Rue de la Roquette at this end is lined with fashionable eating-places and has little in common with the '*rue dégueulasse*' described by Léon Daudet in 1882 as the home of Verlaine, who lived with his mother at no. 17. As for RUE DE LAPPE, on your right, most of its rickety houses have, miraculously, not as yet been torn down, only renovated, but the accordions and *bals-musette* have long been silenced. The Balajo at no. 9 is now a fashionable nightclub, quite different from the place visited by Edith Piaf or Arletty. Le Bouscat, which used to be at no. 13, has regrettably disappeared, as well as the one-storeyed house where it stood before being turned into a garage. A sorry disappearance, for this was the birthplace of the *bal-musette*, introduced by Antoine Bouscatel in 1905. Before then one danced the *cabrette*, accompanied by the Auvergnat bagpipe. The despicable accordion brought over by the *Ritals* (Italians) was absolutely taboo – but not for long. In 1904 Charles Peguri braced himself, walked over to rue de Lappe with  his accordion and ended up by persuading Bouscatel that it was not such a bad instrument after all. The marriage between the two cultures was sealed the following year, to be followed in 1913 by the real-life wedding of Charles Peguri to Monsieur Bouscatel's daughter.

Only one scrap iron-dealer, at no. 25, has survived on rue de Lappe, once the centre of the trade. Back in the 18th century this proved a useful commodity to deal in for the newly arrived Auvergnats, whilst during the French Revolution the *sans-culottes* used the iron to forge their notorious pikes with which they stormed the Bastille and on which they impaled the heads of victims such as the fair Princesse de Lamballe. A café-restaurant at no. 29, Les Sans-Culottes, evokes their presence in these parts, but has otherwise bartered French insignia for modern Anglo-Saxon music and Spanish tapas. At no. 41, however, La Galoche d'Aurillac is standing its ground with its genuine Auvergnat fare of ham and sausages and its forest of Auvergnat clogs (*galoches*) hanging from the ceiling. On the other hand, the old neighbourhood dance-hall at no. 47 has been replaced by an art gallery.

Cross over and retrace your steps. At no. 34 is a lovely courtyard with vines and honeysuckle, while more green creepers welcome you at no. 26, and especially at no. 24 – a shady Eden enhanced by the song of birds, all the more delightful when the wistaria is in bloom. There was a notice outside on one of our visits, reading 'nothing to sell, nothing to let. . .' probably hung up by a pestered resident. Hopefully, no digicode will bar your way in. La Boule Rouge at no. 8, was the haunt of roughnecks – *apaches* or *julots* who would swagger in accompanied by their girls, *les gonzesses*. However, they had to watch their step, for the massive boss of the place would stand no nonsense. He had an imposing walrus moustache and always wore a basque beret and he made short shrift of troublemakers. Today the Cactus Bleu, a clinically sleek American establishment stands in its place, shining with stainless-steel trimmings and equipped with a TV set over the bar. French popular music has given way to the Beatles and the Beach Boys who will enliven your Tex-Mex meals. After 100 odd years **les Produits d'Auvergne** at no. 6 is still going strong and selling wonderful regional wines, sausages and cheeses – not, however, without waging a fierce battle against their landlord who wanted them out. Determined neighbours got together 500 signatures in 1992 in support of this last Auvergnat grocery shop of the Bastille area. After all, the Auvergnats have become an endangered species around the Bastille and need to be preserved.

You may wind up at one of the crowded cafés around rue de la Roquette and **PLACE DE LA BASTILLE**. Opposite you is the winged *génie de la Liberté* ('spirit of Liberty') stuck up on one leg in mid air on top of its tall column, ready to take off, all shiny since 1989 when it was freshly gilded for the Bicentennial of the Revolution.

This is a good opportunity to meditate on this mythical place where the birth pangs of modern France began, at least in the consciousness of its people, who therefore kept alive its emblem for nearly 200 years. Thus, although the storming of the Bastille by the *sans-culottes* of Faubourg Saint-Antoine was largely an act of mock-heroism, the victims of the 1830 July Revolution were brought back to this place of liberation and laid to rest under the column in July 1840. Likewise, on 24 February 1871, on the eve of yet another storm, the people of Paris gathered here to commemorate the 1848 revolution. The column was decked with red flags and one child climbed to the top and stuck another flag in the graceful hand of the *génie*, while the cheering crowds below, bellowed out the *Marseillaise*.

Le Genie de la Bastille

Meanwhile, a straw puppet had been set up at the foot of the column bearing the inscription, *'Je suis Thiers l'Orléaniste.'* Soon it was consumed by crackling flames, as befitted the traitor who had sold France to the Prussians. On 14 July 1935 and 1936, the victory of the *Front Populaire* was celebrated at the Bastille. Bourgeois Paris, however, was quite indifferent to the emblem and Daniel Halévy, the son of the famous Belle-Epoque writer and librettist Ludovig, and a well-known chronicler and member of Tout-Paris in his own right, exclaimed, *'La Bastille, mais où est-ce donc?'* ('The Bastille, but where is it then?').

He would probably have had the same reaction in 1981, when the socialist voters rallied at this oversized roundabout to celebrate François Mitterand's election as president. Except that this time the partying was lubricated with champagne! Parisians had already moved up the social scale and the Bastille would soon follow suit. Which explains why, as you sip your Manhattan cocktail in one of the cafés of the north-eastern edge of Place de la Bastille, you will find yourself surrounded by the beautiful people of today's Western cross-bred culture, as remote from their French roots as they can possibly be, yet intrinsically Parisian in their own way.

THE 12TH ARRONDISSEMENT

La forme d'une ville change plus vite, hélas!
Que le coeur d'un mortel.

The face of a city changes faster, alas!
than a mortal heart.

Charles Baudelaire

NO arrondissement illustrates Baudelaire's comment better than the 12th. Until a few years ago this was an area of small tradesmen – carpenters in Faubourg Saint-Antoine, coopers at the wine warehouses of Bercy and railwaymen who cultivated their little kitchen gardens along rue de Reuilly. All this industrious world laboured to the sound of rattling railway tracks and the ringing of church bells. For, this being the gateway to the south east, the railway developed here rapidly in the 19th century and the presence of religious institutions went all the way back to the Middle Ages, first and foremost the Abbey of Saint-Antoine-des-Champs (now the Saint-Antoine hospital), founded in 1198, the pivot of the future Faubourg Saint-Antoine.

During the Counter-Reformation that followed the Wars of Religion in the 17th century, new Catholic institutions were founded in these tranquil, outlying parts. Charitable institutions followed suit and the 12th arrondissement became the hospital and charity arrondissement *par excellence*. Among them was the internationally renowned ophthalmological hospital, les Quinze-Vingts, originally founded by Saint Louis in homage to 300 (15 x 20) crusaders, whose eyes had been gouged out by the Moslems in Egypt. In the 17th century Saint Vincent de Paul, the most charitable churchman of his time, founded a foundling hospice, setting an example to other religious groups – the Protestants on rue du Sergent-Bauchat, and the Rothschild hospital and orphanage, founded initially for the Jewish community. More recently, the Empress Eugénie founded the Fondation Eugène-Napoléon, using for that purpose the 600,000 francs she had been given as a wedding gift for the purchase of a set of diamonds. Although, in contrast to her husband, Eugénie on the whole showed little concern for social issues, on this occasion she preferred to use this huge sum for a constructive purpose and set up an educational establishment where destitute girls were taught a trade and were provided with shelter until they found employment.

At present the church bells of the arrondissement can hardly be heard, as their sound is drowned by the din of contemporary living, and the market on Place d'Aligre, where the humble local people could buy the cheapest second-hand clothes in the capital, has somewhat lost its provincial charm, being imprisoned by high-rise buildings that have sprung up around it overnight.

All the upheaval began with the construction of a gigantic interchange, the largest 'automobile circus or funnel' in Europe, which, under its own impetus, tore off a chunk of the Bois de Vincennes in the process. It was built at the Porte de Bercy in the early 1970s in an effort to cope with the daily influx of commuter traffic, but the nightly queues of cars heading east along the Seine have not shortened.

Next followed railway reconstruction. A large portion of the 19th-century network was scrapped, La Bastille and other stations were demolished, having lost their *raison d'être* when the RER, the express network, was put into service. The RER in its turn did not prove adequate in coping with the ever-growing number of commuters and, at the time of writing, construction of an automatic, unmanned Métro network is in progress between Tolbiac (in the 13th arr.) and the Madeleine. France's officials, always in raptures over technological feats, have blessed it enthusiastically with the promising name of Météore. It is hoped that the daily nightmare of commuting in these eastern parts will be somewhat alleviated when it is put into service in 1998, exactly 100 years after the first Métro was opened in this very arrondissement. It ran from Nation to Reuilly-Diderot, underneath Boulevard Diderot. On 19 July 1900 the first Métro line, line no. 1 Vincennes-Neuilly, was inaugurated in the 12th arrondissement on the occasion of the Universal Exposition. The 12th arrondissement also boasts the first Métro murder in Paris. The victim was an elegant, young woman returning from a ball, the sole occupant of a first-class carriage, who was murdered between the Porte Dorée and Porte de Charenton stations, on 16 May 1937. The murder was carried out with masterly precision, the victim was never identified – although it was inferred she may have been a spy – and the mystery was never solved.

The 1900 Universal Exposition brought other changes to the arrondissement. First of all, the horrific prison of Mazas, at no. 23–27 Boulevard Diderot, had to disappear so as not to hurt public sensitivity and was removed to the more discreet location of Fresnes, a modest suburb south of Paris. The Gare de Lyon had to be enlarged and renovated to accommodate visitors, who, it was hoped, would alight here in great numbers. Originally built in the late 1840s, the station was inaugurated on 12 August 1849 with a single line that linked Paris with the town of Tonnerre. Beautiful murals decorated the new station, enticing the visitor to embark to other destinations – the vineyards of Bourgogne, Lamartine's cherished Lake of Bourget, the awe-inspiring Alps, the sunny Mediterranean shores, and exotic Algeria and Tunisia beyond . . . all lay on the route of the PLM (Paris–Lyons–Marseilles) much used by wealthy travellers. At the same time the magnificent restaurant Le Train Bleu was opened to cater for them. It has preserved both its sumptuous period decorations (including Flameng's fabulous ceiling) and its excellent food and remains an exciting address.

The huge station clock-tower – 64 metres high – stood proudly against the sky, embodying the achievements of mechanical progress. Today it is more of a period piece, drowned in a cluttered skyline of office-blocks, nostalgically recalling the age of the steam engine. In 1982 the Gare de Lyon entered a new era, when the revolutionary TGV was put into service, linking Paris to Lyons in a record time of two hours. Fortunately, the tremendous expansion of the reconstructed station has been carried out entirely underground and has caused no further damage to the neighbourhood. With its 140,000 daily passengers, the Gare de Lyon became the largest station in Paris (and in France), only recently overtaken by Montparnasse, a new business centre, now also served by the TGV. As this is the departure point of all trains leaving for the Alps and the south of France, on the eve of school holidays the station becomes a bedlam, especially before the winter holidays, when the crush is compounded by the clutter of thousands of skis.

With the massive demolition of so much of the old railway network, and also of the neighbouring infested slums (specifically the
drug-ridden Ilôt Chalon, where several generations of desperadoes
huddled together when alighting at the Gare de Lyon), the public
authorities now had plenty of space at their disposal. The 12th was
consequently picked out to serve as a beach-head for the development of the eastern part of the city known as *l'Est parisien*, a particularly propitious area for such experimentation since the land was
cheap. Jacques Chirac and François Mitterand, then respectively
Mayor of Paris and President of the Republic, were able to hand
over huge tracts of land (by contemporary urban standards) on
which the architects of the future could let loose their creative
impulses. They began with the 20,000-seat Palais Omnisports at
Bercy, referred to simply as 'Bercy'. This curiously shaped, overpowering monument (less so now that its sloping sides have been
covered with lawn), topped by a steel structure, rests on four concrete stumps, the components of which recall Pei's Pyramid, La
Villette and other recent constructions. Besides sports events, for
which it was originally designed, 'Bercy' hosts pop concerts and,
before the opening of the neighbouring Bastille Opera House,
operas, which attracted huge audiences, undeterred by its appalling
acoustics.

The Bastille Opera, the most controversial of President Mitter-
and's '*grands projets*' and a bottomless financial pit, was decided
upon in 1982, a year after Mitterand's triumphant first election.
The choice of the Bastille as the location of '*un opéra populaire*' ('a
people's opera') as against the Second Empire bourgeois Palais
Garnier in the 9th arrondissement, was not fortuitious. After all,
it was on this symbolic spot that the socialists chose to celebrate
François Mitterand's first victory. Throngs of excited supporters,
wild with joy, flocked to the *bal populaire* organised at the Bastille
on the night of his election. From the time of the Revolution until
the recent collapse of the Soviet Union and its Eastern European
satellites, the Bastille was the symbol of class struggle and the
rallying point of many working-class protest marches (*manifes-
tations*) which periodically paralysed the city. Today they are
played down by the media as '*mouvement social*' but the havoc
they cause can be even worse than before because, in the present
context of ideological confusion, they take place all over Paris,

rendering the entire city vulnerable, shop owners edgy and tourists bewildered.

There was a more pragmatic, if not wildly trumpeted reason for the choice of site: the plot of land on which the old Bastille railway station had stood was, quite simply, cheap. Originally 6 billion francs were poured into the 2,716-seat Opera House, built by the Canadian architect Carl Ott. It was going to be the largest opera house in the world and the largest Parisian monument, capable of accommodating the entire Cathedral of Notre-Dame in its interior. The enterprise was also the outcome of one of the largest architectural contests ever held – 756 projects from 1,200 contestants in more than 40 countries were submitted to President Mitterand. Originally, the post of artistic director was to have gone to Daniel Barenboim, undoubtedly the most accomplished musician residing in France at the time, who for ten years had shaped the Orchestre de Paris into a top-ranking body. But French politicians are often more intent on showing off architectural and technological prowess than on the nurturing of art. The head of a leading *haute couture* house was appointed to preside over the destiny of the Opera. Financial considerations prevailed, to the detriment of artistic standards, and Daniel Barenboim was compelled to resign, a sorry situation made worse by anti-Semitic insinuations in some of the media. In 1989 the Korean Myung Whun Chung was ushered in as music director with an unrestrained welcome, but he too stumbled and in 1994 resigned from the post.

For the time being one rose to the occasion – the Opera House was inaugurated in July 1889 with Berlioz's *Les Troyens*, a French work as befitting the Bicentennial of the French Revolution

The initial 6-billion-franc budget had been dissipated in no time and had more than doubled by the time the building was completed. Willy-nilly, prices of tickets had to be raised to help meet the deficit, so that when the opera was ready to open to the public, the people of Paris, for whom it was initially built, had to pay up to 520 francs per ticket for regular performances – not much less than at the denigrated, bourgeois Palais Garnier – and much more for special events. True, there were some seats at 40 francs, but those were located on the lateral walls with no view of the stage. These were in fact added at a later stage, not as a concession to opera-goers but to improve the quality of the acoustics and as such might as well have been offered free of charge, just as kings of yore distributed free wine to everyone on special occasions.

In 1989 the Ministry of Economy and Finance also moved to its new gigantic premises at Bercy – a 400-metre-long, L-shaped, concrete block stretching all the way from the Gare de Lyon to the Seine, opposite the Palais Omnisports. Although its old premises in one of the wings of the Louvre were by no means comfortable or adequate for modern office work, the neighbourhood was certainly more congenial than the surreal no-man's-land to which the Ministry's 7,000 employees have been exiled. By 1995 the new 12,000-square-metre American Center was also completed on the other side of the Palais Omnisports, on the edge of the new Parc de Bercy. The old 4,000-square-metre American Center on Boulevard Raspail (in the 14th arr.) was deemed inadequate and despite its old-world charm and its century-old trees and beautiful grounds, was, scandalously, allowed to be torn down. Turning their back on nostalgia, the directors of the new centre entrusted the Californian Frank Gehry (the architect of the Museum of Contemporary Art in Los Angeles) with this gigantic hi-tech project on an area three times the size of its predecessor, meant to house a library, a book store, music, dance and theatre workshops, a private radio station, an art gallery and much else besides. At present, however, owing to financial difficulties, the place is lifeless most of the time, activities are few and far between and opening hours are at a minimum. None of the planned amenities has materialised: there is not even a basic coffee shop. Drinks can be had across the street, in a shiny new café on the ground floor of a shiny new block of flats, overlooking the characterless buildings of a Novotel, a Hôtel Ibis and some office-blocks. Gone are Chez Claude, Chez Jojo and the other neighbourhood cafés.

Before the French Revolution, life in the 12th arrondissement rotated around the Abbey of Saint-Antoine-des-Champs, the rich and powerful women's abbey, like the Abbey of Montmartre. A hermitage was already mentioned here in 1180, but it was from the 13th century onwards that the Order became prosperous. In 1471 Louis XI enfanchised the craftsmen of Saint-Antoine, which gave their guild a tremendous economic boost and soon allowed its members to gain worldwide renown as cabinet-makers. The craft began here because the wood, floated down the river to Paris, often as rafts, was unloaded and 'torn up' at the Port de la Rapée at Bercy, conveniently near the Faubourg Saint-Antoine. By the 16th century ebony was the most favoured wood, hence the term *ébénisterie* (cabinet-making), derived from *ébène* (ebony). It was here in Faubourg Saint-Antoine that the Renaissance style was born, largely owing to the contact with Italy during the Italian campaigns led by François I and reaching its peak at the time of Henri II, when the Faubourg enjoyed an influx of expert craftsmen from Italy, Flanders and Germany. Today students at the top-flight Ecole Boulle, at 57 rue de Reuilly, still spend hours making copies of *style Henri II* pieces. *Style Henri IV*, however, never came into being, his reign having been cut short by his assassination, before the Faubourg had time to recover from the Wars of Religion. Indeed, because of their predominantly Flemish and Germanic origins, the Faubourg's craftsmen had converted to Protestantism *en masse* and were either massacred on the night of Saint Bartholomew or persecuted thereafter. On 12 October 1561 the first gathering of 6,000 Protestants took place in a makeshift temple on rue de Charenton, in the presence of Jeanne d'Albrets, Queen of Navarre and mother of the future Henri IV, a gathering that turned into a violent confrontation with the Catholics.

In 1657 the Abbess of Saint-Antoine won the right for the craftsmen of the Faubourg to be free from the tutelage of the guild, and from then on they were able to give vent to their own inspiration and create works of art. New techniques were now used for decoration, including veneering, tortoiseshell and brass inlaying. At the end of the 17th century the dresser and the chest of drawers were invented here and in 1720, when Paris was bursting with new mansions built for the playful Regency crowd who were now back in the city, as many as 200 workshops, specialising in marquetry, varnishing and lacquering were to be found in the Faubourg, the most famous ones on rue du Faubourg Saint-Antoine, rue de Charenton and rue Saint-Nicolas. Throughout the 18th century the furniture of the Faubourg supplied all the courts and mansions of Europe and many samples of its works of art can still be seen in the stately homes of Britain. Other crafts connected with interior decoration naturally developed at the same time, notably china and porcelain, as well as the Saint-Gobain glass workshop at 20 rue de Reuilly, first established in 1634. Some of the craftsmen were extremely successful and founded dynasties, among them Caffieri and Boulle (it was Charles Boulle who invented the chest of drawers). The more opulent built themselves beautiful dwellings alongside what was then the royal route leading from the King's residence at Vincennes to Paris. The prestigious architect of the colonnade of the Louvre, Claude Perrault (brother of the story-teller Charles), was even commissioned to erect a triumphal arch on Place du Trône (now Nation), a project which never materialised.

Royalty began to frequent Vincennes in the 7th century, when the area was entirely covered by an immense forest, Lanchonia Silva, bountiful ground for hunting, their favourite recreation. Over the centuries, the expanding religious orders encroached upon the forest, but it remained vast enough for hunting, which was its only purpose until the time of Louis XV, who turned it into a park and even opened it to the public. However, it suffered during the violent convulsions of the Revolution, especially when the troops set up camp on its grounds. By the time Napoleon III came to power, it was all but a shambles. The Emperor loved gardens and took it upon himself to repeat here the renovation undertaken at the Bois de Boulogne. He commissioned his usual team of Alphand (for the landscaping) and Davioud (for the ornamentation) to embellish this eastern border of Paris, taking Hyde Park, Kensington Gardens and London's other renowned parks as models. However, eastern Paris had little time to enjoy the beautiful newly laid-out grounds, for these were devastated once more in 1871 by the upheavals of the *Commune*. The Bois de Vincennes was incorporated into Paris in 1926 and equipped with new attractions in 1931, when it was chosen to play host to the Colonial Exhibition. It was for that occasion that the Zoo of Vincennes was set up, as well as the lovely Parc Floral with its ever-changing display of flowers reflecting the cycle of nature. Today, the statue of La France Colonisatrice still stands at the Porte Dorée entrance to the park, a vestige of a time when colonialism was a cause for national pride.

It was at Faubourg Saint-Antoine that the wind of revolt began to blow on 28 April 1789, when rumours had it that the paper manufacturer Réveillon, on rue de Montreuil (now in the 11th arr.), was planning to lower his workers' wages. Some claim that the riots were instigated by the King's cousin, the Duc d'Orléans, later to become Philippe Egalité, in the hope of overthrowing the present dynasty and securing the throne for himself. Be that as it may, it was at the *'Faubourg de la gloire'* that the Revolution recruited its most determined troops of *sans-culottes*, with San-terre, *'Le Roi du Faubourg'*, the rich Flemish brewer of 11 rue de Reuilly riding on horseback at their head. His booming voice, reported to carry from Place du Trône to Porte Saint-Antoine, and his massive frame clad in a jacket with epaulettes, gave him an awesome presence.

The crowd loved him, especially when they were the benefic-iaries of his largesse, or rather that of the Orleanist party which was funded by the Duc d'Orléans. Having bartered their chisels and planes for pikes, they sported the red phryngian cap – symbol of liberty – and set out to annihilate the decadent aristocracy whose homes they had hitherto been employed to adorn. Because they had been organised into a strong guild for several centuries, they had a deeper class awareness than other inhabitants of Paris, as a result of which the Faubourg became the focal point of all the successive insurrections that shook Paris during the social upheav-als of the next 100 years – 1792, 1793, 1795, 1830, 1848 and 1871. The Faubourg had already witnessed fierce fighting during the *Fronde*, the princely revolt against the young Louis XIV on 1 and 2 August 1652, a battle engaged on the high street between the supporters of the loyalitst Turenne and of the rebel Condé, and watched by the King from one of the turrets of the Château de Charonne (now in the 20th arr.). Condé, in his turn, watched the battle from the church-tower of the abbey. Mlle de Montpensier, La Grande Mademoiselle, the King's cousin and one of the instigators of the revolt, opened the gate of Saint-Antoine to the defeated rebels, to help them escape. It has been suggested that she had been intended as a wife for Louis XIV but that this misguided political step on her part cost her the throne.

In 1789, it was their own destiny the inhabitants of the Faubourg took in hand – and not the least the women – at least that is what the *Montagnards*, with Robespierre at their head, led them to believe. Well aware of their revolutionary spirit, Robespierre used their support to hound down the *Girondins* and the rich in their 'golden breeches'. When the one-billion-franc loan was voted by the Convention on 20 May 1793 to save the bankrupt Republic, Robespierre stood up in their defence: 'You have an immense people of *sans-culottes* ('without breeches'), very pure, very vigorous; they cannot abandon their work. Let the rich pay.' Whether a sincere Republican or an impostor, Philippe Egalité, who had goaded them on at the outset, was among those sent to their deaths during the staged witch-hunt of autumn 1793. He was guillotined on 6 November 1793, less than a year after his cousin the King and three weeks after the Queen. But the Revolution did not live up to its promises and the disappearance of the aristocracy entailed the economic ruin of Faubourg Saint-Antoine. From 21,000 on the eve of the Revolution, the number of its inhabitants dropped to 15,000 in 1800.

It was on Place du Trône (now Nation) that the Revolution took the heaviest toll. The name commemorated the throne erected on the site on 26 August 1660, on the occasion of the wedding procession of Louis XIV and Marie-Thérèse of Spain, which stopped there on its way from Vincennes to the Louvre. With the removal of royalty, it was now realistically renamed Place du Trône Renversé ('the overturned throne') and was picked up during the Terror as the site of the guillotine.

It is often assumed that there were three guillotines in operation, one at Place de la Révolution (Concorde), one at the Bastille and one at Place du Trône (Renversé). As a matter of fact there was only one guillotine, which was dismantled, shifted around and re-erected according to circumstances. It was first transferred from Place de la Concorde to the Bastille, when, after the initial excitement, the inhabitants of the neighbouring Faubourg Saint-Honoré became exasperated by its gory presence. The neighbours round the Bastille were just as opposed to its presence and had it removed further east, to the remote Place du Trône, where there were no neighbours and no-one to protest. 1,306 heads were chopped off at Place du Trône within just two months (15 June – 16 August 1794) and out of the 1,109 male victims 579 were commoners. The figures for the women are even more striking – 123 out of 197 were commoners. Among the victims were 108 monks and 23 nuns. Thus the 12th arrondissement was the place where, thanks to the 'national razor', efficient productivity was applied to mass murder for the first time in history.

Throughout the 19th century Place du Trône was to reflect the shaky plight of France. In 1805 Napoleon, having completed the sabotage of the young Republic and established himself on the imperial throne, again renamed it Place du Trône, emulating the megalomaniac sovereign of a century before, whose ghost haunted him throughout his career. But when the monarchy was ousted in 1848 it became once more Place du Trône Renversé. In a symbolic re-enactment of the people's first Revolution, a throne was erected here and set on fire. The Third Republic finally put an end to all this shilly-shallying: in 1880 the place was named Place de la Nation, to which, obviously, no one could object. In 1889 a bombastic monument was set up in the centre – an allegorical figure of the Republic standing on a chariot pulled by two lions. In front are the three figures of Work, Law and Justice; behind, Peace is strewing flowers along her way!

La Foire du Trône, the annual spring funfair on the edge of the Bois de Vincennes, was located at Place de la Nation until as recently as 1965, hence its name. Few contemporary Parisians are aware of the origin of the name or that the gigantic Ferris wheel, the thrilling switchback rides, the giddying roundabouts, the shooting-stands and candy-floss all had their roots in the old medieval fair, the only one to have survived within the boundaries of Paris. The year 1957 in fact marked the millennium of the first embryonic fair, authorised by King Lothaire, then held in front of the old church that preceded the Cathedral of Notre-Dame. In 1222 Philippe Auguste granted the privilege of the fair to the Order of Saint-Antoine, on its traditional location on the Ile de la Cité, but some 100 years later Philippe le Bel allowed the Order to transfer the fair to the outlying site of the present Place du Trône, which was also closer to their abbey. By the same token they gained freedom from the tutelage of Notre Dame. Bacon and gingerbread were the two traditional specialities of the fair, together with the customary entertainment provided by tumblers and jugglers. The fair's success lasted throughout the generations and in the 19th century Thomas Cook advertised it to English tourists as one of the entertainments of the City of Light.

Meanwhile, on the southern edge of the arrondissement, along the river at Bercy, people led a life of bucolic idleness. Part of the area was still marshland, which accounts for the presence of a large pond – *l'étang de Bercy* – and a multitude of market gardens (*marais*). The Romans had already roamed the area and rue de Charenton was known at the time as *Via Carentonis*. In January 1990, however, during the overall renovation of the area, it was discovered that, well before them, between four and five millennia before the present era, a riverfaring people – the earliest Parisians yet known – inhabited Bercy. Three oak pirogues, dating from the Neolithic times, were dug up, one with a prow in the shape of a spoon.

For centuries the main attraction of Bercy remained as a recreational site and some of the privileged members of society owned magnificent estates and dwellings here. Back in the 7th century, King Dagobert – the first King of France to be buried in the Basilica of Saint-Denis – already had a manor in the vicinity, not quite in Bercy, but on the site of today's rue de Reuilly, probably opposite rue Erard. The manor was known as *Rutiliacum*, later distorted to *Reuilly*. The first *chatel de Bercy* goes back to the early 14th century, and was offered by Philippe V to his mother-in-law, the Comtesse d'Artois, as a gift. It was even occupied by the English during the Hundred Years' War and Jean de Berry, brother of Charles V, is said to have loved Bercy, which is no small recommendation, for he was the great patron of the arts who had commissioned the fabulous Book of Hours, and his home, the Hôtel de Nesle, across the Seine from the Louvre (now the 6th arr.), was one of the most beautiful dwellings in the kingdom.

In 1658 a new palace, in a pure classical style, was erected here by François Le Vau, brother of Louis, comparable in magnificence to the Palace of Versailles. Its graceful terrace ran along the Seine, like the one at the Louvre, and the grounds stretched as far as the present lake of Daumesnil in the Bois de Vincennes. It was largely reconstructed in 1715 and the magnificent gardens were altered to slope gracefully towards the river. The lords of the estate, wealthy though they were, were also notorious misers. The one who lived at the time of Molière is said to have been his model for Harpagon in *l'Avare* (*The Miser*), and an 18th-century satirist wrote about his own contemporary:

Que le Bercy, dans l'or fondu
Satisfasse son avarice.

Would Bercy, cast in gold,
satisfy his avarice.

A number of aristocrats built themselves country houses in the area in the 17th century, among them the Duc de Rohan and Nicolas Fouquet, Louis XIV's Minister. His house here was much more modest than the one at Vaux-le-Vicomte, which caused his downfall. Fouquet patronised La Fontaine and paid him a regular pension, in return for which the writer came to read to his benefactor his new fables. The Marquise de la Sablière, wife of Antoine de Rambouillet, another patron and great friend of La Fontaine, also owned a place here, la Folie Rambouillet, said to be the most beautiful house in the vicinity, where the non-Catholic foreign ambassadors would stay before making their official entry into Paris by way of the gate of Saint-Antoine. Although she was one of the most enlightened women of 17th-century society, praised by La Fontaine for her 'heaven-begotten mind', she also led a thoroughly dissolute life in these enchanting surroundings. The notorious mass-poisoner, la Marquise de Brinvilliers, owned a house on the site of the present no. 39 rue de Reuilly. The skeletons that were found there may have belonged to her murdered brothers. By the early 18th century, owning a house at Bercy had become the vogue and the financier Law bought the Folie Rambouillet in 1719, before the collapse of his financial venture. The Marquis de Marigny, the Pompadour's brother, also owned a dwelling here, overlooking the Seine and nicknamed le Pâté-Paris because of its massive shape. Even the bandit Cartouche, his notorious contemporary, owned a place here at the time, by no means palatial, but with an underground passage leading to it, which enabled him to avoid the police.

All this beautiful world fell into decline in the wake of the Revolution. The Château de Bercy as such was spared, perhaps because Robespierre liked to come to rest here, but it suffered from the economic transformation of France, her political plight and, finally, from the natural extinction of the Nicolaï family. By then Haussmann had incorporated most of the grounds into Paris, largely as wine warehouses. That process began in 1809, when the landlord conceded a plot of land to a wine merchant for the storage of his wine after it was unloaded at the Port de la Rapée, then the eastern fringe of Paris, beyond which taxes were levied. In 1841 the estate was deprived of a substantial stretch to the east, when Thiers decided to gird Paris with defensive walls. In 1861, the last lord, the Marquis Nicolaï, died without leaving an heir and the mansion was delivered up for demolition. Its magnificent woodwork was scattered among several purchasers, from France and elsewhere, among them the imperial couple, who transferred their acquisition to the Palais de l'Elysée, where it can still be seen. Other samples of woodwork are kept at the Musée d'Arts Décoratifs, still others decorate the Italian Embassy on rue de Varenne.

Wine was transported to Bercy already at the end of the 15th century, alongside wood, and in 1787 a guidebook to Paris mentions its open-air *guinguettes* (taverns) by the Seine and its water jousts. It was in 1819, however, that the vicinity was metamorphosed, when the warehouses were laid out and the Port de la Rapée accommodated as many as 2,000 boats per year. By the second half of the 19th century it became France's wine store-room, across the Seine from the wine market, la Halle aux Vins, at Jussieu, where the University of Paris VI/VII is now located. But it was more than a storeroom. If the wine of France was the best of wines – '*il n'est bon vin que de France*', as the saying went – Bercy was the place to savour it, especially in warm weather, in the pleasing setting of its open-air *guinguettes* along the Seine, where it was untaxed and cheaper. Colourful jousts often took place on the river by day, adding to the pleasure, while at night one could be entertained by music played aboard lit-up boats and often also by fireworks.

Before the industrial age, much of the Paris area was covered with vineyards and the local vintages often enjoyed a high reputation. A doctor at the Sorbonne submitted a thesis in 1724 to prove the superiority of the wines of Suresnes – today a suburb lying west of Paris – over those of Champagne and Bourgogne (a vineyard still exists in Suresnes and grape-picking celebrations take place there every October to commemorate a happy past). But with the industrialisation and urbanisation of Paris, the vineyards shrank to pocket-size, giving way to shacks and hovels, to factories surmounted by smoke-belching chimney-stacks or to long stretches of railway tracks.

The railway at least permitted the supply of wines from the provinces to be speeded up and increased, and choice ones at that – those of Champagne and Bourgogne, south-east of Paris, had been hitherto transported to Bercy down the Seine in a journey that took several days. Within two decades Bercy became the largest alcohol warehouse in the world, enjoying both a favourable geographic position and huge demand. This was not the usual ugly 19th-century development, but a 'wine village' unique in the world, the home of wine-traders and coopers, with long, low, one-storeyed, red-tiled houses lying along shady alleys that were lined with beautiful plane trees and rejoiced in such names as rue de Médoc and rue de Sauternes.

No more. Like Les Halles, the demolished warehouses are bemoaned by those who knew them. Admittedly, the old plane trees have been preserved – owing to recent public awakening to ecological issues – and integrated into the new Parc de Bercy, and likewise it is too early to pass a verdict on the gardens, which at the time of writing have not yet been completed. But the modern blocks that surround them are there to stay, and the Seine is completely hidden from the view by a wall, supposed to deaden the noise of traffic from the Georges Pompidou motorway which runs along the river. Ultimately the wall will be topped with vegetation and serve as a belvedere overlooking the Seine, but for the present all the stroller below can see are the four glass towers of the new Bibliothèque de France (the new national library) sticking out above the wall, on the opposite bank. A clinical, soulless atmosphere prevails in new Bercy, encompassing also the new American Center and La Maison des Vins Français, an impersonal substitute for yet another slice of old Paris that has been wiped out.

However, even in this age of high-tech modernity, some architects have committed themselves to preserving human aspirations and the quality of life in the 12th arrondissement, tending to its 150,000 trees, extracting as much land as possible from the jaws of concrete mixers and delivering it to landscape gardeners, sometimes in ingeniously imaginative ways. Thus a riband of gardens 4km long, la Coulée Verte, has been planted across the arrondissement, all the way from the Bastille soon to reach the Bois de Vincennes, much of it on the viaduct that previously supported the railway.

Spacious workshops have also been installed beneath its arches to perpetuate the tradition of crafts in the arrondissement. In the Bois de Vincennes 100 km of foot trail and 19 km of bridle paths are to be laid out; the Parc Floral is to be enlarged and the time-worn zoo is to be entirely renovated. In fine weather the Bassin de l'Arsenal, which connects the Seine with the Canal Saint-Martin on the western edge of the arrondissement, resembles nothing so much as a summer resort, with its festive marina and its sunny shore. To think that 20-odd years ago, in order to ease the flow of traffic, some town-planners suggested building a motorway over the Bassin de l'Arsenal and the Canal Saint-Martin, all the way to the north of Paris!

WHERE TO WALK

THROUGH FAUBOURG SAINT-ANTOINE TO PLACE FELIX EBOUE

You should aim for the western part of the 12th arrondissement in the morning – except on a Monday – and preferably on a sunny morning, if you are to include the bustling Marché d'Aligre in this walk. Start out from the new **Opera House** on the site of the old Bastille/Vincennes railway station, which served the south-eastern suburbs of Paris. Centuries earlier there was a very small Jewish ghetto here, known as la Cour de la Juiverie. Group visits to the Opera House, in French, are available. You may also like to attend an opera or a concert. If you do so, you will find out that prices at this 'people's Opera' are almost as prohibitive as in any bourgeois establishment and that first nights are often reserved for top-drawer people and are awash with champagne. In the early seasons of the new establishment, when the Socialist Party was in power, its members and friends who attended those first nights were dubbed 'caviar socialists' by their disillusioned supporters. So much for mass culture. As for the building itself, a poll conducted among Parisians in 1990, ranked the Centre Georges Pompidou as the first monument they wished to see pulled down, the Bastille Opera as the second!

Adjacent to the Opera House is a well-known brasserie, Les

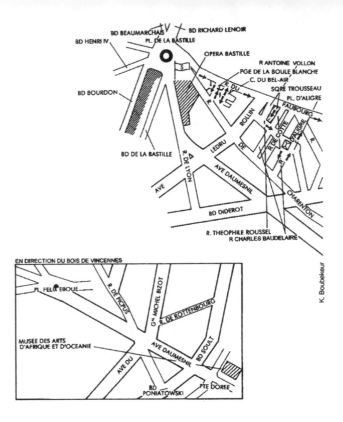

Grands Marches, known until recently as La Tour d'Argent. In June 1990 it lost a law case, and by the same token its previous name, to that other Tour d'Argent, Claude Terrail's world-famous restaurant. Legality apart, the name was historically justifiable, as it evoked the memory of La Tour du Trésor, one of the eight towers of the Bastille fortress, on the other side of Place de la Bastille, where Henri IV deposited all his savings – 15,875,000 pounds, according to his minister Sully. An inn was already mentioned here in 1640, an obvious location at the heavily frequented eastern gateway of Paris and on the edge of the active Faubourg Saint-Antoine. During the French Revolution, it became an important meeting-place of the *patriotes* and its proprietor, Gilbert Gaillard, was captain of the armed forces of the First Company. The establishment was in the front line of all the revolutions and convulsions of the 19th century, at times an entrenched camp, at times a makeshift hospital. In 1914 its memorabilia were given to the City of Paris and are now in the Musée Carnavalet, while documents

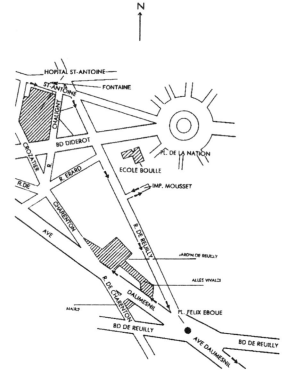

N

HOPITAL ST-ANTOINE
ST-ANTOINE — FONTAINE
CHALIGNY
BD DIDEROT
CROZATIER
R.
R. ERARD
ECOLE BOULLE
R. DE
PL. DE LA NATION
IMP. MOUSSET
CHARENTON
AVE
R. DE REUILLY
JARDIN DE REUILLY
ALLEE VIVALDI
R. DE CHARENTON
DAUMESNIL
MAIRE
BD DE REUILLY
PL. FELIX EBOUE
AVE DAUMESNIL
BD DE REUILLY

relating to its history are kept in the National Archives. At present the restaurant serves opera-goers and other middle-class Parisians with a traditional dish of oysters, whilst its new name honours the unconvincing staircase of the new Opera House.

Turn right into **RUE DU FAUBOURG SAINT-ANTOINE**. In the 18th century some 80 workshops of cabinetmakers were scattered throughout the Faubourg's courtyards and alleys; they are all gone, although carpentry and woodworking still thrive here. The craftsmen of Saint-Antoine formed a strong economic community, where political consciousness and class awareness first developed, coming to a head in 1789 with the French Revolution: '*le cratère d'où s'échappa la lave révolutionnaire*' ('the crater from which the revolutionary lava erupted'). The site of many insurrections, of barricades and shootings, it took a heavy toll on its own people, but also on both enemies and friends. Thus, during the June 1848 riots, the Archbishop of Paris, Monsieur Denis Affre, tragically lost his life here. The prelate had come to appease the infuriated people and climbed up the barricade erected level with no. 2 Faubourg Saint-Antoine to address the insurgents. '*Mes amis, mes amis!*' he called out. A bullet struck him down in reply. '*Que mon sang soit le dernier versé,*' ('May my blood be the last to be shed'), were his dying words. Two and a half years later, on 2 December 1851, the deputy Baudin, an opponent of Louis Napoleon's coup, also died on a barricade of Faubourg Saint-Antoine, an incident described in the chapter on the 11th arrondissement.

La Cour de la Boule Blanche at no. 50 was the scene of one of Lacenaire's first crimes in 1829. The notorious, gentlemanly criminal committed a series of crimes between 1829 and 1835 and ended up ascending the guillotine in January 1836. He was a charismatic culprit, who appeared in court dressed with impeccable elegance and spoke immaculate French (he had been a poet on occasions) interspersed with witticisms. His trial fascinated Paris, and one lady sent a letter to him in prison requesting his autograph to add to her collection. Like all dark, unfathomable souls, he continues to intrigue, so much so that his *Memoirs* were sold out in no time when they were republished in 1988. By the end of the *Memoirs* Lacenaire gains the reader's sympathy as a victim of the wickedness of society rather than a cause of evil. On one occasion, Lacenaire writes, he even risked his life to rescue a child from a fire. Of his sentence to death he confides, 'I reach death by the wrong route, I climb up the steps [of the guillotine] to it. . . I wished to explain the reasons for this journey, of this deathly ascent.' In 1968 Catherine Sauvage, a respected interpreter of *la chanson française*, sang one of Lacenaire's poems at the Bobino music hall, then the shrine of this type of music – *Pétition d'un voleur à un roi son voisin* ('Petition from a Thief to a King his Neighbour') – which was specially put to music for the occasion and followed in the same vein as that other villainous, medieval poet, François Villon.

La Cour de la Boule Blanche leads to the world-renowned eye hospital, **les Quinze-Vingts**, at no. 28 rue de Charenton, a rural way in the 18th century, leading to the village of Charenton. A countrified house still stands at no. 45, redolent of those days.

'*La Maison des tras cens aveugles de Paris*' ('the house of the three hundred blind men of Paris') was first founded by his 'Lordship Louis the Ninth for three hundred of his valiant knights whose eyes

Faubourg Saint-Antoine

were gouged out by the wicked Saracens, during the Crusade.' The number was calculated at fifteen per day, for twenty days, exacted in retribution for his delay in paying the ransom demanded. The institution was first set up in the central area of the Louvre, which enabled its tenants to collect alms from passers-by. The Cardinal de Rohan was the Great Chaplain of France at the time of Louis XVI, and in that capacity head of the institution. A shrewd businessman, he had considerations in mind other than the well-being of the blind inmates. Pleading the healthier air of the outskirts of Paris, he bought the present premises at a very low cost from the Mousquetaires Noirs, who had settled here in 1704, and, having sold the old premises by the Louvre for ten times that sum, made a substantial profit. The vehement protests of his blind tenants –

justly worried about making a living in a scantily populated area –
were of no avail and in 1775 they were transferred to their new
home on the premises of the celebrated Mousquetaires Noirs, so
called because of the black coats of their horses. The Marquis de La
Fayette had begun his military career as one of their members.

The *Quinze-Vingts* had become so prominent in the 17th century that eminent figures wished to be buried in its chapel. Thus,
the remains of the Cardinal de Gondi, better known as the
Cardinal de Retz, were transferred here from the old premises and
lie in the crypt of the chapel. Little is left of the gorgeous building
designed by Jules Hardouin Mansart, the famous architect of
Versailles. It was converted into a hospital by Gambetta in 1880,
but by the 1950s was deemed unsuitable to house a modern
hospital and in 1957 was simply pulled down, admittedly at a time
when conservation of historical treasures was given even less
thought than it is today. Only the entrance portal, the Master's
home and the chapel have been rescued from the wreckage.

Retrace your steps to **RUE DU FAUBOURG SAINT-ANTOINE**
and turn into the **Cour du Bel-Air** at no. 56 – the most attractive
example of upgrading on this side of the street. The nature-loving
residents have planted the two successive courtyards with a proliferation of creepers and a riot of flowers. Lavender adds a touch of
Provence and tomatoes an air of rusticity, counterbalanced, however, by a photographer's gallery, an exciting bookshop and the
offices of Encyclopedia Universalis. A beautiful staircase at
entrance D, known as les Mousquetaires Noirs, is worth a glimpse
before you leave. The **Passage du Chantier**, at no. 66, goes back to
the Middle Ages, while no. 74 provides an architectural example of
a workers' compound in early industrial days. At the back of the
courtyard is the spacious, bourgeois home of the boss, from where
he could watch over them paternalistically. It is decorated with
wrought iron in keeping with his social superiority.

At no. 80 Rémy Sendar, a cabinetmaker, still carries on the traditional calling of the neighbourhood. His premises too have been
somewhat smartened up and profuse vegetation grows around the
old pebbled courtyard; but Rémy Sendar remains a true *fau-
bourien*, turning out reproductions, especially of Art Nouveau
pieces, that are works of art. His marquetry is also noteworthy.

Needless to say, he caters to an upmarket clientele, as indeed the Faubourg did in the past. No. 94 is another working-class compound, with its typical 19th-century architecture. Here too the boss's house stands at the back of the courtyard.

You will now reach the corner of Avenue Ledru-Rollin, where a lively open-air furniture market – *la trôle* – was held every Saturday before World War I. Craftsmen exempted from trading dues could sell their goods here at competitive prices, a serious threat to the tradesmen of Faubourg Saint-Antoine, who managed to have it closed down in 1914.

Ahead is the pleasant **SQUARE TROUSSEAU** with its typical turn-of-the-century kiosk. The square lies on the site of a children's hospital, l'Hôpital Trousseau, which was transferred to rue du Général Michel Bizot further east in 1904. The original institution, founded by Saint Vincent de Paul in 1638, was an orphanage for foundlings, hence its name '*Les Enfants Trouvés*'. The King could not ignore the dramatic level of homelessness that afflicted 10 per cent of the population of Paris, and clearing the streets of the capital became a major item on his agenda. Several institutions were founded to absorb the homeless and it is significant that in 1674 Queen Marie-Thérèse was dispatched to lay the cornerstone of this hospice, marking the sympathy of the throne for Saint Vincent de Paul's initiative. It was in the cemetery of the orphanage that the body of the wretched Princesse de Lamballe was dumped on 3 September 1792 after she had been massacred outside the prison of La Force (in the present 4th arr.), except for her fair-haired head, which was impaled on a pike and carried to the Temple, to be displayed in front of the window of her close friend, Marie-Antoinette. At the other end of the square, at no. 7 rue Théophile Roussel, is the Rothschild Foundation, as indicated by a plaque, testifying yet again to the charitable aspect of the arrondissement.

Rue Théophile Roussel leads to the **Marché Saint-Antoine-Beauvau** on **PLACE D'ALIGRE**, known to locals as Marché d'Aligre.

Originally this was a haymarket. It was held at the entrance gate to the abbey, where it caused a considerable obstruction. In 1788 Madame de Craon-Beauvau, the last abbess of Saint-Antoine, obtained permission from the King to transfer it to the present location, then an outlying marshy enclosure. It was stipulated, however, that the vendors must also sell cheap clothing to the poor. By 1885 there were 200 of them, so numerous were the needy. A thriving flea market later took its place, which has unfortunately declined in the last ten years, the number of stalls having dropped from 75 to 35.

In front of the indoor section of the market, built in 1843, a picturesque guard-room topped by a small bell-turret creates a nostalgic villagey touch, compensating somewhat for the recent high-rises. Somebody has even decorated the façade with artificial wistaria hanging down in perpetual bloom. The bustling market spills beyond Place d'Aligre, stretching along rue d'Aligre both south and north, an exciting sight when the sun shines, a piece of the genuine Paris of pre-Yuppy days, when such knowledgeable Americans as Eisenhower and Clark Gable visited La Boule d'Or in search of authenticity. Piles of cheap clothes here, a jumble of cheap secondhand goods there, fruit, vegetables, flowers – a riot of colours! On a fine day a street-organ emits langorous French melodies on the sunny corner of rue d'Aligre and rue Théophile Roussel, delighting kids and mothers. Street-organs for the funfairs and roundabouts of Paris were actually made in the 12th arrondissement, at 116 Avenue Daumesnil, by the brothers Limonaire. The current owner of the street-organ at Place d'Aligre performs with friends at the century-old Limonaire, a neighbourhood bistro at no. 88, rue de Charenton. Few outsiders have heard of the place, but those who have and go in there are made to feel very welcome.

As you make your way back to rue du Faubourg Saint-Antoine along rue d'Aligre and its colourful stalls, you will notice the North African grocery shops and the ethnic melting-pot of which both vendors and customers are part. With the opening of the Gare de Lyon in the 19th century, the 12th arrondissement became the immigrant harbour *par excellence*, connecting Paris with Marseilles and beyond it with Italy and Africa. Mingling with the descendants of the *sans-culottes*, they keep alive a vibrant atmosphere which, one hopes, will be preserved.

Back on RUE DU FAUBOURG SAINT-ANTOINE, turn right. At no. 170 the old lodge of the abbey's porter is still standing on the site of the former entrance to the abbey. The entrance to the **hospital of Saint-Antoine**, which has replaced the abbey, is now at no. 184. The Abbey of Saint-Antoine was founded in 1198 to offer shelter to penitent women who wished to give up their life of dissolution and make penance in monastic conditions for the rest of their lives. The golden sash they wore is the origin of the French proverb, '*Mieux vaut bonne renomée que ceinture dorée*' ('a good reputation is better than a golden belt'). When Saint Louis returned from the First Crusade in 1241, he deposited the crown of thorns here, before taking it over to Notre-Dame where it was kept until the completion of the Sainte-Chapelle. True, the abbey lay on his way to the capital, but there was more to it than convenience, for the abbey had distinguished ties with the royal authorities, as a result of which it enjoyed centuries of economic prosperity. With the authorities' consent its grounds gradually extended over the better part of the 12th arrondissement and even over parts of the 11th and the 20th. The entire Faubourg was under the protection and jurisdiction of the abbey and its walls were guarded by armed soldiers under the command of the all-powerful Abbess, '*la Dame du Faubourg*' who also dispensed justice. Forty-two abbesses had ruled over the Faubourg up until the Revolution, when the abbey was confiscated and turned into a hospital. The old church was razed to the ground in the heat of anticlerical fury, but the 18th-century buildings of the convent were to a large extent preserved.

Opposite the hospital stands an early 18th-century fountain which used to supply water to the Faubourg and especially to the market that was located here before its transfer to the present Place d'Aligre. Adjoining it until 1946 was a small meat market which had first been set up at the time of Louis XIII and from which derived the name of the fountain, la Fontaine de la Petite Halle. It was at this junction of **rue du Faubourg Saint-Antoine and rue de Montreuil** that the first Revolutionary eruption was sparked off on 27 and 28 April 1789, when the entire Faubourg rose against the paper manufacturer Réveillon, who was rumoured to be planning wage cuts. Being the employer of 400 *faubouriens* – an enormous figure for those days, equalled only by the Gobelins workshops – their economic fate could not fail to have repercussions on the entire neighbourhood.

Next to the hospital, stands a watchmaker's shop, which has

been carrying on the same trade on the same premises since the 18th century. The three bells of the original clock outside the shop still punctuate the rhythm of the neighbourhood every quarter of an hour, better still at midday, when they chime the hour and echo the past of Faubourg Saint-Antoine. If you decide to wait for this to happen, you can meanwhile walk into no. 207 across the street – a brief excursion into the 11th arrondissement – and into a lovely courtyard with an unusual Louis XVI building at the back. Another charming courtyard is situated at no. 173, together with an interesting Louis XIV staircase.

RUE DE REUILLY to your right has little to offer by way of aesthetics or picturesque atmosphere, but is worth seeing if you are interested in recapturing the past.

A plaque at no. 11 indicates the site of the brewer Santerre's famous *brasserie*, l'Hortentia. This was where Santerre, with the help of the butcher Legendre and the abbot Lareynie, prepared the assault on the Palais des Tuileries, which took place on 20 June 1792 and was to alter the destiny of France. In the same year Santerre met the King's cousin here, the formerly Duc d'Orléans, now Citizen Philippe Egalité, who, it is suggested, had hoped to take the place of the deposed monarch by gaining the support of the Faubourg. Santerre became commander-in-chief of the National Guard, but was known familiarly as '*le Roi du Faubourg*'.

The prestigious Saint-Gobain workshops were located at no. 20 rue de Reuilly, having been set up here during the more peaceful reign of Louis XIV. Somehow, the premises were spared by the Revolution and the workshops were still standing in 1830. Founded by Colbert in 1666, in order to compete with the world-renowned Venetian glass and to produce items to complement the furniture and tapestry made by the Gobelins, which Colbert had set up on the Left Bank at the same time, the workshops enjoyed a reputation for unsurpassable workmanship and artistry, worthy of the reign of the Sun King. The name of the workshops derives from the town of Saint-Gobain where much of the glass was melted down before being brought to Paris to be polished and silvered.

Further on, probably somewhere level with rue Erard, stood the manor house of King Dagobert in ancient times, the great statesman who reorganised and reunited the Merovingian Kingdom, and the first King of France to have been buried in the Basilica of Saint Denis (638 AD). He is also remembered as the hero of the song, *Le Bon Roi Dagobert*, known to every French child.

An alleyway at no. 57 leads to the cabinetmaking school, l'**Ecole Boulle**, founded in 1866 and named after the famous family of cabinetmakers. The school is known for specialising in reproductions with a partiality for the period of Henri II. In fact, it has been diversifying for some time and now teaches interior decoration and design at large. As such, it was one of its alumni who designed the 'muzzle' of the TGV train.

A succession of workshops and picturesque little houses huddle together in the **Impasse Mousset**, at no. 81, bringing to life a recent past that existed before the eruption of high-rise buildings and of urbanisation in general. At the back of the countrified alley is an indoor tennis-court, hidden from the public eye and used by locals only.

Continue to **PLACE FÉLIX EBOUÉ**, a residential, leafy round-about with Davioud's elegant fountain standing in the centre, spurting water energetically through its proud lions' jaws. It was moved here from Place de la République in 1874, to make room for the more emblematic allegorical statue of the Republic, which was accordingly inaugurated on 14 July. **AVENUE DAUMESNIL** runs west and east of the roundabout. If you head west, you will come to the old railway station of Reuilly. Behind it is l'**Allée Vivaldi**, a pleasant section of the leafy strip, **la Coulée Verte**, that now runs through the arrondissement. It opens up into a spacious garden, beyond the **Mairie** on your left. Avenue Daumesnil continues along the old railway viaduct, which now has the new attractions of workshops installed underneath the arches and suspended gardens above. A **copper and silver museum** stands at no. 113, complete with a guided tour and a film about the historic city of copper, Villedieu-les-Poêles. There you will see traditional silverware and learn about its usage not only in the kitchen and on the dining table but also in fashion, hunting and travelling. However, the idea of perpetuating the arrondissement's traditions of crafts in this 'Viaduct des Arts' feels contrived, which explains, perhaps, why the picturesque café, **Au Père Tranquil**, at no. 79, is currently the only animated spot. If you wish to avoid the crowd, climb the staircase to the secluded and relaxing gardens. You can also walk (or cycle) through them as far as the ring road to the east, although not quite yet to the Bois de Vincennes.

If you wish to visit the **Bois de Vincennes**, head for the PORTE DORÉE, its main entrance. Drivier's shining gilt statue, La France Colonisatrice, stands at Place Edouard-Renard, bearing the mark of the 1931 Colonial Exposition that took place here. To your left, at no. 293 Avenue Daumesnil, the **Musée des Arts d'Afrique et d'Océanie** was also built in 1931 for the occasion. At that time, when colonialism was by no means taboo, it was known as the Musée des Colonies, a name later exchanged for the less offensive Musée de la France d'Outre-Mer, and in 1990, with one minor other change intervening, for the present name. Besides its display of works of art from South-East Asia, Africa, the West Indies and Oceania, the museum contains an underground aquarium and a crocodile pit. The spectacular interior architecture by Laprade and Joussely also deserves special mention.

FROM PLACE DE LA NATION
TO THE CIMETIERE DE PICPUS

PLACE DE LA NATION, the eastern royal gateway to the capital, is the starting point of our next walk. In pre-Revolution days, when the Château de Vincennes was used by royalty during the hunting season, it was through Place de la Nation, then Place du Trône, that, having taken the Cours de Vincennes, they made their entry into the high street of Faubourg Saint-Antoine and on to the city. This was the itinerary followed by the royal wedding procession on 15 August 1660, which had come up to Paris from Saint-Jean-de-Luz near the Spanish border, where Louis XIV had been married to the Infanta of Spain, Marie-Thérèse. A throne was set up here for the occasion, magnificently decorated with a taffeta canopy studded with *fleurs-de-lis*, as befitting a glorious reign that was about to commence. The place was consequently named Place du Trône. The extravagant festivities continued along Faubourg and rue Saint-Antoine, and especially at the Louvre. Ten years later there were plans for Claude Perrault to build a colossal triumphal arch surmounted by an equestrial statue of the Sun King, but His Majesty was too busy with other grand constructions and the project never got beyond the socles of its columns.

A century passed before the Place du Trône was again accorded attention, when in 1784 Nicolas Ledoux was commissioned to build a toll-gate, which he flanked by two elegant pavilions and by the two tall columns still standing on its eastern edge. The statues of Saint Louis and Philippe Auguste surmounting the columns, standing guard above the city and facing Vincennes, date from the reign of Louis-Philippe and were designed by Etex and Dumont. These colossal monuments were erected for no other purpose than to serve as a setting for the toll-gate, where goods entering Paris were taxed. When Charles X acceded to the throne in 1824, he wished to revive the old traditions of the *Ancien Régime* and chose the Cathedral of Reims for his coronation ceremony. But instead of entering Paris by the medieval route of rue Saint-Denis, he entered through Place du Trône – where there was no throne – and he had to make do with Ledoux's monumental toll-gate as a substitute for a triumphal arch. On the other hand Napoleon III was honoured with a triumphal arch in 1862 but it was a makeshift construction of wood and canvas, erected between the two columns and which disappeared before long.

The emblem of the Third Republic, on the other hand, erected by Dalou in 1899, has been standing for nearly 100 years, bearing the unequivocal name *Le Triomphe de la République*. No other monument in the French capital expresses such grandiloquent emotions. All the clichés are here: the spirit of Liberty brandishing a torch, the energetic features of the blacksmith – the allegorical figure of Work – the inevitable Justice and her pair of scales, the opulence of the female nude, surrounded by the bucolic idyll of infants playing gaily, the Horn of Abundance overflowing with fruit, Marianne perched on a chariot drawn by lions – all the stereotyped values the Third Republic stood for, carved into the stone.

Place du Trône was by and large an uneventful place, being situated too far out from the centre of action. But when on 14 June 1794 the 'national razor' made an appearance on Place du Trône Renversé, as it was then renamed, it entered the history of France in a big way. In the early stages of the Revolution, when the guillo-

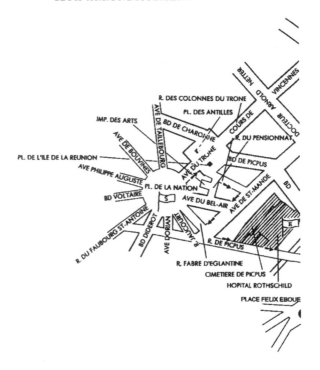

tine had been set up at the Place de la Révolution (now Concorde), it operated sporadically and its presence therefore did not seem bothersome. By spring 1794, however, when its activitiy had been intensified, the inhabitants of Faubourg Saint-Honoré could no longer tolerate the stench of blood nor the sight of the bloody tumbrils rolling past their Faubourg on their way to the cemetery of the Madeleine. After energetic protestations on their part the guillotine was moved to Place de La Bastille on 9 June 1794 where it remained in service for just three days, the inhabitants of Faubourg Saint-Antoine proving to have the same delicate sensibility as those of Saint-Honoré. 73 heads were chopped off at Place de la Bastille, nonetheless, after which the guillotine was removed to Place du Trône Renversé, an uninhabited rural area on the eastern edge of the city, where it caused no further outcry.

Erected roughly on the corner of the present Avenue du Trône and rue des Colonnes du Trône, east of Place de la Nation, the guillotine could operate with complete impunity in these remote parts. It became the instrument of a conveyor-belt industry which,

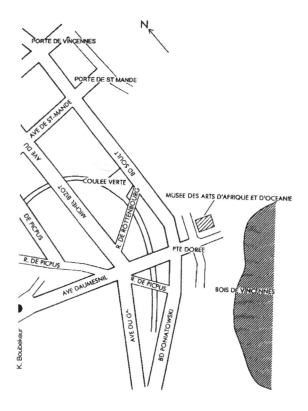

between 14 June and 27 July 1794, eliminated 1,306 human beings, a huge number for those days. This was, of course, the peak of the Terror, when the guillotine operated in bulk, chopping off heads tirelessly, irrespective of age or social rank. The age of the victims varied from 17 to 80 and 702 of them – more than half – were pure commoners. Among the dead too were 16 harmless Carmelites from Compiègne, who walked to the guillotine chanting prayers and praising the Lord. On one occasion Sanson the executioner surpassed himself and chopped off 54 heads in the record time of 24 minutes, a feat for which he was specially rewarded. It was not just Sanson but the entire process that demonstrated exemplary efficiency and was lubricated to perfection at every stage of the operation, from the preparation of the victims at the Conciergerie to their annihilation which took place in the nearby Jardin de Picpus, where we shall now head.

Leave Place de la Nation by way of rue des Colonnes du Trône and Avenue Saint-Mandé to your right, south of Ledoux's pair of columns, so as to walk past the site of the guillotine. Next to it stood the ghastly red tumbril (a tip-cart covered with lead and painted red so as to camouflage the blood), into which were piled the mutilated bodies and chopped heads. As you follow the route of the red tumbril, perhaps paying silent homage to those martyrs, bear in mind that the sinister procession plodded through muddy fields of what was then a rural area and that, unlike you, they made their way to the garden of Picpus by night to avoid being seen, for the goings-on in the garden, now also known as the **Cemetery of the Revolution**, at 35 RUE PICPUS, to your left, were kept secret from the public.

Rue Picpus follows the medieval route that linked the Abbeys of Saint-Denis and Saint-Maure and for centuries was studded with religious institutions. The hamlet of Picpus is first mentioned in 1478, a name possibly derived from *pique puces*, alluding to a flea-infested inn.

A few other sites on rue Picpus are of historical interest. At no. 4 stood a detention house where Saint-Just, the man of moral principles with a predestined name, the 'Archangel' of the Terror, was kept from 30 September 1786 to 30 March 1789 by order of a sealed letter from the King, which had been sent at the request of his mother. Having found himself short of money, the future apostle of virtue thought nothing of burgling his own mother's house and stealing and selling all her silver! 'He has ill paid me for all the tenderness and affection I have always poured on him,' she said, with admirable understatement. Yet on 30 May 1793 he would become member of the *Comité du salut public* and send to their deaths all the corruptible enemies of the virtuous and egalitarian Republic. Another detention house was located at no. 10, which may have been a hunting lodge of Henri IV, near the Bois de Vincennes. On the site of the present no. 12 stood a country residence belonging to the notorious Ninon de Lenclos, then having a short break from her life of dissolution. It was in her grounds that the Marquis de Sévigné was killed by his rival, le Chevalier d'Albret, in a duel over Madame de Gondran. Ninon, who had bestowed her charms on the entire Marais, had also shared her bed with the Marquis de Sévigné. However, she did not remember him as an enlightening figure, unlike his distinguished wife, but rather, in her words, as 'an empty pumpkin-head'. No. 61, now an old people's home, used to belong to the very strict reformed Franciscan Order, who nonetheless disposed of some lavish apartments where the Roman Catholic Ambassadors lodged while waiting to be received by the King. The highest-ranking princesses and princes would come here to pay their respects, before the Ambassadors were escorted to the King in a state coach by an eminent prince or Maréchal de France.

The old convent of the Augustinian Order, on the site of the present no. 35, was confiscated during the Revolution and converted into yet another detention house – *une maison de santé et détention* – whose detainees were protected from going to the guillotine so long as monthly payments were received from their relatives. Once their financial resources were exhausted, the inmates were transferred to the Conciergerie and from there to certain death. Both Monsieur Riédain, who had leased the place, and Monsieur Coignard, the director of the institution, were displeased to discover one morning in June 1794 that during the night a considerable part of their garden had been confiscated by order of the Republic and shut off with a fence without any further justification. They were even more alarmed to find out that this new allotment was intended as a mass grave for the guillotined victims from Place du Trône Renversé. What would become of their 'nursing home' and of the substantial profits they drew from their sinister trade? The Republic turned a deaf ear to their protestations, deeming the location most suitable for the disposal of bodies and heads, owing both to its proximity to the guillotine and to the surrounding high walls which would conceal the evil deed from the public eye. Night after night the sinister red tumbril made its way to the garden of Picpus to tip out its load. Once out of sight behind the garden walls, the men set to work, stripping off the bodies, meticulously sorting all the different items, then throwing the anonymous remains into two mass graves. For the Revolution wished not only to obliterate the evil deed, but also to eradicate every trace of the victims, even their memory:

Point de cercueil, point de linceul, pas une marque qui pût un jour permettre aux familles de reconnaître leurs morts et de leur procurer une autre sepulture.

No coffin, no shroud, no mark that would enable the families to recognise their dead some day and find another burial place for them

Chilling associations come to mind to anyone aware of 20th-century European history. . .

Provision had been made for a third grave and you can still see the boundary markers of its site, but the age of Terror came to an end on 27 July, when the last load of victims, 45 in all, were taken from the Conciergerie to Place du Trône Renversé. Two days later Robespierre's head fell on Place de la Révolution (Concorde), where the royal couple had died the previous year.

In 1796, the Princess Amélie de Hohenzollern, sister of the Prince of Salm-Kyrburg, bought the plot of ground that surrounded the mass graves of the victims, among whom was her brother. A few years later, another *émigrée*, the Marquise de Montagu, returned to Paris in search of the grave of her guillotined relatives. She was helped by a young commoner, a lacemaker by the name of Mlle Paris, who, having followed her innocent father and brother to the guillotine and to their burial-place, knew where they lay. With other members of the victims' families, they bought up the entire property and turned it into a graveyard for the relatives of the guillotined and their descendants, while keeping intact the site of the common graves. Thus many great names of the *Ancien Régime* nobility are to be found here – the Broglie, the Montalembert, La Rochefoucauld, the Montmorency, including the last abbess of the flourishing Abbey of Montmartre, a descendant of that illustrious house. The venerable abbess, by then decrepit and nearly blind and deaf, had been brought to trial before the formidable judges of the Committee of Public Salute and had barely been able to hear the indictment that she had plotted against the Republic 'blindly and deafly'. She too went the way of many others. No cemetery in France contains so many remains of the old nobility.

A plaque in memory of André Chénier, the greatest poet of the time, can also be seen in the cemetery. A fervent friend of the Republic, but not of its excesses, he was among the last load to travel to the guillotine. Members of the nobility who joined the ranks of the Resistance during the Nazi occupation and died in concentration camps are also buried or commemorated here, such as Anne,

Princesse de Bauffremont Courtenay, who died in Ravensbrück, the Comte de Montalembert who died in Mauthausen on 16 December 1944 and the Marquis de Grammont who died in Dachau on 5 February 1945. But for the American visitor the most meaningful tomb is that of the Marquis de La Fayette, placed here because he was himself a relative of guillotined victims. The American flag flies over it perpetually. For some reason the Germans did not remove it during World War II. Every year on 4 July a ceremony is held by the tomb, the most memorable occasion being in 1917 when General Pershing delivered a patriotic speech before a distinguished assembly which included the Maréchal Joffre and the American Ambassador Mr Sharp. It was on that occasion that Colonel Stanton uttered the famous phrase, '*La Fayette nous voici*'.

All that is left today of the old convent is a small pavilion dating from the time of Louis XIII, and the house occupied by Monsieur Riédain. Adjoining the cemetery is a lovely, peaceful garden, conducive to quiet meditation on the hapless victims of man's inexplicable mind.

FROM BERCY
TO THE BASSIN DE L'ARSENAL

Our last walk through the renovated neighbourhood of Bercy starts at Métro station Bercy. As you come out you are greeted by the colossal, fortress-like premises of the Ministry of Finance on one side, the gigantic lawn-covered Palais Omnisports on the other, and, perhaps to your relief, two rows of humble, red-tiled cottages, on your left, as you make your way east along rue de Bercy. These cottages accommodated the railway workers of the Gare de Lyon and Gare de Bercy.

At no. 51 RUE DE BERCY stands Frank Gehry's new **American Center** whose deconstructed architecture is unquestionably a stunning achievement. However unconventional it looks at first sight, the building respects Parisian traditions through its use of limestone and the zinc of its roof. Ironically, this is the very aspect that some Parisians find fault with, because they would have liked it to be more daring and more Californian. You can never win in

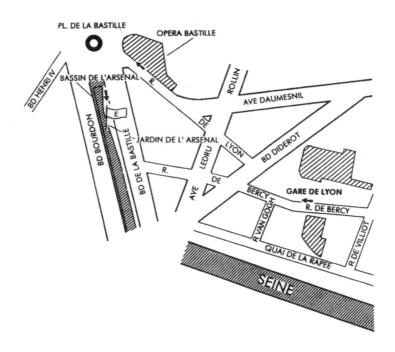

Paris! Artistically successful though the Center is, it is currently a numb, empty shell – alas, for lack of funds – in an outlying, impersonal neighbourhood.* How shameful that its construction entailed the sale and demolition of the old homely and lovely American Center of Boulevard Raspail.

The American Center stands on the edge of the new **Parc de Bercy**, which is being created on the site of the old wine warehouses and is due to be completed in 1996. Like so many aspects of Paris, these gardens reflect the French temperament insofar as their design is motivated wholly by intellectual considerations. Thus they are interspersed with various symbols the stroller is supposed to decipher, such as the criss-cross pattern of alleys differentiating between the old paved ones, which run perpendicular to the Seine and belonged to the wine warehouses, and the new alleys covered with limestone, running parallel to the river. The idea was to perpetuate the memory of the warehouses through this intellectual exercise, which is obviously impossible, because only the informed visitor will have the tools with which to decode the symbols. Dubbing the gardens 'Le Jardin de la Mémoire' is of little consolation

* The American Center closed down altogether in February 1996

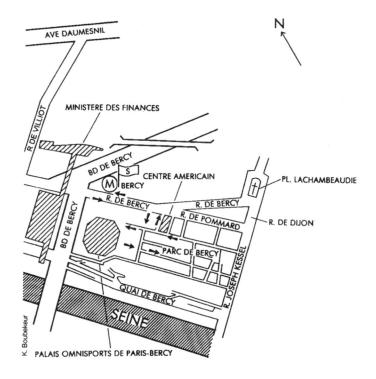

and is in fact almost cynical on the part of a city that has lately wiped out so much of its memory for reasons of financial gain or for lack of sensitivity for the past. Still, one welcomes the fact that Bercy's 2,500 trees have been preserved and integrated into the gardens: cutting down trees has become taboo in Paris, of which every politician is well aware.

In order to maintain a semblance of Bercy's past, a railtrack used for transporting wine barrels from the Seine has also been preserved, as well as a brick storehouse, a guard's house and even the scanty ruins of the Petit Château de Bercy. The park is divided into three sections – the lawns, the flower beds and the romantic gardens. The latter have a canal, a basin with an island and a lovely footbridge over rue de Dijon. Among the great variety of plants in the park, which include miscellaneous roses, heather, herbs and rhododendron, the vine has not been forgotten. Indeed, it has been an indispensable addition to all the recently created parks of Paris, following the example of the inhabitants of Montmartre, who, in

The American Center

1934 planted a vineyard on their hill in order to revive the memory of Paris's traditional life-giving beverage.

At the time of writing, the belvedere overlooking the Seine is nearing completion; it promises to afford a sweeping view of this section of the Seine. Opposite is the new national library, la Bibliothèque de France. Distinguished by its four controversial glass towers, it provides once more food for thought about Charles Baudelaire's verse cited above.

Leave the gardens by way of **RUE DE BERCY** and head west towards the **Gare de Lyon** and the **Bastille**. The station's clock-tower looks like an antiquated period piece now that contemporary constructions have stolen the show in commanding the skyline, but the restaurant Le Train Bleu inside has preserved its spectacular setting from glamorous days gone by. To spare your feet, take the no. 91 bus from in front of the station, on rue de Lyon, to the Bastille, a short ride away. When you get off the bus, you will notice the Fouquet's restaurant on this side of the Opera House. The celebrated establishment of the Champs-Elysées, wishing to be part of the party when it moved east, opened a branch in this strategic location.

The party, however, proved a financial black hole for the Bastille Opera and its chaotic management. Despite the early bragging, the technological wizardry proved a fiasco, and few people were ever fond of the building. Many, not least Luciano Pavarotti, wish the troupe would retrace its steps west and return to the Palais Garnier.*

The younger generation, however, seem quite settled in the *Est parisien* – after all, they had not moved here for the Opera. Its spacious pavement provides the more energetic youths with ample space for skateboarding, while the junction of Place de la Bastille and rue de la Roquette (in the 11th arr.) is a fine, sunny place for café-goers. On the 12th-arrondissement side of Place de la Bastille, the Bassin de l'Arsenal, overlooking the cheerful marina, reflects another aspect of the leisurely lifestyle of modern Paris.

To this spot the Socialist Party and their supporters flocked once more on 10 January 1996 to pay a last homage to François Mitterand on the eve of his funeral, in an ultimate gesture to remind the world and themselves that, despite the marina, the trendy cafés and the Opera House, the Socialist rose has not wilted in this most gentrified area of Paris, the one-time home of the *sans culottes*. And just as Jessye Norman was called upon to strike up the *Marseillaise* at Place de la Concorde on the bicentennial anniversary of the Revolution, it was Barbara Hendricks who now lent her voice to honour the late President, reminding us, once more, that Paris belongs to all those who call it their own – foreigners and natives alike – even on historic commemorations and on the territory most sacred to the nation.

If the sun has greeted you today, you may like to end your walk in the Arsenal's gardens. Here there are several secluded nooks where no one will disturb your privacy, as you muse over the moat of Charles V's formidable fortifications that ran on the site of the marina in less peaceful times.

* Which they now have – since 1 March 1996 smaller scale productions take place at Palais Garnier.

INDEX

AROUND AND ABOUT PARIS
VOLUMES 1, 2 & 3

Volume 1 takes you from the 1st to the 7th arrondissement, the territory of Paris before the French Revolution.

Volume 3 covers the 13th to the 20th arrondissements which were annexed to Paris in 1860.

Thirza Vallois brings Paris to life in a way that enthralls her readers and provides them with a detailed knowledge of the city which exceeds that of most Parisians, while her fast moving style disguises a depth of historical fact that is normally only found in academic tomes.

ORDER FORM

To order your copy, either check or insert the number of copies you want in the appropriate box and return this order form (or a photocopy of it) along with your cheque to the address below. Alternatively you can phone your order through on (+44/0) 973 325 468 and pay by credit card.

Volume 1: From the Dawn of Time to the Eiffel Tower
Arrondisements 1 to 7   £14.95   ☐

Volume 2: From the Guillotine to the Bastille Opera
Arrondisements 8 to 12   £14.95   ☐

Volume 3: New Horizons: Haussmann's Annexation
Arrondisements 13 to 20   £15.95   ☐

Add £2.90 per copy for post and packing

Send your order to:
Iliad Books, 5 Nevern Road, London SW5 9PG

Name: _____

Address: _____

_____

_____

Enclosed is my cheque payable to Iliad Books, amount: _____

Please bill my credit card. Specify type of card _____

Card No _____   Expiry date _____

Signature _____